The Elusive Quest for
Growth

The Elusive Quest for Growth

Economists' Adventures and Misadventures in the Tropics

William Easterly

The MIT Press
Cambridge, Massachusetts
London, England

Fourth printing, 2002

This book was set in Palatino by Asco Typesetters, Hong Kong, in '3B2'.

Printed and bound in the United States of America.

Library of Congress Cataloging-in-Publication Data

Easterly, William.
    The elusive quest for growth : economists' adventures and misadventures in the tropics / William Easterly.
        p.   cm.
    Includes bibliographical references and index.
    ISBN 0-262-05065-X (hc. : alk. paper)
    1. Poor—Developing countries. 2. Poverty—Developing countries. 3. Developing countries—Economic policy.   I. Title.
HC59.72.P6 E17   2001
338.9'009172'4—dc21   00-068382

To Debbie, Rachel, Caleb, and Grace

Contents

Acknowledgments

I am very grateful to Ross Levine and Lant Pritchett, who made comments on various drafts and provided many insights through numerous discussions of growth. I am also grateful for comments to my editors at MIT Press, five anonymous referees, Alberto Alesina, Reza Baqir, Roberta Gatti, Ricardo Hausmann, Charles Kenny, Michael Kremer, Susan Rabiner, Sergio Rebelo, Sergio Schmukler, Michael Woolcock, to my coauthors of various studies I use here, from whom I have learned much, including the late Michael Bruno, Shanta Devarajan, David Dollar, Allan Drazen, Stanley Fischer, Roumeen Islam, Robert King, Aart Kraay, Paolo Mauro, Peter Montiel, Howard Pack, Jo Ritzen, Klaus Schmidt-Hebbel, Lawrence Summers, Joseph Stiglitz, Holger Wolf, and David Yuravlivker, to the organizers of the very educational National Bureau of Economic Research meetings on growth, including Robert Barro, Charles Jones, Paul Romer, Jeffrey Sachs, and Alwyn Young, and to the many participants in seminars, classes at Georgetown and Johns Hopkins School of Advanced International Studies, and training courses where I have presented parts of the draft of this book. I alone am responsible for views expressed here.

Prologue: The Quest

The theme of the quest is ancient. In many versions, it is the search for a precious object with magical properties: the Golden Fleece, the Holy Grail, the Elixir of Life. The precious object in most of the stories either remains elusive or is a disappointment when found. Jason got the Golden Fleece with the help of Medea, who betrayed her own father, but Jason and Medea's subsequent marriage was rather dysfunctional. Jason betrayed Medea in turn for another princess; she worked out her disappointment by killing Jason's new bride and her own children.

Fifty years ago, in the aftermath of World War II, we economists began our own audacious quest: to discover the means by which poor countries in the tropics could become rich like the rich countries in Europe and North America. Observing the sufferings of the poor and the comforts of the rich motivated us on our quest. If our ambitious quest were successful, it would be one of humankind's great intellectual triumphs.

Like the ancient questors, we economists have tried to find the precious object, the key that would enable the poor tropics to become rich. We thought we had found the elixir many different times. The precious objects we offered ranged from foreign aid to investment in machines, from fostering education to controlling population growth, from giving loans conditional on reforms to giving debt relief conditional on reforms. None has delivered as promised.

The poor countries that we treated with these remedies failed to achieve the growth we expected. The region we treated most intensively, sub-Saharan Africa, failed to grow at all. Latin America and the Middle East grew for awhile, but then spiraled into a growth crash in the 1980s and 1990s. South Asia, another recipient of intensive attention from economists, has suffered from erratic growth that has still left it the home to a huge proportion of the world's poor. And most recently, East Asia, the shining success we celebrated over and over, went into its own growth crash (from which some, but not all, East Asian nations are now recovering). Outside the tropics, we tried applying some of the tropical remedies to the ex-communist countries—with very disappointing results.

Just as various claims to have found the elixir of life proved groundless, we economists have too often peddled formulas that violated the basic principle of economics. The problem was not the failure of economics, but the failure to apply the principles of economics in practical policy work. What is the basic principle of economics? As a wise elder once told me, "People do what they get paid to do; what they don't get paid to do, they don't do." A wonderful book by Steven Landsburg, *The Armchair Economist*, distills the principle more concisely: "People respond to incentives; all the rest is commentary."

Economists have done of lot of research over the past two decades on how economic growth responds to incentives. This work has variously detailed how private businesses and individuals respond to incentives, how government officials respond to incentives, and even how aid donors respond to incentives. This research shows that a society's economic growth does not always pay off at the individual level for government officials, aid donors, and private businesses and households. Incentives often lead them in other, unproductive, directions. This research makes clear how unfortunately misguided, with the benefit of hindsight, were the past panaceas—including some still in force today—for economic growth in the tropics.

To find their way from poverty to riches, we need reminding that people do what they get paid to do. If we do the hard work of ensuring that the trinity of First World aid donors, Third World governments, and ordinary Third World citizens have the right incentives, development will happen. If they don't, it won't. We will see that the trinity often did not have the right incentives, following formulas that violated the basic principle of economics, and so the expected growth did not happen.

This is a sad story, but it can be a hopeful one. We now have statistical evidence to back up theories of how the panaceas failed and how incentive-based policies can work. Incentives can change and start countries on the road to prosperity. It won't be easy. Incentives are not themselves a facile panacea. We will see how the interlocking

incentives of aid donors, governments, and citizens form a compli-
cated web that is not easily untangled.

Moreover, there is already widespread disappointment that the
quest has not been more successful. Protesters from Seattle to Prague
call for abandoning the quest altogether. That is not acceptable. As
long as there are poor nations suffering from pestilence, oppression,
and hunger, as I describe in the first part of the book, and as long as
human intellectual efforts can devise ways to make them richer, the
quest must go on.

Four notes before I begin. First, what I say here is my own opinion
and not that of my employer, the World Bank. Occasionally I am
even critical of what my employer has done in the past. One thing I
admire about the World Bank is that it encourages gadflies like me to
exercise intellectual freedom and doesn't stifle internal debate on
World Bank policies.

Second, I am not going to say anything about the environment. I
tried to say something about the environment in early drafts of this
book, but found I didn't have anything useful to say. There is a
big issue about how growth affects the environment, but that's a
different book. Most economists believe that any negative effects of
growth on the environment can be alleviated with wise environmental policies, like making polluters bear the costs of their delete-
rious effects on human welfare, and so we don't actually have to stop
economic growth to preserve the environment. This is a good thing,
because stopping growth would be very bad news for the poor
everywhere, as I discuss in the first chapter.

Third, I am not trying to do a general survey of all of economists'
research on growth. This research has exploded in the past decade
and a half, following the seminal work of Stanford Business School
professor Paul Romer and, later, the inspirational work of Nobel
Prize winner Robert Lucas. There is not yet a scholarly consensus on
some issues, although I think the evidence is strong on others. I try to
follow the thread of work that specifically relates to the efforts of
economists to figure out how to make poor tropical countries rich.

Fourth, I am going to insert snapshots of daily life in the Third
World, "intermezzos," between chapters to remind us that behind
the quest for growth are the sufferings and joys of real people, and it
is for them we go on the quest for growth.

I

Why Growth Matters

As I pursue my career as a self-anointed expert on poor countries, the differences in the lives of the poor and the rich supply motivation. We experts don't care about rising gross domestic product for its own sake. We care because it betters the lot of the poor and reduces the proportion of people who are poor. We care because richer people can eat more and buy more medicines for their babies. In this part, I review the evidence on growth and relief from poverty.

1   To Help the Poor

When I see another child eating, I watch him, and if he doesn't give me something I think I'm going to die of hunger.
—A ten-year-old child in Gabon, 1997

I am in Lahore, a city of 6 million people in Pakistan, on a World Bank trip as I write this chapter. Last weekend I went with a guide to the village of Gulvera, not far outside Lahore. We entered the village on an impossibly narrow paved road, which the driver drove at top speed except on the frequent occasions that cattle were crossing the road. We continued as the road turned into a dirt track, where there was barely enough space between the village houses for the car. Then the road seemed to dead-end. But although I could not detect any road, the guide pointed out to the driver how he could make a sharp right across an open field, then regain a sort of a road—flat dirt anyway. I hated to think what would happen to these dirt roads in rainy season.

The "road" brought us to the community center for the village, where a number of young and old men were hanging out (no women, on which more in a moment). The village smelled of manure. The men were expecting us and were extremely hospitable, welcoming us in to the brick-and-mortar community center, everyone grasping each of our right hands with their two hands and seating us on some rattan benches. They provided pillows for us to lean on or with which to otherwise make ourselves comfortable. They served us a drink of lassi, a sort of yogurt-milk mixture. The lassi pitcher was thickly covered with flies, but I drank my lassi anyway.

The men said that during the week, they worked all day in the fields, then came to the community center in the evenings to play cards and talk. The women couldn't come, they said, because they still had work to do in the evenings. Flocks of flies hummed everywhere, and some of the men had open sores on their legs. There was one youngish but dignified man nicknamed Deenu to whom everyone seemed to defer. Most of the men were barefoot, wearing long dusty robes. A crowd of children hung around the entrance watching us—only boys, no girls.

I asked Deenu what the main problems of Gulvera village were. Deenu said they were glad to have gotten electricity just six months before. Imagine getting electricity after generations spent in darkness. They were glad to have a boys' elementary school. However, they still lacked many things: a girls' elementary school, a doctor, drainage or sewerage (everything was dumped into a pool of rancid water outside the community center), telephone connections, paved roads. The poor sanitary conditions and lack of access to medical care in villages like Gulvera may help explain why a hundred out of every thousand babies die before their first birthday in Pakistan.

I asked Deenu if we could see a house. He walked with us over to his brother's house. It was an adobe-walled dirt-floor compound, which had two small rooms where they lived, stalls for the cattle, an outside dung-fired oven built into a wall, piles of cattle dung stacked up to dry, and a hand pump hooked up to a well. Children were everywhere, including a few girls finally, staring curiously at us. Deenu said his brother had seven children. Deenu himself had six brothers and seven sisters. The brothers all lived in the village; the sisters had married into other villages. The women in the household hung back near the two small rooms. We were not introduced to them.

Women's rights have not yet come to rural Pakistan, a fact reflected in some grim statistics: there are 108 men for every 100 women in Pakistan. In rich countries, women slightly outnumber men because of their greater longevity. In Pakistan, there are what Nobel Prize winner Amartya Sen called "missing women," reflecting some combination of discrimination against girls in nutrition, medical care, or even female infanticide. Oppression of women sometimes takes an even more violent turn. There was a story in the Lahore newspaper of a brother who had killed his sister to preserve the family honor; he had suspected her of an illicit affair.

Violence in the countryside is widespread in Pakistan, despite the peaceful appearance of Gulvera. Another story in the Lahore paper described a village feud in which one family killed seven members of another family. Bandits and kidnappers prey on travelers in parts of the countryside in Pakistan.

We walked back to the community center, passing a group of boys playing a game, where they threw four walnuts on the ground and then tried to hit one of the walnuts with another one. Deenu asked us if we would like to stay for lunch, but we politely declined (I didn't want to take any of their scarce food), said our good-byes, and drove away. One of the villagers rode away with us, just to have an adventure. He told us that they had arranged for two cooks to prepare our lunch. I felt bad about having declined the lunch invitation.

We drove across the fields to where four brothers had grouped their compounds into a sort of a village and went through the same routine: the men greeting us warmly with two hands and seating us on rattan benches outside. No women were to be seen. The children were even more numerous and uninhibited than in Gulvera; they were mostly boys but this time also a few girls. They crowded around us watching everything we did, frequently breaking into laughter at some unknown faux pas by one of us. The men served us some very good milky sweet tea. I saw a woman peeking out from inside the house, but when I looked in her direction, she pulled back out of sight.

We walked into one of the brothers' compounds. Many women stood at the doors into their rooms, hanging back but watching us. The men showed us a churn that they used to make butter and yogurt. One of the men tried to show us how to use it, but he himself didn't know; this was woman's work. The children nearly passed out from laughing. The men brought us some butter to taste. They said they melted the butter to make ghee—clarified butter—which was an important ingredient in their cooking. They said if you ate a lot of ghee, it made you stronger. Then they gave us some ghee to taste. Most of their food seemed to consist of dairy products.

I asked what problems they faced. They had gotten electricity just one month before. They otherwise had the same unfulfilled needs as Gulvera: no telephone, no running water, no doctor, no sewerage, no roads. This was only a kilometer off the main road just outside Lahore, so we weren't in the middle of nowhere. They were poor, but these were relatively well-off villagers compared to more remote villages in Pakistan. The road leading to their minivillage was a half-lane track constructed of bricks that they had made themselves.

The majority of people in Pakistan are poor: 85 percent live on less than two dollars a day and 31 percent live in extreme poverty at less than one dollar a day. The majority of the world's people live in poor nations like Pakistan, where people live in isolated poverty even close to a major city. The majority of the world's people live in poor nations where women are oppressed, far too many babies die, and far too many people don't have enough to eat. We care about economic growth for the poor nations because it makes the lives of poor people like those in Gulvera better. Economic growth frees the poor from hunger and disease. Economy-wide GDP growth per capita translates into rising incomes for the poorest of the poor, lifting them out of poverty.

The Deaths of the Innocents

The typical rate of infant mortality in the richest fifth of countries is 4 out of every 1,000 births; in the poorest fifth of countries, it is 200 out of every 1,000 births. Parents in the poorest countries are fifty times more likely than in the richest countries to know grief rather than joy from the birth of a child. Researchers have found that a 10 percent decrease in income is associated with about a 6 percent higher infant mortality rate.[1]

The higher rates of babies dying in the poorest countries reflect in part the higher rates of communicable and often easily preventable diseases such as tuberculosis, syphillis, diarrhea, polio, measles, tetanus, meningitis, hepatitis, sleeping sickness, schistosomiasis, river blindness, leprosy, trachoma, intestinal worms, and lower respiratory infections.[2] At low incomes, disease is more dangerous because of lower medical knowledge, lower nutrition, and lower access to medical care.

Two million children die every year of dehydration from diarrhea.[3] Another 2 million children die annually from pertussis, polio, diphtheria, tetanus, and measles.[4]

Three million children die annually from bacterial pneumonia. Overcrowding of housing and indoor wood or cigarette smoke make pneumonia among children more likely. Malnourished children are also more likely to develop pneumonia than well-fed children.[5] Bacterial pneumonia can be cured by a five-day course of antibiotics, like cotrimoxazole, that costs about twenty-five cents.[6]

Between 170 million and 400 million children annually are infected with intestinal parasites like hookworm and roundworm, which impair cognition and cause anemia and failure to thrive.[7]

Deficiency of iodine causes goiters—swelling of the thyroid gland at the throat—and lowered mental capacity. About 120,000 children born each year suffer from mental retardation and physical paralysis caused by iodine deficiency. About 10 percent of the world's population, adults and children both, suffer from goiter.[8]

Vitamin A deficiency causes blindness in about half a million children and contributes to the deaths of about 8 million children each year.[9] It is not independent of the other diseases discussed here; it makes death more likely from diarrhea, measles, and pneumonia.

Medicines that would alleviate these diseases are sometimes surprisingly inexpensive, a fact that UNICEF often uses to dramatize the depths of poverty of these suffering people. Oral rehydration therapy, at a cost of less than ten cents for each dose, can alleviate dehydration.[10] Vaccination against pertussis, polio, diphtheria, measles, and tetanus costs about fifteen dollars per child.[11] Vitamin A can be added to diets through processing of salt or sugar or administered directly through vitamin A capsules every six months. Vitamin A capsules cost about two cents each.[12] Iodizing salt supplies, which costs about five cents per affected person per year, alleviates iodine deficiency.[13] Intestinal parasites can be cured with inexpensive drugs like albendazole and praziquantel.[14]

Wealthier and Healthier

Lant Pritchett, from Harvard's Kennedy School of Government, and Larry Summers, the former U.S. secretary of the treasury, found a strong association between economic growth and changes in infant mortality. They pointed out that a third factor that was unchanging over time for each country, like "culture" or "institutions," could not be explaining the simultaneous change in income and change in infant mortality. Going further, they argued that the rise in income was causing the fall in mortality rather than the other way around. They used a statistical argument that we will see more of later in this book. They observed some income increases that were probably unrelated to mortality, like income increases due to rises in a country's export prices. They traced through the effect of such an income increase, finding that it still did result in a fall in infant mortality. If an income increase that has nothing to do with mortality changes is still associated with a fall in mortality, this suggests that income increases are causing reduced mortality.

Pritchett and Summers's findings, if we can take them literally, imply huge effects of income growth on the death of children. The deaths of about half a million children in 1990 would have been averted if Africa's growth in the 1980s had been 1.5 percentage points higher.

The Poorest of the Poor

The statistics presented so far are national averages. Behind the averages of even the poorest nation, there is still regional variation. Mali is one of the poorest nations on earth. The countryside along the Niger River around the city of Tombouctou (Timbuktu) is one of the poorest regions in Mali and thus one of the poorest places on earth. At the time of a survey in 1987, over a third of the children under age five had had diarrhea in the preceding two weeks. Very few of them were on simple and cheap oral rehydration therapy. None had been vaccinated for diphtheria, pertussis, or typhoid. Forty-one percent of children born do not live to the age of five, three times the mortality rate in the capital of Bamako and one of the highest child mortality rates ever recorded.[15]

As in Tomboctou, there are some regions or peoples at the very bottom of the economic pyramid, despised even by other poor. "In Egypt they were *madfoun*—the buried or buried alive; in Ghana, *ohiabrubro*—the miserably poor, with no work, sick with no one to care for them; in Indonesia, *endek arak tadah*; in Brazil, *miseraveis* —the deprived; in Russia, *bomzhi*—the homeless; in Bangladesh *ghrino gorib*—the despised/hated poor." In Zambia the *balandana sana* or *bapina* were described in these terms: "Lack food, eat once or twice; poor hygiene, flies fall over them, cannot afford school and health costs, lead miserable lives, poor dirty clothing, poor sanitation, access to water, look like made people, live on vegetables and sweet potatoes." In Malawi, the bottom poor were *osaukitsitsa*, "mainly households headed by the aged, the sick, disabled, orphans and widows." Some were described as *onyentchera*, "the stunted poor, with thin bodies, short stature and thin hairs, bodies that did not shine even after bathing, and who experience frequent illnesses and a severe lack of food."[16]

Eating

High mortality in the poorest countries also reflects the continuing problem of hunger. Daily calorie intake is one-third lower in the poorest fifth of countries than in the richest fifth.

A quarter of the poorest countries had famines in the past three decades; none of the richest countries faced a famine. In the poorest nations like Burundi, Madagascar, and Uganda, nearly half of all children under the age of three are abnormally short because of nutritional deficiency.[17]

An Indian family housed in a thatched hut seldom "could have two square meals a day. The lunch would be finished munching some sugarcane. Once in a while they would taste 'sattu' (made of flour), pulses [dried beans], potatoes etc. but for occasions only."[18]

In Malawi, the poorest families "stay without food for 2–3 days or even the whole week ... and may simply cook vegetables for a meal ... some households literally eat bitter maize bran (*gaga/deya owawa*) and *gmelina* sawdust mixed with a little maize flour especially during the hunger months of January and February."[19]

Oppression of the Poor

Poor societies sometimes have some form of debt bondage. To take one example, observers of India report "a vicious cycle of indebtedness in which a debtor may work in a moneylender's house as a servant, on his farm as a laborer.... The debt may accumulate substantially due to high interest rates, absence due to illness, and expenses incurred for food or accommodations."[20]

Ethnic minorities are particularly prone to oppression. In Pakistan in 1993, the Bengali community of Rehmanabad in Karachi "had been subject to evictions and bulldozing, and on returning to the settlement and constructing temporary housing of reeds and sacks, have faced on-going harassment by land speculators, the police and political movements."[21]

Poor children are particularly vulnerable to oppression. Forty-two percent of children aged ten to fourteen are workers in the poorest countries. Less than 2 percent of children aged ten to fourteen are workers in the richest countries. Although most countries have laws forbidding child labor, the U.S. State Department classifies many countries as not enforcing these laws. Eighty-eight percent of the poorest countries are in this no-enforcement category; none of the richest countries is.[22] For example, we have this story of Pachawak in western Orissa state in India: "Pachawak dropped out of class 3 when one day his teacher caned him severely. Since then he has been working as child labor with a number of rich households. Pachawak's father owns 1.5 acres of land and works as a laborer. His younger brother of 11-years-old also became a bonded laborer when the family had to take a loan for the marriage of the eldest son. The system is closely linked to credit, as many families take loans from landlords, who in lieu of that obligation keep the children as 'kuthia.' Pachawak worked as a cattle grazer from 6 A.M. to 6 P.M. and got paid two to four sacks of paddy a year, two meals a day, and one lungi [wrap-around clothing]."

One particularly unsavory kind of child labor is prostitution. In Benin, for example, "the girls have no choice but to prostitute themselves, starting at 14, even at 12. They do it for 50 francs, or just for dinner."[23]

Another occupation in which children work in poor countries is particularly dangerous: war. As many as 200,000 child soldiers from the ages of six to sixteen fought wars in poor countries like Myanmar, Angola, Somalia, Liberia, Uganda, and Mozambique.[24]

Women are also vulnerable to oppression in poor countries. Over four-fifths of the richest fifth of countries have social and economic equality for women most of the time, according to the *World Human Rights Guide* by Charles Humana. None of the poorest fifth of countries has social and economic equality for women.[25] In Cameroon, "Women in some regions require a husband's, father's, or brother's permission to go out. In addition, a woman's husband or brother has access to her bank accounts, but not vice versa." A 1997 survey in Jamaica found that "in all communities, wife-beating was perceived as a common experience in daily life." In Georgia in the Caucasus, "women confessed that frequent household arguments resulted in being beaten." In Uganda in 1998, when women were asked, "What kind of work do men in your area do?" they laughed and said, "Eat and sleep then wake up and go drinking again."[26]

Growth and Poverty

My World Bank colleagues Martin Ravallion and Shaohua Chen collected data on spells of economic growth and changes in poverty covering the years 1981 to 1999. They get their data from national surveys of household income or expenditure. They require that the methodology of the survey be unchanged over the period that they are examining so as to exclude spurious changes due to changing definitions. They found 154 periods of change in 65 developing countries with data that met this requirement.

Ravallion and Chen defined poverty as an absolute concept within each country: the poor were defined as the part of the population that had incomes below $1 a day at the beginning of each period they were examining. Ravallion and Chen keep this poverty line fixed within each country during the period they analyze. So the question was, How did aggregate economic growth change the share of people below this poverty line?

The answer was quite clear: fast growth went with fast poverty reduction, and overall economic contraction went with increased poverty. Here I summarize Ravallion and Chen's data by dividing the number of episodes into four equally sized groups from the fastest growing to the fastest declining. I compare the change in poverty in countries with the fastest growth to the poverty change in countries with the fastest decline:[27]

	Percentage change in average incomes per year	Percent change in poverty rate per year
Strong contraction	−9.8	23.9
Moderate contraction	−1.9	1.5
Moderate expansion	1.6	−0.6
Strong expansion	8.2	−6.1

The increases in poverty were extremely acute in the economies with severe economic declines—most of them in Eastern Europe and Central Asia. These were economies that declined with the death of the old communist system and kept declining while awaiting the birth of a new system. Several of these poverty-increasing declines also occurred in Africa. Poverty shot up during severe recessions in Zambia, Mali, and Côte d'Ivoire, for example.

Countries with positive income growth had a decline in the proportion of people below the poverty line. The fastest average growth was associated with the fastest poverty reductions. Growth was reaching the poor in Indonesia, for example, which had average income growth of 76 percent from 1984 to 1996. The proportion of Indonesians beneath the poverty line in 1993 was one-quarter of what it was in 1984. (A bad reversal came with Indonesia's crisis over 1997–1999, with average income falling by 12 percent and the poverty rate shooting up 65 percent, again confirming that income and poverty move together.)

All of this in retrospect seems unsurprising. For poverty to get worse with economic growth, the distribution of income would have to get much more unequal as incomes increased. There is no evidence for such disastrous deteriorations in income inequality as income rises. In Ravallion and Chen's data set, for example, measures of inequality show no tendency to get either better or worse with economic growth. If the degree of inequality stays about the same, then income of the poor and the rich must be rising together or falling together.

This is indeed what my World Bank colleagues David Dollar and Aart Kraay have found. A 1 percent increase in average income of the society translates one for one into a 1 percent increase in the incomes of the poorest 20 percent of the population. Again using statistical techniques to isolate direction of causation, they found that an additional one percentage point per capita growth *causes* a 1 percent rise in the poor's incomes.[28]

There are two ways the poor could become better off: income could be redistributed from the rich to the poor, and the income of both the poor and the rich could rise with overall economic growth. Ravallion and Chen's and Dollar and Kraay's findings suggest that on average, growth has been much more of a lifesaver to the poor than redistribution.

To Begin the Quest

The improvement in hunger, mortality, and poverty as GDP per capita rises over time motivates us on our quest for growth. Poverty is not just low GDP; it is dying babies, starving children, and oppression of women and the downtrodden. The well-being of the next generation in poor countries depends on whether our quest to make poor countries rich is successful. I think again back to the woman I saw peering out at me from a house in a village in Pakistan. To that unknown woman I dedicate the elusive quest for growth as we economists, from rich countries and from poor countries, trek the tropics trying to make poor countries rich.

Intermezzo: In Search of a River

In 1710, a fifteen-year-old English boy named Thomas Cresap got off a boat at Havre de Grace, Maryland. Thomas was emigrating to America from Yorkshire in northern England.[1]

Thomas knew what he wanted in America: some land on a river. Riverside land was fertile for growing crops, and the river provided transportation to get the crops to market. He settled on the Susquehanna River that ran through Havre de Grace.

We next hear of Thomas a decade and a half later. In 1727, when he married Hannah Johnson, he had just defaulted on a debt of nine pounds sterling.[2] Thomas struggled to support Hannah and their first child, Daniel, born in 1728. Thomas and Hannah experienced early America's health crisis firsthand as two of their children died in infancy.

Trying to escape his debtors, Thomas decided to move. In his next attempt at getting land on a river, he rented some land from George Washington's father on the Virginia side of the Potomac, not far from what is today Washington, D.C., and began building a log cabin. But he was an outsider, and as he was chopping down trees, a posse of armed neighbors suggested he might want to investigate housing opportunities elsewhere. Thomas turned his ax on his attackers, killed a man in the ensuing battle, then went back home to Maryland to pack up for the move to Virginia and tell Hannah about their new neighbors. "For some reason," the record reports, "she refused to go."[3]

They decided to move to Pennsylvania instead, settling in March 1730 upriver on the Susquehanna near what is now Wrightsville, Pennsylvania. Thomas thought he had finally found his riverside homeplace. But he once again got into trouble with the neighbors in Pennsylvania. Lord Baltimore, the owner of Maryland, and William Penn, the proprietor of Pennsylvania, were disputing the border between their colonies, and Thomas was loyal to what turned out to be the losing side. He got a grant of two hundred acres of Pennsylvania riverfront land from Lord Baltimore, for which he paid two dollars a year. It appeared to be good deal, except that the land turned out not to belong to Baltimore, and the Pennsylvanians resolved to drive off these Marylanders.

In October 1730, two Pennsylvanians ambushed Thomas, hit him on the head, and threw him into the Susquehanna. Thomas somehow managed to swim ashore. He appealed for justice to the nearest Pennsylvania judge, who told him that Marylanders were ineligible for justice from Pennsylvania courts.[4]

A couple of hours after dark on January 29, 1733, a mob of twenty Pennsylvanians surrounded Thomas's house and asked him to surrender so they could hang him. Thomas was inside with several other Maryland loyalists, son Daniel, and Hannah, who was eight months pregnant with Thomas Jr. When the mob broke down the door, Thomas opened fire, wounding one Pennsylvanian. The Pennsylvanians wounded one of the children of the Maryland loyalists. Finally, the Pennsylvanians retreated.

The next battle came a year later, in January 1734, when the sheriff of Lancaster County and sent an armed posse to arrest Thomas. The posse again broke down the door, and Thomas again opened fire. One of Thomas's men shot one of the attackers, Knoles Daunt. The Pennsylvanians begged Hannah for a candle to attend to Daunt's wound in the leg. The gentle Hannah said she had rather the wound "had been his heart."⁵ Knoles Daunt later died of his wounds. The posse again failed to capture Thomas.

Finally in November 1736, a new sheriff of Lancaster Country decided to resolve the Thomas Cresap problem. At midnight on November 23, the sheriff took a well-armed posse of twenty-four men to serve Thomas with an arrest warrant for the murder of Knoles Daunt. They knocked at the door of the Cresaps'. Inside was the usual assortment of Maryland supporters and the family—Hannah again very pregnant, now with their third child. Thomas asked those peaceable Pennsylvania Quakers what the "Damn'd Quakeing Sons of Bitches" wanted.⁶ They wanted to burn down Thomas's house. The Marylanders fled the burning house, and the Pennsylvanians finally captured Thomas.⁷

They put Thomas in irons and marched him off to jail in Philadelphia (a city Thomas called "one of the prettiest towns in Maryland"), where he spent a year in jail. The guards occasionally took him out for fresh air, like the time they exhibited him to a jeering Philadelphia mob as the "Maryland monster."

Finally Thomas's supporters got the Maryland monster released by petitioning the king in London. Having had enough of Pennsylvania, Thomas loaded his family on a wagon and moved back to Maryland, to the western frontier in what is now Oldtown, Maryland, on the banks of the Potomac. They arrived just in time for Hannah to give birth to their fifth, and last, child, Michael.

Thomas kept quarreling with his neighbors, one of whom noted that "Cresap is a person of hot Resentm't and great Acrimony."⁸ But this time the quarreling stopped short of battle, and Oldtown finally became his home for the rest of his life.⁹ He built his house on a rise overlooking the

Potomac river floodplain, which made for good farmland. Unfortunately this particular riverside property lacked transportation because the Potomac was not navigable until Georgetown, 150 miles downstream. The nonnavigable Potomac was fuel to Thomas's continued transportation obsession.

Thomas in the 1740s participated in a group of land and transportation investors, including the Washington family, who explored the idea of building a canal along the unnavigable parts of the Potomac, but the project ran afoul of the threat of war with the French. The canal would eventually be built early in the next century.

Canals and rivers were in hot demand because colonial roads were often choked by mud, and when they were dry, they were deeply rutted. To cope with the suffering, whiskey was passed around frequently to both driver and passengers during the journey. "The horses," said a passenger gratefully, "were sober."[10]

Thwarted by the river, Thomas turned to building his own roads. His road building standards, however, were quite low; his idea of making a road was simply to remove some of the "most difficult obstructions."[11] A son of Thomas's old landlords and investment partners, George Washington, passed through in 1747 on a surveying trip. He described the road leading up to Thomas Cresap's as "ye worst road that ever was trod by Man or Beast."[12]

If Thomas thought he had escaped border wars by moving to the remote frontier, he was wrong. He was now in the midst of the biggest war of his life—the war between the French and the English that lasted from 1754 to 1763.

The war started in part because Thomas (and other English settlers) was not satisfied with his riverside land and looked to the west, where there was much more fertile land along the navigable Ohio River. So Thomas joined the Washingtons and other Virginians in an Ohio River land grab known as the Ohio Company, which gave short shrift to the actual owners of the land, the Shawnees and the Mingoes. And when the Ohio Company tried to build a trading post and fort at the forks of the Ohio (today's Pittsburgh), they ran smack into another enemy, the French from Quebec, who also wanted to steal the Ohio River land. The French chased away the Ohio Company's local military commander, twenty-one-year-old George Washington, after a brief battle in 1754, which started what became known as the French and Indian War. Thomas and his sons Daniel and Thomas, Jr., volunteered to fight against the French as part of the colonial militia, a collection of rural hoodlums known more for their *"unruly licentiousness" than for any military skills.*[13] *Thomas also commanded one of his African-American slaves, Nemesis, to join the militia. On April 23, 1757, in a battle near what is now Frostburg, Maryland, Thomas, Jr., was killed. A few weeks later, Nemesis was also killed in battle.*[14]

But in the end, with a lot of help from the British, the colonials defeated the French and their Indian allies. That was not the end of Thomas's wartime suffering, however. In 1775, the Revolutionary War broke out. Thomas's youngest son, Michael, was killed early in the war. Thomas and Hannah had lost two of their children to war and two to infant diseases. Thomas's life had been filled with violence, heartbreak, and the struggle to make a living.

Yet in the end, Thomas's quest for a river was successful. Before Michael died, he had staked out land on the Ohio River. Thomas' heirs would farm fertile lands and later work in manufacturing plants along the Ohio River. The growing American economy, throwing out its tentacles along rivers, canals, and railroads, pulled the Cresaps along out of poverty into prosperity. Life has changed since the days of Thomas, who was my great-great-great-great-great-great-grandfather.

The majority of the world's population have not yet said goodbye to the bad old days before development. The majority of the world's population is not as fortunate as I to be borne along on rivers of prosperity. When those of us from rich countries look at poor countries today, we see our own past poverty. We are all the descendants of poverty. In the long run, we all come from the lower class. We embarked on the quest for growth to try to make poor countries grow out of poverty into riches.

II   Panaceas That Failed

Many times over the past fifty years, we economists thought we had found the right answer to economic growth. It started with foreign aid to fill the gap between "necessary" investment and saving. Even after some of us abandoned the rigidity of the "necessary" investment idea, we still thought investment in machines was the key to growth. Supplementing this idea was the notion that education was a form of accumulating "human machinery" that would bring growth. Next, concerned about how "excess" population might overwhelm the productive capacity of the economy, we promoted population control. Then, when we realized that government policies hindered growth, we promoted official loans to induce countries to do policy reforms. Finally, when countries had trouble repaying the loans they incurred to do policy reforms, we offered debt forgiveness.

None of these elixirs has worked as promised, because not all the participants in the creation of economic growth had the right incentives. In this part, we look at these failed panaceas. In part III, we examine how to go about the hard work of getting everybody to buy in to economic growth.

2   Aid for Investment

How use doth breed a habit in a man!
Shakespeare, *Two Gentleman of Verona*

On March 6, 1957, the Gold Coast, a small British colony, became the first nation of sub-Saharan Africa to gain its independence. It renamed itself Ghana. Delegations from both sides of the iron curtain, including from Moscow and Washington, vied to be the first to extend loans and technical assistance to the new nation. Vice President Richard Nixon led the American delegation. (According to one source, Nixon asked a group of black journalists, "What does it feel like to be free?" "We don't know," they replied, "we're from Alabama.")[1]

A later writer commented about Ghana's independence day, "Few former colonies can have had a more auspicious start."[2] Ghana supplied two-thirds of the world's cocoa. It had the best schools in Africa, and economists thought education was one of the keys to growth. It had a good amount of investment, and economists thought investment was another of the keys to growth. Under limited self-government in the 1950s, the Nkrumah government and the British had built new roads, health clinics, and schools. American, British, and German companies expressed interest in investing in the new nation.[3] The whole nation seemed to share an excitement about economic development. As one Ghanaian wrote at the time, "Let us now seek the economic kingdom."[4]

Nkrumah had the services of many of the world's economists— Arthur Lewis, Nicholas Kaldor, Dudley Seers, Albert Hirschman, and Tony Killick—who shared the optimism that Dudley Seers had already expressed in a report in 1952: that assistance to Ghana would yield very high returns. As Seers put it in 1952, "Surfacing the road from Tarkwa to Takoradi would increase total output" by much more "than applying the same materials to almost any road in the United Kingdom."[5]

Miracle on the Volta

Nkrumah had bigger goals than paving a few roads. He had already begun plans to build a large hydroelectric dam on the Volta River, which would provide enough electricity to build an aluminum smelter.[6] Nkrumah anticipated that once the smelter was operational, an integrated aluminum industry would develop. The new smelter would process alumina, which would come from a new alumina refinery, which would process bauxite from new bauxite mines. Railways and a caustic soda plant would complete this dynamic industrial complex. A report prepared by expatriate advisers was enthusiastic that the lake created by damming the Volta would also provide a water transportation link between north and south in Ghana. The project would lead to "a major new fishing industry in the lake." Large-scale irrigated agriculture using lake water would make the loss due to flooding of 3,500 square miles of agricultural land "small in comparison."[7]

The Ghanaians indeed built Akosombo Dam within a few years, with support from the American and British governments and the World Bank. The dam created the world's largest man-made lake, Lake Volta. They built an aluminum smelter quickly as well, owned 90 percent by the multinational giant Kaiser Aluminum. Nkrumah ceremonially lowered the dam gates to start filling the great Volta Lake on May 19, 1964.[8]

I remember visiting Akosombo Dam when I lived in Ghana for a year in 1969–1970. The big pile blocking the Volta River was indeed a stunning achievement.

I was optimistic in 1969 about the prospects of Ghana, but my projections did not receive a great deal of public notice, perhaps because I had just finished elementary school.

Other more mature observers shared my precocious optimism. The head of the World Bank's Economics Department in 1967, Andrew Kamarck, thought that Ghana's Volta project gave it the potential to reach growth of 7 percent per annum.[9]

Back to the Volta

In April 1982, a Ghanaian student at the University of Pittsburgh named Agyei Frempong handed in his Ph.D. dissertation, which compared the performance of the Volta River project to the high hopes held by Nkrumah and his foreign and domestic advisers for industrialization, transport, agriculture, and overall economic development. Lake Volta was there, an electricity generator was there, and an aluminum smelter was there. Production of aluminum in the smelter had fluctuated up and down, but did grow on average about 1.5 percent a year from 1969 to 1992.

But that was it for the project's benefits. Frempong noted in 1982, "There is no bauxite mine nor alumina refinery nor caustic soda plant nor railways." The efforts to create a lake fishery were "plagued by poor administration and mechanical equipment failures." People living next to the lake, including the 80,000 whose old homes had been submerged, suffered from waterborne illnesses like river blindness, hookworm, malaria, and schistosomiasis. The large-scale irrigation projects that the planners had envisioned never worked. The lake transport from north to south that was going to solve "the nation's transport difficulties" had "ended up in complete failure."[10]

The saddest part was that the Volta River project was the most successful investment project in Ghanaian history. Frempong agreed with other analysts like Tony Killick that the core part of the project had been a success. The electricity generator and aluminum smelter continue to operate today, the latter with subsidized electricity and imported alumina.

The real disaster is that the Ghanaians are still about as poor as they were in the early 1950s. Ghana had a half-century of stagnation in growth. How did this happen? Just about everything went wrong. The military overthrew Nkrumah in a coup in 1966, the first of five successful military coups over the next decade and a half. His overthrow set off street celebrations in Accra, because Nkrumah's development ambitions had brought little but food shortages and high inflation.

Ghanaians would have celebrated less if they had known how much worse their situation would get over the next two decades. The military briefly restored democracy between 1969 and 1971 under the presidency of Kofi Busia. After the army overthrew Busia in 1971, economics and politics alike fell apart. Ghana even had a famine in the 1970s.[11]

The nadir came in 1983 during the new military government of Flight Lieutenant Jerry Rawlings. In 1983, the income of the average Ghanaian was two-thirds of what it had been in 1971. A drought lowered Lake Volta so much that the hydro plant had to cut off electricity to the Volta Aluminum Company for a year. Ghanaians in 1983 were getting only two-thirds of their recommended daily calorie supply.[12] In 1983, even relatively well-off Ghanaian civil servants made macabre jokes about their "Rawlings necklaces"—the collarbones protruding from their underfed bodies.[13] Malnutrition caused nearly half of all child deaths in 1983.[14] Per capita income in 1983 was below that at independence in 1957.

The crisis in 1983 provoked the Rawlings government to new efforts to bring Ghana back, and economic growth did recover, but it was a long and slow road after a quarter-century of decline.

The Harrod-Domar Model, 1946–2000

The idea that aid-financed investment in dams, roads, and machines would yield growth goes back a long way. In April 1946, economics professor Evsey Domar published an article on economic growth, "Capital Expansion, Rate of Growth, and Employment," which discussed the relationship between short-term recessions and investment in the United States. Although Domar assumed that production capacity was proportional to the stock of machinery, he admitted the assumption was unrealistic and eleven years later, in 1957, complaining of an "ever-guilty conscience," he disavowed the theory.[15] He said his earlier purpose was to comment on an esoteric debate on business cycles, not to derive "an empirically meaningful rate of growth." He said his theory made no sense for long-run growth, and instead he endorsed the new growth theory of Robert Solow (which I discuss in the next chapter).

To sum up, Domar's model was not intended as a growth model, made no sense as a growth model, and was repudiated as a growth model over forty years ago by its creator. So it was ironic that Domar's growth model became, and continues to be today, the most widely applied growth model in economic history.

How did Domar's model survive its supposed demise in the 1950s? We economists applied it (and still do) to poor countries from

Albania to Zimbabwe to determine a "required" investment rate for a target growth rate. The difference between the required investment and the country's own savings is called the *financing gap*. Private financing is assumed to be unavailable to fill the gap, so donors fill the financing gap with foreign aid to attain target growth. This is a model that promised poor countries growth right away through aid-financed investment. It was aid to investment to growth.

With the benefit of hindsight, the use of Domar's model for determining aid requirements and growth projections was (and still is) a big mistake. But let's not be too unkind to the proponents of the model (I was one, earlier in my career), who did not have the benefit of hindsight. The experiences we observed at the time of the model's heyday seemed to support a rigid link from aid to investment to growth. It was only as more data became available that the model's failings became ghastly apparent.

Domar's approach to growth became popular because it had a wonderfully simple prediction: *GDP growth will be proportional to the share of investment spending in GDP.* Domar assumed that output (GDP) is proportional to machines, so the change in output will be proportional to the change in machines, that is, last year's investment. Divide both sides by last year's output. So GDP growth this year is just proportional to last year's investment/GDP ratio.[16]

How did Domar get the idea that production was proportional to machines? Did not labor play some role in production? Domar was writing in the aftermath of the Great Depression, in which many people running the machines lost jobs. Domar and many other economists expected a repeat of the depression after World War II unless the government did something to avoid it. Domar took high unemployment as a given, so there were always people available to run any additional machines that were built. Domar's theory became known as the Harrod-Domar model. (A British economist named Roy Harrod had published in 1939 a similar but more convoluted article.)

Clearly Domar's interest was the short-run business cycle in rich countries. So how did Domar's fixed ratio of production to machines make it into the analysis of poor countries' growth?

The Invention of Development

The quest for a theory of growth and development has tormented us economists as long as there have been economists. In 1776, economics' founding father, Adam Smith, asked what determined the wealth of nations. In 1890, the great English economist Alfred Marshall said the quest for growth "gives to economic studies their chief and their highest interest."[17] Nobel Prize winner Robert Lucas confessed in a 1988 article that once one starts to think about economic growth, "It is hard to think about anything else." But this constant interest in a theory of growth was focused on the rich countries only. No economists paid much attention to the problems of poor countries. The League of Nations's 1938 *World Economic Survey*, prepared by the future Nobel Prize winner James Meade, included one paragraph on South America. Poor areas in Asia and Africa received no coverage at all.[18]

Suddenly after World War II, we policy experts, having ignored poor countries for centuries, now called for attention to their "urgent problems."[19] Economists had many theories as to how the newly independent poor countries could grow and catch up to the rich.

It was the bad luck of poor countries that the first generation of the development experts was influenced by two simultaneous historical events: the Great Depression and the industrialization of the Soviet Union through forced saving and investment. The depression and the large number of underemployed rural people in poor countries motivated development economist Sir Arthur Lewis to suggest a "surplus labor" model, in which only machinery was a constraint. Lewis suggested that building factories would soak up this labor without causing a decline in rural production.

Lewis and other development economists in the 1950s assumed a fixed ratio between people and machines, like one person per each machine. Because of surplus labor, machines (not labor) were the binding constraint on production. Production was proportional to machines, just as in Domar's theory. Lewis suggested that the supply of available workers was "unlimited" and cited a particular example of an economy that had grown through pulling in excess labor from the countryside: the Soviet Union.

Lewis said that "the central fact of economic development is rapid capital accumulation."[20] Since growth was proportional to investment, you could estimate that proportion and get a required amount of investment for a given growth target. For example, suppose that you got one percentage point of growth for every four percentage points of investment. A country that wanted to triple growth from 1 percent to 4 percent had to raise its investment rate from 4 percent of GDP to 16 percent of GDP. The 4 percent GDP growth would give a per capita growth rate of 2 percent if population growth was 2 percent. At a 2 percent per year rate of growth, income per capita would double every thirty-six years. Investment had to keep ahead of population growth. Development was a race between machines and motherhood.

How do you get investment high enough? Say that current national saving is 4 percent of GDP. The early development economists thought that poor countries were so poor they had little hope of increasing their saving. There was thus a "financing gap" of 12 percent of GDP between the "required investment" (16 percent of GDP) and the current 4 percent of GDP level of national savings. So Western donors should fill the "financing gap" with foreign aid, which will make the required investment happen, which in turn will make the target output growth happen. (I will henceforth use *financing gap approach* as equivalent nomenclature to *Harrod-Domar model*.)

The early development economists were hazy about how long it took for aid to increase investment and in turn increase growth, but in practice they expected quick payoff: this year's aid will go into this year's investment, which will go into next year's GDP growth.

The idea that growth was proportional to investment was not new. Domar ruefully mentioned in his 1957 book that an earlier set of economists very concerned about growth, Soviet economists of the 1920s, had already used the same idea. N. A. Kovalevskii, the editor of *Planned Economy*, in March 1930 used the growth-proportional-to-investment idea to project Soviet growth, exactly the way that economists were going to use it from the 1950s through the 1990s.[21] Not only had the Soviet experience inspired the Harrod-Domar model, but the Soviets themselves should get some of the credit (or debit, as it turned out) for the invention of the model.

The Stages of Rostow

The next step in the evolution of the financing gap was to persuade rich nations to fill the gap with aid. In 1960, W. W. Rostow published his best-selling book, *The Stages of Economic Growth*. Of the five stages he projected, the stage that stuck in peoples' minds was the "takeoff into self-sustained growth." Yet the only determinant of output take-off that Rostow cited was investment increasing from 5 to 10 percent of income. Since this was almost exactly what Sir Arthur Lewis had said six years earlier, "takeoff" just reasserted Domar and Lewis with vivid images of planes swooping off runways.

Rostow tried to show that the investment-led takeoff fit the stylized facts. Stalin's Russia influenced Rostow a great deal, as it had everyone else; it fit the takeoff story. Then Rostow considered a number of historical and Third World cases. His own evidence was weak, however: only three of fifteen cases he cited fit the story of an investment-led takeoff. Nobel laureate Simon Kuznets in 1963 found his own independent historical evidence even less supportive of Rostow's story: "In no case do we find during the takeoff periods the acceleration in the rate of growth of total national product implied in Professor Rostow's assumptions of a doubling (or more) in the net capital formation proportion."[22] (But stylized facts never die. Three decades later, a leading economist would write: "One of the important stylized facts of world history is that massive increases in saving precede significant takeoffs in economic growth.")[23]

The Soviet Scare and Foreign Aid

Regardless of the evidence, Rostow's *Stages* drew a lot of attention to the poor nations. Rostow was not the only or even the most important advocate for foreign aid, but his arguments are illustrative.

Rostow played on cold war fears in *Stages*. (The subtitle was *A Non-Communist Manifesto*). Rostow saw in Russia "a nation surging, under Communism, into a long-delayed status as an industrial power of the first order," a common view of that time. Hard as it is to imagine today, many American opinion makers thought that the Soviet system was superior for sheer output production, even if inferior in individual freedoms. In issues of *Foreign Affairs* in the 1950s, writers noted the Soviet willingness to "extract large forced savings," the advantage of which "it is difficult to overemphasize." In "economic power," they will "grow faster than we do." Observers warned that the competitor derived "certain advantages" from the "centralized character of the operation." There was danger that the Third World, attracted by "certain advantages," would go communist.[24]

It is too easy today in hindsight to mock these fears. When I first visited the Soviet Union in August 1990, almost everyone by then had belatedly realized that the Soviet Union was still a poor country, not "an industrial power of the first order." As I sat sweating in a tiny Intourist hotel room with sealed windows, with air-conditioning that had broken down under Khruschev and hadn't been fixed yet, with less than irresistible prostitutes trying to break down my door ("Hello I Natasha, I lonely"), I wondered how the Soviets managed to fool us for so long. Today Russian per capita income is estimated to be less than one-sixth of American per capita income. (With an economist's gift for prophecy, I said to my companions in 1990, "This place will be booming in no time!" Actually growth has been negative every year since 1990.)

Nevertheless, at the time Rostow felt the need to demonstrate to the Third World that communism was not "the only form of effective state organization that can ... launch a take-off" and offered in its place a noncommunist way: Western nations could provide Third World nations with aid to fill the "financing gap" between the necessary investment for takeoff and actual national saving. Rostow used the financing gap approach to figure out the necessary investment for "takeoff."[25] The role of private financing was ignored, since international capital flows to the poor countries were minuscule.

The Soviet scare worked. U.S. foreign aid had already increased a lot under Eisenhower in the late 1950s, to whom Rostow was an adviser. Rostow had also caught the eye of an ambitious senator named John F. Kennedy, who, with advice from Rostow, successfully got the Senate to pass a foreign aid resolution in 1959. After Kennedy became president, he sent a message to Congress in 1961 calling for increased foreign aid: "In our time these new nations need help ... to reach the stage of self-sustaining growth ... for a special reason. Without exception, they are all under Communist pressure."

Rostow was in government throughout the administrations of Kennedy and Johnson. Under Kennedy, foreign aid increased by 25 percent in constant dollars. Under Johnson, American foreign aid reached its historical maximum of $14 billion in 1985 dollars, equivalent to 0.6 percent of American GDP. Rostow and other like-minded economists had triumphed on aid.

The United States decreased its foreign aid after that peak under Johnson, but other rich countries more than compensated. Between 1950 and 1995, Western countries gave $1 trillion (measured in 1985 dollars) in aid.[26] Since virtually all of the aid advocates used the financing gap approach, this was one of the largest policy experiments ever based on a single economic theory.

Don't Forget to Save

There was a remarkable degree of consensus that the aid to investment to growth dogma "was substantially valid," as a popular text
by Jagdish Bhagwati in 1966 put it. But there were warnings about
excessive indebtedness to donors on the low-interest loans that made
up part of the aid. Turkey had already developed debt servicing
problems on its past aid loans, this early text noted. One early aid
critic, P. T. Bauer, sarcastically (but presciently) noted in 1972 that
"foreign aid is necessary to enable underdeveloped countries to service the subsidized loans ... under earlier foreign aid agreements."[27]

The obvious way to avoid a debt problem with official donors was
to increase national saving. Bhagwati said this was a job for the state:
the state had to raise taxes to generate public savings.[28] Rostow predicted the recipient country would naturally increase its savings as it
took off, so that after "ten or fifteen years" the donors could anticipate that aid would be "discontinued." (We are still waiting for that
apotheosis forty years later.)

Hollis Chenery stressed the need for national saving even more
heavily in his application of the financing gap approach. Chenery
and Alan Strout in 1966 started off in the usual way with a model in
which aid will "fill the temporary gap between investment ability
and saving ability."[29] Investment then goes into growth. But they
also assumed a high rate of saving out of the increase in income. This
saving rate had to be high enough for the country eventually to
move into "self-sustained" growth, in which it financed its investment needs out of its own savings. They suggested that donors
relate "the amount of aid supplied to the recipient's effectiveness in
increasing the rate of domestic saving." (Donors have yet to follow
this suggestion thirty-four years later.)

The Financing Gap Meets the Computer

Economists computerized Chenery's version of the financing gap at
the World Bank in 1971, where Chenery was now the chief economic
adviser to Bank president Robert McNamara, who was delighted to
get a tool that gave precise aid requirements for each country.

A Bank economist, John Holsen, developed over a long weekend
what he called the minimum standard model (MSM). Holsen expected
the "minimum" model to have a useful life of about six weeks.[30]

He expected country economists to build more elaborate country-specific models to supplant it. (As it turned out, it is still being used today, twenty-nine years later. I was part of a unsuccessful attempt to revise it fundamentally eleven years ago, so it's partly my fault.) World Bank economists revised the MSM a couple of years later and renamed it the revised minimum standard model (RMSM).[31] The growth part of the RMSM was Harrod-Domar: the growth rate of GDP was proportional to last year's investment/GDP. Foreign aid and private finance were to fill the financing gap between saving and the necessary investment to get high growth.

The financing gap informed discussions with other donors over how much aid or other financing that country needed. Following Chenery—and equally unheeded—the RMSM creators cautioned that saving out of the additional income had to be high to avoid unsustainable debt. (Much Latin American and African debt indeed turned out to be unsustainable in the 1980s and 1990s.)

The failure of growth to respond to aid-financed investment did give economists pause, but there was a logical fallback for defenders of the financing gap approach. One leading development textbook (both recently and in earlier versions) gave what quickly became a new dogma: "Although physical capital accumulation may be considered a *necessary* condition of development, it has not proved *sufficient*."[32] Another leading development textbook echoed, "The basic reason why [the investment-led takeoff] didn't work was not because more saving and investment isn't a *necessary* condition—it is—but rather because it is not a *sufficient* condition."[33] We will see how the idea that investment is necessary but not sufficient works out in the data.

The Financing Gap Forever

The financing gap approach had a curious fate after its heyday in the 1960s and 1970s. It died out of the academic literature altogether, yet the ghost of it lives on. We economists in the international financial institutions (IFIs) today still use it to make aid, investment, and growth projections.

We IFI economists used the financing gap approach even when it clearly wasn't working. Total GDP in Guyana fell sharply from 1980 to 1990, as investment was increasing from 30 percent to 42 percent of GDP,[34] and while foreign aid every year was 8 percent of Guyana's GDP.[35] This was no triumph for the financing gap approach. Yet another World Bank report in 1993 argued that Guyana "will continue to need substantial levels of foreign capital inflows ... to provide sufficient resources to sustain economic growth."[36] The idea seems to be, "That didn't work, so let's try it again."

We IFI economists used the financing gap approach amid recovery from civil war. We World Bank economists programmed the Ugandan economy in 1996 to grow rapidly (at the ubiquitous growth target of 7 percent). With little savings and substantial investment requirements, this implied high foreign aid inflows. The report argued for the high aid because anything less "could be harmful for medium-term growth in Uganda, which requires external inflows."[37]

We IFI economists used the financing gap approach in the aftermath of macroeconomic crises. A World Bank report in 1995 told Latin Americans that "enhancing savings and investment by 8 percentage points of GDP would raise the annual growth figure by around 2 percentage points."[38] An Inter-American Bank report in 1995 worried about the Latin American "challenge of sustaining the level of investment necessary for continued output growth."[39] A World Bank report on Thailand in 2000 told the country that was the epicenter of the East Asian crisis that "private investment is the key to the resumption of growth."[40]

We IFI economists used the financing gap approach to train developing country officials. Courses still given today at the International Monetary Fund (IMF) and World Bank train developing-country officials to project investment requirements as proportional to the "target growth rate."[41]

We IFI economists used the financing gap approach amid the chaotic transition from communism to capitalism. A 1993 World Bank report on Lithuania said that "large amounts of external assistance will be required" in order to "provide the resources for critical investments" to stem the output decline.[42] A 1998 World Bank on Lithuania was still using the assumption that growth was proportional to investment. A 1997 report on war-ravaged Croatia said that "to achieve sustainable growth of 5–6 percent ... within the next three years ... [it] must achieve investment levels of 21–22 percent of GDP."[43]

How much aid and investment is needed to reach a growth target? A report by the European Bank for Reconstruction and Development (EBRD) in 1995 adroitly notes that these are central planners' questions—and then goes on to answer them anyway. The EBRD announced it was using the "Harrod-Domar growth equation" to project investment requirements. This equation warned the ex-communist countries that "investment finance of the order of 20 percent or more of GDP will be required" to reach "growth rates of 5 percent" The report noted that "conditional official assistance ... contributes to cover the gap between domestic savings and investment."[44]

So the circle of irony closes. The communist economies had inspired the financing gap approach, the cold war inspired the filling of the gap with aid, and now the capitalist economies strove to fill the financing gap for the ex-communist economies.[45]

Aid to Investment in the Light of Experience

As far as I know, nobody has checked the financing gap approach against actual experience. By the time that sufficient cross-country data became available, the model had already fallen out of favor in the academic literature. Yet as we have seen, the ghost of the model lives on in the determination of aid requirements and growth prospects of poor countries. Let's now test this model.

When we financing gap users calculated aid requirements as the excess of "required" investment over actual saving, our presumption was that aid would go one for one into investment. Moreover, aid givers talked about conditions that would require countries to increase their rate of national saving at the same time, which some like Rostow thought would even happen naturally. So aid combined with savings conditions should increase investment by even more than one to one. Let's see what actually happened.

We have eighty-eight countries on which data are available spanning the period 1965 to 1995.[46] The aid to investment link has to pass two tests for us to take it seriously. First, there should be a positive statistical association between aid and investment. Second, aid should pass into investment at least one for one: an additional 1 percent of GDP in aid should cause an increase of 1 percent of GDP in investment. (Rostow predicted investment would rise by even more than one for one because of increased saving by the aid recipient.) How did the aid to investment do on these tests? On the first test, only seventeen of eighty-eight countries show a positive statistical association between aid and investment.

Just six of these seventeen countries also pass the test of investment increasing at least one for one with aid. The magic six include two economies with trivial amounts of aid: Hong Kong (which got an average of 0.07 percent of GDP in aid, 1965–1995) and China (average of 0.2 percent of GDP). The other four—Tunisia, Morocco, Malta, and Sri Lanka—did have nontrivial amounts of aid. The other eighty-two countries fail the two tests.

These country-by-country results are reminiscent of the results of a 1994 study that found no relationship between aid and investment across countries. Unlike this study, I do not intend here to make a general statement about whether foreign aid is effective. There are many problems in doing such an evaluation, most of all the possibility that both aid and investment could be responding to some third factor. It could be that in any given country there was bad luck like a drought that caused investment to fall and aid to increase. I am only asking whether investment and aid jointly evolved the way that the users of the financing gap model expected. We financing gap advocates anticipated that aid would go into investment, not into tiding countries over droughts. According to my results, investment and aid did not evolve the way we expected.

The financing gap approach failed badly as a panacea because it violated this book's official motto: People respond to incentives. Think of the incentives facing the recipients of foreign aid. They invest in the future when they get a high return to their investments. They do not invest in the future when they do not get a high return to their investments. There is no reason to think that aid given just because the recipient is poor changes the incentives to invest in the future. Aid will not cause its recipients to increase their investment; they will use aid to buy more consumption goods. This is exactly what we found when we checked the aid-investment relationship: on balance there is no relationship.

Aid could have promoted investment instead of all going into consumption. As many aid advocates suggested, aid should have been made conditional on matching increases in a country's savings rate. That would have given the governments in poor countries incentives to increase their own savings (for example, cutting government consumption so as to increase government saving) and to promote private savings. The latter can be done by a combination of tax breaks for income that is devoted to saving and taxes on consumption. The increase in saving would have kept the aid recipients out of debt troubles and would have promoted as increase in investment. Having aid increase with country saving is the opposite of the current system, where a country with lower saving has a higher financing gap and so gets more aid.

Investment to Growth

The second link in the financing gap approach is the link from investment to growth. Does investment have a quick growth payoff, as the financing gap model assumed?

I start assuming the same short-run investment-growth relationship across all countries. I tried using four-year averages to assess the growth-investment relationship. (Five years is a common forecast horizon on country desks in the IFIs. Country economists usually project the first year from current business conditions, so four years is de facto the common horizon for projections.) The results with four-year averages do not bode well for the financing gap approach: there is no statistical association between growth in one four-year period and investment in the previous four-year period.[47]

Let's now allow the investment-growth relationship to vary across countries by examining the link from investment to growth individually for each country. We have 138 countries with at least ten observations on growth and investment. Again there are two tests of the investment-to-growth link. First, countries should display a positive statistical association between growth and last year's investment. Second, the investment-growth relationships should be in the "usual" range to give reasonable "financing gaps." The four economies that pass both tests are an unusual assortment: Israel, Liberia, Réunion (a tiny French colony), and Tunisia.[48]

Remembering the few countries where the aid-to-investment link worked as expected, I can now say that the financing gap approach fits one country: Tunisia. Before Tunisians throw a national celebration, I should point out that 1 success out of 138 countries is likely to have occurred by chance even if the model made no sense, which so far the evidence says it doesn't.

Is Investment Necessary in the Short Run?

For the other 137 countries, the ritual incantation of us practitioners at this point is that investment is necessary but not sufficient. I can test this idea by checking how many four-year-long high-growth episodes (7 percent and above) were accompanied by the necessary investment rates in the previous four years. Nine-tenths of the countries violate the "necessary" condition. At the short-run horizons at which we IFI economists work, there is no evidence that investment is either a necessary or a sufficient condition for high growth. In the longer run, accumulation of machines does go along with growth, but I will discuss in the next chapter how investment is not the causal force; instead it is technology.

Using the four-year averages for both growth and investment, let's also look at episodes where growth increased and see how often investment increased by the "required amount." During episodes of increased growth with four-year periods, investment increased by the "required amount" only 6 percent of the time. The other 94 percent of the episodes violated the "necessary condition." Empirically, increases in investment are neither necessary nor sufficient for increases in growth over the short to medium run.

To understand why the idea that growth is proportional to last period's investment doesn't work out in practice, remember that such a relationship assumed that machines were the constraint on production, because it assumed that laborers were perpetually in excess supply. Nobel laureate Robert Solow, whose model of growth I discuss in the next chapter, pointed out the problem with this assumption as long ago as 1956 (although his insight went unheeded by those of us in the IFIs for the succeeding four decades). If there is an abundant supply of laborers and a limited supply of machines, then companies will have a strong incentive to use technology that uses a lot of workers and few machines. For example, road construction projects in the labor-scarce United States use many jackhammers and relatively few workers. By contrast, road construction projects in labor-abundant India use many workers with picks breaking up rocks. The idea that investment is a rigid constraint on growth is incompatible with "people respond to incentives."

The surplus labor idea led to another cause for urgency to fill the gap for the "necessary" investment—if the investment is not forthcoming to generate enough output growth to absorb more of this excess labor, unemployment will increase. For example, a 1998 World Bank report on Egypt used the usual growth-proportional-to-investment idea, and then noted the alarming possibility that unemployment would shoot up to 20 percent of the labor force in 2002 (as opposed to 9.5 percent in 1998) if growth was only 2 percent. If on the other hand, growth were 6.5 percent (with the accompanying higher investment), unemployment in 2002 would be only 6.4 percent of the labor force.[49] The idea of low investment mechanically increasing unemployment is silly—it ignores again the possibility of substituting labor for machinery. If machines increase slowly because of low investment, then the presumably abundant workers will be substituted for the scarce machines. The surplus labor idea suggests that additional people have no effect on production at a given rate of investment, an idea strongly rejected by the evidence.

How could we have gotten more of a growth response from investment? It is true that as an economy grows, it will need more machines. But the reason that the rigid investment-and-growth relationship has not worked is that machinery investment is just one of many forms of increasing future production, and all the forms are responsive to incentives. If incentives to invest in the future are strong, then there will be more investment in machines, but also more adaptation of new technology (an important component of growth, as we will see in the next chapter). There will be more investment in machines, but also more investment in education and training. There will be more investment in machines, but also more investment in organizational capital (designing efficient institutions).

The multiple factors that affect growth cause the relationship between growth and investment to be loose and unstable. Growth fluctuates around an average for each country, while investment rates drift all over the place. Nevertheless, it is common in the IFIs to use the ratio of investment to growth (called the jaw-breaking name of Incremental Capital to Output Ratio, or ICOR) as an inverse measure of the "productivity" of investment. For example, the World Bank in a 2000 report on Thailand saw that one of the harbingers of the 1997–98 financial crisis was that the ICOR "was almost at its historical high in 1996."[50] Likewise a World Bank 2000 report on Africa attributed Africa's low and declining growth over 1970 to 1997 to low and declining investment productivity "as measured by the incremental capital-output ratio."[51] The ICOR is reified to the extent that it is seen as an independent causal factor, when it really is just the ratio of two things only loosely related. Even if growth declined for reasons totally unrelated to investment (like mismanaged banking systems in Thailand or kleptocratic governments in Africa), we could still tautologically say growth fell for an unchanged investment rate because the ICOR rose—that is, the ratio of growth to investment fell. We could equally say the price of apples fell because the price of oranges was unchanged and the price ratio of apples to oranges fell!

Rather than worrying about how much investment is "needed" to sustain a given growth rate, we should concentrate on strengthening incentives to invest in the future and let the various forms of investment play out how they may. (I talk more about how to do this at the end of this chapter and in future chapters.)

Jointly Checking the Aid-to-Investment and Investment-to-Growth Links

I can construct a scenario of what income a country would have achieved if the predictions of the financing gap approach had been correct and then compare the prediction to the actual outcome. The financing gap model predicts that aid goes into investment one to one, or more. I stick to the one-to-one prediction to be conservative. So investment to GDP will increase over the initial year by the amount that aid to GDP increases over the initial year. Then this investment will increase growth in the next period. This predicts total GDP growth. To get per capita growth, I subtract actual population growth.

I start with a comparison of what Zambians' actual average income to what would have been, $2 billion of aid later, if filling the financing gap had worked as predicted (figure 2.1). Zambia today would be an industrialized country with a per capita income of $20,000, instead of its actual condition as one of the poorest countries in the world with a per capita income of $600 (which is one-third lower than at independence). Zambia is one of the worst cases for the financing gap approach, because it already had a high investment rate before aid and it got a lot of aid. But Zambia's investment rate went down, not up, as the aid increased, and the investment in any case did not yield growth.[52]

What about the financing gap approach's predicted growth for all of the aid recipients? First, the countries' actual growth was more often than not lower than predicted growth. Second, the financing gap model did not successfully pick out the growth superstars. The most notable examples are the predicted superstars like Guinea-Bissau, Jamaica, Zambia, Guyana, Comoros, Chad, Mauritania,

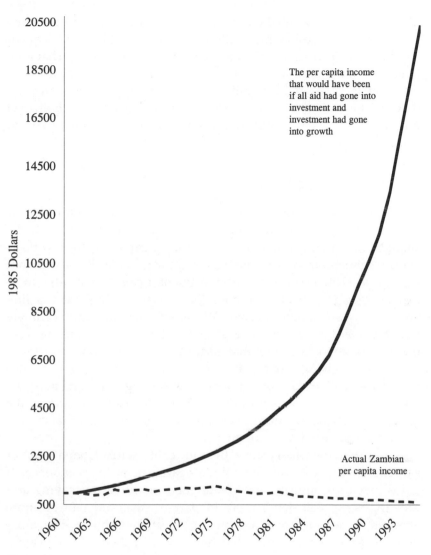

The per capita income
that would have been
if all aid had gone into
investment and
investment had gone
into growth

Actual Zambian
per capita income

Figure 2.1
The gap between the financing gap model and the actual outcome in Zambia

Mozambique, and Zimbabwe, countries that instead turned out to be growth disasters despite high initial investment and high subsequent aid. We have real superstars like Singapore, Hong Kong, Thailand, Malaysia, and Indonesia (superstars until very recently, at least) that the financing gap predictions did not pick up. These were countries that had low initial investment or low subsequent aid (or both) yet grew rapidly. There is virtually no association between predicted and actual growth.

Fifty Years Is Enough

The aid-financed investment fetish has led us astray on our quest for growth for fifty years. The model should finally be laid to rest. We should eliminate the notion of the financing gap altogether, with its spurious precision on how much aid a country needs. We should not attempt to estimate how much investment a country "needs" for a given target growth rate, because there is no stable short-run link between investment and growth. We should not attempt to estimate how much aid a country "needs" for a given growth rate, because there is no economic model that addresses that question.

Moreover, giving aid on the basis of the financing gap creates perverse incentives for the recipient, as was recognized long ago. The financing gap is larger, and aid larger, the lower the saving of the recipient. This creates incentives against the recipient's marshaling its own resources for development.

To return to the Ghana story, the sad reality is that Ghana is about as poor today as it was forty-three years ago at independence. If aid is given to countries that create good incentives for saving and growth, as we will detail more in part III, then aid will be more effective at helping countries on the quest for growth. The more hopeful reality is that Ghana has had a healthy 2 percent per capita growth rate since reforms (and fresh aid inflows) began after the low point in 1983.

Still, the fetish for achieving growth by building factories and machines proved amazingly resistant to blasted hopes. In the next chapter, we will see how a more flexible version of the machine fetish would be held out as a panacea for growth.

Intermezzo: Parmila

Parmila is an Indian widow in her early thirties. Her husband passed away last year after a prolonged illness, leaving her to fend for her seven-year-old son and three-year-old daughter. The land that her husband once owned had to be sold off to raise money for his expensive treatment. Today Parmila is left with no land and finds it extremely difficult to make ends meet.

Parmila comes from a well-off family in Khairplan village of Singhbhum district, but destitution has forced her to take up menial work despite her lineage. She earns her living by selling firewood, dehusking rice grains, and working as a daily laborer for local contractors. She collects wood from the nearby forests and dries it, then twice a week walks 8 kilometers to sell the wood at Jamshedpur market. She finds employment on farms in the months of Agrahayan and Poush (from mid-November to mid-January) dehusking rice. She dehusks 36 kilograms of rice a day working for nine hours; one-twelfth of her daily output is paid to her as wage. Thus, two weeks of work in each of the two months fetches her about 90 kilograms of rice in wages. Her daily household consumption of rice amounts to about 1 kilo, so the rice she earns as wages lasts for nearly three months. In addition, Parmila works for a local contractor and gets about ten days of work a month at a construction site. For this work, she is paid 25 rupees daily, which is less than half of the minimum wages set by the Minimum Wages Act. This work, however, is not available during the four months of the rainy season.

Parmila does not receive any support from her relatives or in-laws. Nevertheless, in spite of her destitution, she has high hopes for her two children, whom she regularly sends to the local village school. She even has plans to send them to Dimna Higher Middle School when they grow up. She plans to take up making puffed rice to save enough money to be able to send her two children to school.

Parmila has great self-respect and despite her woes refuses to be looked at with sympathy. "Even in times of acute crisis, I held my nerves and did not give in to circumstances. My God has always stood with me," says Parmila in a confident tone.[1]

3 Solow's Surprise: Investment Is Not the Key to Growth

Politicians are the same all over. They promise to build bridges, even where there are no rivers.

Nikita Khrushchev

Nobel laureate Robert Solow published his theory of growth in a couple of articles in 1956 and 1957. His conclusion surprised many, and still surprises many today: investment in machinery cannot be a source of growth in the long run. Solow argued that the only possible source of growth in the long run is technological change. Solow in the 1957 article calculated that technological change accounted for seventh-eighths of U.S. growth per worker over the first half of the twentieth century.

While economists applied (and still apply) Solow's model of growth to many poor countries, many are reluctant to accept his view that technological change, not investment, drives long-run growth. While development practitioners slowly weaned themselves from the Harrod-Domar conclusion that growth was proportional to investment in the short run, they continued to believe that investment was the dominant determinant of growth in the long run.

Economists call the belief that increasing buildings and machinery is the fundamental determinant of growth *capital fundamentalism.* Whether capital fundamentalism holds is fiercely debated in the academic literature on growth; we will see in the next chapter what happens when the notion of "capital" is extended to include skills and education—human capital. In this chapter, we will see that capital fundamentalism is incompatible with "people respond to incentives."

But capital fundamentalism has few doubters in the international financial institutions. Paging through their recent reports, one finds statements like these: "The adjustment experience of sub-Saharan Africa has demonstrated that to achieve gains in real per capita GDP an expansion in private saving and investment is key" (International Monetary Fund, 1996).[1] Latin America too must meet "the challenge of sustaining the level of investment necessary for continued output growth" (Inter-American Development Bank, 1995).[2] In the Middle East, "Improving the investment performance—in both human and physical assets—is an important determinant of the ... region's ability to grow" (IMF, 1996).[3] In East Asia, "accumulation of productive assets is the foundation of economic growth" (World Bank, 1993).[4] In case you have any remaining doubts, you should know that "additional investment is the answer—or part of the answer—to most policy problems in the economic and social arena" (United Nations 1996).[5]

But the conventional wisdom that investment in buildings and machinery is the key to long-run development is another panacea that has not met expectations.

Solow's Shocker

To see how Solow arrived at his surprising conclusion that investment cannot be the source of growth, let's go back to his original vision of growth in his 1956 article, with the 1957 follow-up article. The more men and machines an economy had, the higher its production was. Over time production would grow as we invested in more machines and had more workers.

When we say "growth," what we mean is that each person's standard of living should keep increasing. The only way that we can have a higher standard living for each of us, on average, is if each of us produces more goods, on average. So what we are interested in is production per worker, sometimes called *labor productivity*.

We want production per worker to increase, and there are only two inputs into production: machines and workers. So you might think that the way to increase production per worker is to increase machines faster than the number of workers is increasing. In other words, the way to increase production per worker is to increase machines per worker.

But increasing machines per worker immediately runs into problems. As we increase machines per worker, eventually each worker will be using more than one machine at once, dashing madly from one machine to another, like Charlie Chaplin in the movie *Modern Times*. It's hard to believe that anything good will happen to production from giving one more machine to a worker who already has eight of them. This is diminishing returns.

Diminishing returns has a simple and unavoidable logic: increasing one ingredient of production relative to another ingredient indefinitely cannot increase production indefinitely. When you increase machines relative to workers, the return to each additional machine will get lower and lower.

To see diminishing returns in action, suppose for a moment that one ingredient is fixed, and you try to increase the other one.

The Flour Next Time

Today I am making my kids' favorite breakfast food, pancakes. My pancake recipe calls for one cup milk and two cups Bisquick flour. These proportions are not totally rigid. I think my pancake connoisseurs will still eat them if I make the pancakes thinner by using more milk than the recipe calls for.

Then I realize that I have just barely the right amount of Bisquick for pancakes sufficient for my three children. Suddenly my daughter Rachel reminds me that her friend Eve is coming over for brunch. I knew this but forgot. Concealing the bowl of pancake batter from her view, I slip another cup of milk into the bowl. Nobody will notice. Then my son, Caleb, reminds me that his friend, pancake-devouring Kevin, is coming over for brunch too. I slip some more milk into the batter. Maybe they won't notice. Then my co-parent comes in and reminds me that my preschooler Grace's friend Colleen is coming too. In desperation I dump yet more milk into the pancake batter. Fifteen minutes later, the eating audience rejects the world's thinnest pancakes in disgust.

This is diminishing returns in action: increasing one ingredient while the other ingredient is unchanged does not enable me to achieve sustained growth in production of pancakes. Diminishing returns sets in to the ingredient that I am trying to increase (milk) while the other ingredient (Bisquick) is unchanged. I indeed have diminishing returns to milk. The effect of the first cup of milk on my pancake production was very favorable. Without that cup of milk I have nothing but dry Bisquick; with it I have at least a thick pancake. But when I have already dumped in three cups of milk for only two cups of flour, adding yet one more cup of milk has a pitiful effect on pancake production.

We can increase production of GDP for a given number of workers by increasing machines per person. If there were no machines to begin with, this is Okay; then an additional machine would increase output a lot. When there were already plenty of machines, an additional machine would increase output very little.

How severe these diminishing returns are going to be depends on how important capital is in production. The diminishing returns in my pancake experiment depended on how important the ingredient was that I tried to expand by itself. My failed attempt to expand pancake production by increasing one ingredient would have been even more disastrous if I had been increasing one of the more minor ingredients, like salt, holding everything else constant. I don't think my customers would like the results if I tried to double pancake production by adding more and more salt to an unchanging amount of flour and milk.

If a minor ingredient like salt had been the only ingredient in fixed supply, on the other hand, I would have had a lot more potential to expand pancake production. If I had run out of salt and still had plenty of flour and milk left, I would have been in fine shape for the demands of the children. I think I could have got away with it if I doubled flour and milk together, leaving salt unchanged. A lot of the debate about capital fundamentalism will turn on how important capital is as an ingredient to production.

The reason that Solow's diminishing returns to investment had particular fury was that buildings and machines are a surprisingly minor ingredient in total GDP. We can get a measure of the importance of capital in the United States by calculating the share of capital income in total income. *Capital income* means all the income that accrues to the direct or indirect owners of the buildings and machines: corporate profits, stock dividends, and interest income on loans (since loans finance part of investment). Solow estimated capital income to be about one-third of total GDP in the United States in his 1957 article.[6] It is still about one-third of total income today.[7] The other two-thirds of income is wage income, that is, income to workers.

Thus, capital accounts for only one-third of total production, and workers account for two-thirds of total production. If capital accounts for only one-third of output, then diminishing returns to investment are going to be severe. When machines are scarce, the additional output from one more machine will be high. When machines are abundant, additional output from one more machine will be low.

Not the Way to Grow

Diminishing returns all seems simple and obvious, but it led to Solow's surprise. Increasing machines was *not* a feasible way to sustain growth. If an economy tried to grow by buying more and more machines, then there might be extremely high growth at the beginning when machines were scarce. But diminishing returns means that growth would fall as machines become abundant relative to the labor force. If machines per person grew at a constant rate, eventually the growth of output per person would drop to zero.

Another surprising implication of Solow's view was that saving will not sustain growth. The saving diverts money from consumption today toward buying machinery for production tomorrow, but this does *not* raise the long-run rate of growth, because machinery cannot be a source of long-run growth. So high saving economies would achieve no higher sustained growth than a low-saving economy would. Growth in both cases would drop to zero as the unavoidable diminishing returns to increasing machines set in. The high-saving economy would have higher income than the low-saving economy, but neither would be able to sustain growth.

Here was Solow's surprise: the simple logic of production suggested that growth of output per worker could not be sustained. Yet the United States and many other industrial economies had already sustained economic growth of 2 percent per worker for two centuries. How did we observe sustained growth of output per worker when such sustained growth is not logically possible?

It's Technology, Stupid

Solow's solution to his surprising paradox was technological change. Technological change would progressively economize on the ingredient in fixed supply: labor. In other words, technological change keeps making a given amount of labor go further.

Solow argued that technological progress happened for noneconomic reasons like advances in basic science. Judging by the steady
advance of the technological frontier in the United States, it was
plausible to assume a constant rate of technological progress. It was
this rate of technological progress that determined long-run growth
of income per person.

Think of technology as a blueprint that arranges the workers and
machines. Technological change means these blueprints get better
and better. Say that the workers first had blueprints telling each of
them to follow the item being manufactured all the way through the
production process. I haul the raw material from the pile out back,
then carry it to the melting-down machine, and I melt it down. I next
carry the molten slop over to the molding machine and mold the slop
into a product. Then I take the molded product over to the finishing
machine, and I finish it. Then I carry it over to the painting machine,
and I paint it. I throw the product into the shipment truck. Then I
get into the shipment truck and drive it over to the house of the
customer who had ordered the product. I take the customer's money
and go to the bank to deposit it and then drive back to the plant.
Then I haul some more raw material from the pile out back, carry it
over to the melting-down machine ...

Then I get a new blueprint in the mail, courtesy of a certain Mr.
H. Ford of Dearborn, Michigan. Mr. Ford suggests that it would be
more efficient to have each worker stay at one machine and have the
product rather than the workers move. Mr. Ford suggests installing
a conveyor belt to carry the product from one machine to the next.
So now I stay put at one machine, the painting machine. All of the
time that I spent running from one machine to the next is eliminated.
I also get very skilled at painting. I can use the extra time and skill to
paint more products. Each of the other workers at the other machines
also has extra time to produce more. The new labor-saving blueprint
allows a given number of workers to produce more with the same
machines.[8]

If the new blueprint comes along at the same time as new machines
are added, then the technical leap forward will stave off diminishing
returns. I am more effective because of the more intelligent way of
arranging my labor time. The new blueprint effectively gives us more
workers, so effectively labor and machinery have both increased, and
there is no diminishing returns to machinery.

This example illustrates the general principle: technical change will avoid diminishing returns if it saves on the ingredient in fixed supply: labor. Each worker becomes more and more efficient thanks to better technology, so it seems as if there were more workers. The effective number of workers keeps up with the increasing number of machines, so diminishing returns never sets in.

In the long run, all of growth of production per worker has to be labor-saving technical change.

An Aside About the Luddite Fallacy

Some people believe labor-saving technological change is bad for the workers because it throws them out of work. This is the Luddite fallacy, one of the silliest ideas to ever come along in the long tradition of silly ideas in economics. Seeing why it's silly is a good way to illustrate further Solow's logic.

The original Luddites were hosiery and lace workers in Nottingham, England, in 1811.[9] They smashed knitting machines that embodied new labor-saving technology as a protest against unemployment (theirs), publicizing their actions in circulars mysteriously signed "King Ludd." Smashing machines was understandable protection of self-interest for the hosiery workers. They had skills specific to the old technology and knew their skills would not be worth much with the new technology. English government officials, after careful study, addressed the Luddites' concerns by hanging fourteen of them in January 1813.

The intellectual silliness came later, when some thinkers generalized the Luddites' plight into the Luddite fallacy: that an economy-wide technical breakthrough enabling production of the same amount of goods with fewer workers will result in an economy with—fewer workers. Somehow it never occurs to believers in Luddism that there's another alternative: produce more goods with the same number of workers. *Labor-saving technology* is another term for *output-per-worker-increasing technology*. All of the incentives of a market economy point toward increasing investment and output rather than decreasing employment; otherwise some extremely dumb factory owners are forgoing profit opportunities. With more output for the same number of workers, there is more income for each worker.

Of course, there could very well be some unemployment of workers who know only the old technology—like the original Luddites—and this unemployment will be excruciating to its victims. But workers *as a whole* are better off with more powerful output-producing technology available to them. Luddites confuse the shift of employment from old to new technologies with an overall decline in employment. The former happens; the latter doesn't. Economies experiencing technical progress, like Germany, the United Kingdom, and the United States, do not show any long-run trend toward increasing unemployment; they do show a long-run trend toward increasing income per worker.[10]

Solow's logic had made clear that labor-saving technical advance was the only way that output per worker could keep increasing in the long run. The neo-Luddites, with unintentional irony, denigrate the only way that workers' incomes can keep increasing in the long run: labor-saving technological progress.

The Luddite fallacy is very much alive today. Just check out such a respectable document as the annual *Human Development Report* of the United Nations Development Program. The 1996 *Human Development Report* frets about "jobless growth" in many countries. The authors say "jobless growth" happens whenever the rate of employment growth is not as high as the rate of output growth, which leads to "very low incomes" for millions of workers. The 1993 *Human Development Report* expressed the same concern about this "problem" of jobless growth, which was especially severe in developing countries between 1960 and 1973: "GDP growth rates were fairly high, but employment growth rates were less than half this."[11] Similarly, a study of Vietnam in 2000 lamented the slow growth of manufacturing employment relative to manufacturing output.[12] The authors of all these reports forgot that having GDP rise faster than employment is called *growth of income per worker*, which happens to be the only way that workers' "very low incomes" can increase.[13]

Transitions

Increases in machinery per worker could not be a source of long-run growth, but they could be a source of growth in the transition to the long-run path. An economy that started with very few machines would have a very high return to each additional machine. Because of these high returns, investment would temporarily bring high growth. As the machines accumulated, diminishing returns would set in, and growth would fall. Eventually the economy would settle down to a comfortable existence at the growth rate of labor-saving technologi-cal progress. So we *could* revive investment as an important source of growth if transitions are important relative to long-run growth.

However, there are problems with the idea that transitions are important relative to the long-run growth rate. If most growth comes from the transition to the long run, then there must have been very few machines originally. The return to those machines must have been very high, because they were so scarce. This means the return on machines—the interest rate—in the economy would be very high at the beginning. In fact, interest rates would have had to be ridicu-lously high; Robert King and Sergio Rebelo calculated that the U.S. interest rate would have had to be over 100 percent a century ago for transitional increases in capital per worker to explain U.S. growth. But the evidence we have on interest rates in the United States sug-gests that they have been relatively constant over time (certainly never 100 percent anyway); this confirms Solow's finding that U.S. growth was a long-run phenomenon, not a transitional movement from low to high capital.

There is also a logical problem with making transitions and in-vestment important in explaining growth. The assumption is that all economies are starting far away from their long-run position. Then investment in machinery will allegedly help the ones that started below their long-run position to grow rapidly (after which they will grow at the rate of technological change). The ones that started above their long-run position will grow slowly or even decline, until they settle back down at their long-run position (after which they will grow at the rate of technological change).

But the proponents of investment as the engine of growth have not supplied a good reason that all countries would be so far away from their long-run position. In the absence of such a reason, the most logical assumption is that most countries are close to the long-run position. After all, what has the long run been doing all this time?

Solow in the Tropics

Solow never mentioned income differences between countries as something that he was trying to explain. He applied his theory only to growth in the United States, where the key fact was constant growth over a long period. He never mentioned tropical countries in any of his writings; in fact, he never applied his model to any other country besides the United States Solow is not to blame for how his model was applied to the tropical countries. However, his model became the basic theory of growth taught in economics classes. Economists in the 1960s did apply the Solow framework to explaining a wide variety of growth experiences, including the poor tropical countries.

Here's how it would work in explaining cross-country differences. All countries are assumed to have access to the same technology and the same rate of technological progress. The thinking is that there is no reason that major technological breakthroughs that happen in one country cannot be implemented in other countries. (That doesn't mean that the countries *do* implement them; it means they *could* implement them). Once the blueprints are available in one country, the same blueprints could be used in any other country.

So we rule out differences in available technology. Then the only reason some countries are poorer than others is that they have started with very little machinery. Poor tropical countries will have higher returns to machines than will the rich temperate countries. Poor tropical countries will have strong incentives to grow more rapidly than the mature temperate economies that are growing at the rate of technical progress. Eventually the poor tropics will catch up to the rich temperate zone, and all will grow at the rate of technical progress.

Any country that starts out with low capital will offset this unlucky heritage with very high returns to capital. Since international finance capital flows to countries with the highest rate of return (people respond to incentives), international finance capital will flow to this high-return, low-capital country. The unlucky country will catch up to the more fortunate countries, erasing the memory of its unlucky beginnings. The incentives guarantee that the poor will grow faster than the rich. You can see how nicely this view fits with the postwar optimism about development I described in the previous chapter.

After the failure of growth in many poor countries, the problems with the application of Solow's vision to explain income differences across countries became apparent. Fellow Nobel laureate Robert Lucas pointed out one of the big problems with the naive application of the Solow vision to cross-country income differences. American income per person is fifteen times larger than Indian income per person. In the Solow framework, with technology the same across countries, this income difference could arise only because U.S. workers have more machines than do Indian workers. How many times more machines would the U.S. workers be required to have to explain an income superiority of 15 times? Since machinery is not very important as an ingredient in production, the answer is: a lot. Lucas's calculation implied that each American worker would have to have around 900 times more machines than each Indian worker.[14] American workers do have many more machines, but not that much more. Those who have done the calculations find that American workers have only about twenty times more capital than Indian workers.

Why is it necessary that Indian workers have such an exorbitant superiority—900 times more machines—to explain an income difference of 15 times? It all goes back to the slight role of capital in production: capital accounts for only about a third of all production. Explaining income differences across countries with a relatively minor ingredient like capital doesn't work. Accounting for all cross-country income differences with Solow's model would require a gargantuan difference in machines per worker.

This should have been—but wasn't—foreseen. After all, Solow himself had shown why machines could not explain differences in income across time for the same country, like the increase in U.S. output per worker over forty years: because machines would have to have been more relatively scarce at the beginning than they really were. It is the same logic that shows why machines cannot explain large differences in income across countries rather than across time.

But the solution to the diminishing-returns problem that Solow advanced for growth in the long run in one country—technical progress determined by noneconomic causes like basic science—does not work across countries. It could make sense to assume that technology changes over time for noneconomic reasons like advances in science. But to say that countries have different growth rates because they have different rates of technological progress for some mysterious noneconomic reason is not very satisfying. This is just answering the question of why growth rates differ by saying that growth rates differ—which leads us back to economic incentives. Technology must vary across countries for economic reasons. If technology is so powerful as to explain sustained income growth over time in the same country, it is the logical candidate to explain big income differences between countries. And if technology differs between countries, there must be strong economic incentives to get better technology. I take up the idea of technology responding to incentives in Part III.

Returns and Flows

We haven't even gotten to the worst part about the idea that machinery was the key to development. Lucas also calculated the implied rate of return to machines. Indian machinery should be 900 times scarcer than U.S. machinery if we explain all of the U.S.-India income difference with differences in machinery. Lucas used the Solow principle that machines have higher returns where they are scarce and calculated that the profit rate yielded by Indian machines should be 58 times larger if they are so much scarcer. These super-returns are the counterpart to King and Rebelo's calculation that the return to capital would have had to be over 100 percent a century ago if we explained U.S. growth with transitional capital accumulation. With such huge incentives to invest in poor countries, Lucas wondered, "Why doesn't capital flow from rich to poor countries?"

An answer might be that poor countries have disadvantages to the investor like political instability, corruption, and the risk of expropriation. But these differences in rates of return are too large to be canceled out by such factors. The foreign investor in India still comes out ahead even if he only can get out of the country two rupees, on average, of every one hundred rupees of profit. Nobody thinks that the probability of expropriation in India is 98 percent. Even spectacularly venal governments do not attain a theft rate, on average over many years, of ninety-eight cents on the dollar. Even allowing for reasonable Indian political risk, Lucas argued, one should observe capital fleeing from New York to New Delhi. People should respond to incentives.

That didn't happen. In the 1990s, the U.S. economy had a gross inflow of new loans and investments from the rest of the world equal to $371 for each and every American every year. Over the same period, the loans and investments coming into India worked out to an inflow every year for each and every Indian of—four cents. The incentives to invest in India were not there.

There was nothing peculiar about India's paucity of foreign capital for a poor country. In 1990, the richest 20 percent of world population received 92 percent of portfolio capital gross inflows; the poorest

20 percent received 0.1 percent of portfolio capital inflows. The richest 20 percent of the world population received 79 percent of foreign direct investment; the poorest 20 percent received 0.7 percent of foreign direct investment. Altogether, the richest 20 percent of the world population received 88 percent of private capital gross inflows; the poorest 20 percent received 1 percent of private capital gross inflows.

The Growth That Wasn't

The most important evidence against the Solow vision applied across countries was the failure of growth in many poor countries. With high returns to scarce capital, the poor countries had every incentive to grow faster than the rich countries. The poorer the country, the faster the growth should have been. The poor shall inherit the growth. It didn't work out that way.

Ironically, the first economists to recognize the failure of growth in many poor countries were not specialists in poor countries at all. Development economists who did follow poor countries were certainly aware that things were going badly wrong in Africa and Latin America, but they didn't seem to notice the challenge to the old growth paradigm. Instead it took a rich-country economist like Paul Romer to look up the data and point out that the old paradigm was not working.

Romer used data on over a hundred countries from the compilation of country incomes by Robert Summers and Alan Heston. At the time of his presentation at the National Bureau of Economic Research Macroeconomics Annual Conference in 1987, he had data for growth between 1960 and 1981. He showed that the poor countries were not growing any faster than the rich countries. He demonstrated that the Solow prediction applied to tropical countries had failed.

Romer was showing 1960–1981 data to illustrate the failure of the prediction that the poor grow faster. Ironically, these were the good years for poor countries. The poor countries did even worse both before and after these years that supplied the original damaging blow to the old Solow paradigm applied to the tropics.

The last year in Romer's data set, 1981, was also the last good year for many poor countries. As we will see in chapter 5, Latin America and sub-Saharan Africa had two lost decades for economic growth after 1981. The Middle East and North Africa went into the tank a little later. Since 1981, poor countries have not only not caught up to rich countries; they have done worse than rich countries. They are losing ground.

The poorest three-fifths of countries have had nearly zero or slightly negative growth of income per person since 1981. The bottom two-fifths of countries, already doing badly over the 1960 to 1981 period, continued to do badly between 1981 and 1998. The middle fifth of countries, which had done well between 1960 and 1981, did badly between 1981 and 1998. The richest 20 percent of countries continue to have a positive growth rate of about 1 percent per person. The next richest fifth of countries, which includes the East Asian super-stars, also had respectable growth on average.

Rich countries had some slowdown in growth. The United States had growth per person of 1.1 percent over the 1981 to 1998 time frame compared to 2.2 percent between 1960 and 1980. But this slowdown is nothing compared to Nigeria's change in per capita growth per year from plus 4.8 percent over the 1960–1980 period to minus 1.5 percent between 1981 and 1998.

Despite all the moaning and groaning by rich peoples about slow growth, they have done much better on average than the poor countries over the last half century. The ratio of the richest country's per capita income to that of the poorest country has risen sharply over that period. The rich have grown richer; the poor have stagnated (figure 3.1).

For the whole period 1960 to 1999, the poorest countries did significantly worse than the rich countries, with the poorest two-fifths barely mastering positive growth. The poorest four-fifths of countries in 1960 (including only those countries on which we have available data) roughly correspond to what later became known as the Third World. Seventy percent of these Third World countries grew more slowly over the whole period than the median growth of 2.4 percent per capita for the richest countries. They were falling behind, not catching up.

The Mark of History

Now that it was apparent that this prediction of faster growth of poor countries was not working out, economists started asking some pointed questions about poor countries in earlier periods. Economists had taken it as a given that poor countries were poor when they started applying the Solow model to the tropics in the 1960s.

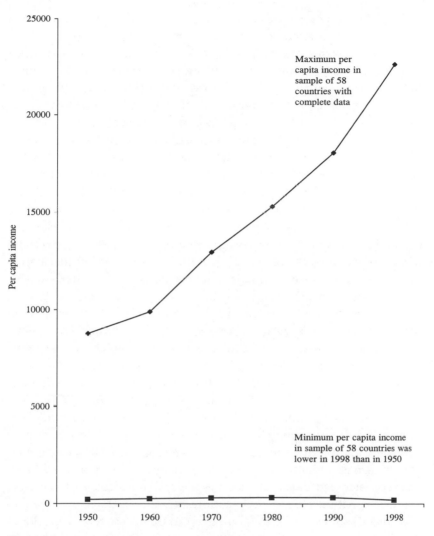

Figure 3.1
The maximum per capita income has grown strongly over the last half century, while the minimum per capita income has stagnated.

Nobody in the 1960s seemed to be asking how the poor nations had gotten to be so much poorer than the rich nations.

A moment's thought supplied the answer, although this moment of thought didn't come along until much later. The poor countries had gotten to be poorer than the rich countries by growing more slowly over some previous period. There had to be some primordial time, back between the Adam and Eve era and now, when the incomes of nations were much more equal. Since the incomes of nations are remarkably unequal now, there must have been a strong process of divergence of national incomes, contradicting the prediction of the Solow model applied across countries that nations' incomes would converge to each other.

Lant Pritchett of the Kennedy School of Government at Harvard crystallized this moment of thought in a recent article.[15] The reasoning is straightforward. The very poor nations today are just barely above the subsistence level in income per person. Subsistence means not starving to death. Therefore, the very poor nations today must have had about the same income a century or two ago as they do today. It couldn't have been less, because that would mean they were below subsistence a century or two ago, which is impossible since they lived to tell the tale. The very rich nations were also much closer to the subsistence level a century or two ago, since we do have data showing they have had substantial growth of income per person over the last century or two. Therefore, the gap between the very richest and the very poorest has grown over the past century or two.

If there's any remaining doubt, you can get data on today's poor countries. An indefatigable economic historian, Angus Maddison, has reconstructed data from 1820 to 1992 on a sample of twenty-six countries. Although the poor countries were underrepresented in Maddison's sample, it is apparent even so that there has been a lot of divergence. The ratio of the richest country—the United States—to the poorest country—Bangladesh—today is about thirty times. The ratio of the richest to poorest in 1820 was only about three times (figure 3.2). All of today's eight poor nations in the Maddison sample were also at or near the bottom in 1820. (The historically highest-ranked nation of today's eighth poorest, Mexico, was already the tenth poorest in 1820.) The countries that were at the bottom in 1820 largely stayed at the bottom; the richest countries increased their incomes by a factor of ten or more.

This is a remarkable outcome. For today's rich countries, more than 90 percent of today's incomes have been created since 1820. Yet

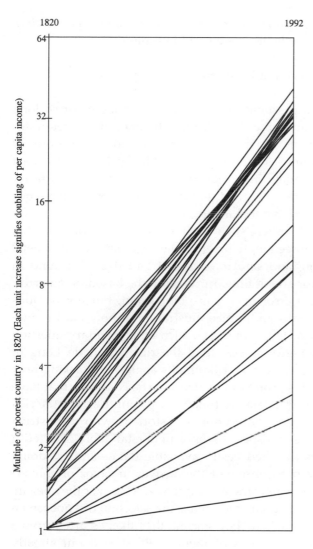

Figure 3.2
The rich got richer, 1820–1992

the income they had attained nearly two centuries ago was already a meaningful predictor whether they would become rich.

The Winners Write Economic History

So why was there a presumption in economic thought for so long that the poor catch up to the rich? William Baumol of Princeton, for example, had a famous paper in which he showed that a group of sixteen industrial countries had caught up to the leader over the past century. The poor among this group of countries had grown faster than the rich. Therefore, he argued that there was a general tendency toward convergence of national incomes.[16]

How had Baumol gotten such a different conclusion to what would later be the seemingly irrefutable argument of Pritchett? Baumol's conclusion, and similar ones that had floated around in economic thought for a long time, turns out to be based on an error. (It's an unmistakable error once you point it out, but not obvious before you point it out—and a nice illustration of how hard economists have to work to figure out even such an elementary question of whether the poor grow faster than the rich.) Brad de Long of Berkeley pointed out the error in Baumol's analysis by asking how Baumol had chosen his group of countries.[17] The countries that have easily available historical data are today's rich countries. It's the rich countries that can afford the economic historians who reconstruct long series of income statistics. Baumol understandably selected a sample of countries that had easily available data—and by doing this unintentionally predetermined the answer in favor of convergence. Naturally these countries, all rich today, wherever they began, will seem to converge to each other. Since the selection did not screen any out on the basis of where they started, they likely started from a variety of circumstances. Some of them likely started out already relatively rich and others relatively poor. Since they all wound up rich at the end—because that's the way Baumol implicitly chose the group—it's a lock that the initially poor in the group of rich-at-the-end countries will have grown faster than the initially rich.

This bias explains why Baumol went astray (as he graciously admitted once de Long pointed it out). More generally, this story helps explain why there was such a bias in economic discussions for so long to assume convergence of national incomes. Economists looked mainly at those that were winners at the end, because those were the countries that had the good-quality data. (Also, economists from rich countries prefer to talk about and visit other rich countries.) The winners write economic history.

Even Maddison's sample suffered a lot from the selection bias toward winners, as it includes only eight countries that the World Bank today classifies as poor—less than a third of the sample. Since poor nations make up the vast majority of all countries in the world, this is still a severe bias in favor of those that have wound up rich today. The Maddison sample whose 1820 income can be guessed has no country from Africa, for example. This Africa data shortage has everything to do with Africa's poverty. Chad today does not support a lot of economic historians rooting around in their country's past. Already poor (and illiterate) Chad in 1820 did not have a government statistics department churning out figures. From the reasoning that today's poor countries cannot have grown much, it is clear that we would see even more evidence for the rich-getting-richer in a more complete sample.

Even my discussion of trends over the 1960 to 1999 period was biased toward the winners at the end. Virtually all winners at the end have good data; the countries that have run into disasters often do not have complete data. I can check this by looking at the World Bank classification of countries at the end of the period as either industrial (members of the Organization of Economic Cooperation and Development) or developing. My calculation of trends over the 1960 to 1999 period, which already showed the poor countries growing more slowly, used only the 100 countries that have data for 1960 and 1999. Only one industrial country lacks complete data: Germany, because of the difficulty of getting consistent data before and after unification. In contrast, half of the countries the World Bank classifies as developing in 1999 lack complete data. So my 1960 to 1999 sample was biased toward the winners at the end.

I already showed that a tendency for the poor countries to grow more slowly over the 1960 to 1999 period and the rich countries to grow faster. Now I know, because of the bias toward the winners, that even this conclusion was understated. There were likely even bigger disasters among poor countries that dropped out of the data altogether—such as Myanmar, Zaire (Congo), Liberia, Chad, and Haiti. Poor economic performance makes it hard to keep statistical offices running. For example, Zaire's statistical office had collapsed by 1999, but earlier data show long-run growth of −2.4 percent per year.

Growth Accounting Meets the Gang of Four

The most straightforward way to assess the importance of capital accumulation is to account for how much of output growth per worker is explained by capital growth per worker. The contribution of capital growth per worker to output growth per worker is equal to the share of capital in production times the growth rate of capital. As I have already noted, the share of capital in production is about one-third, so if capital per worker were growing at 3 percent, then the contribution of capital to growth would be one percentage point. If growth of output per worker were 3 percent, then we would say that capital accounted for one-third of the growth per worker. The part of growth that is unexplained by capital accumulation will be the part explained by technological progress. The contribution of labor-saving technological progress to growth is equal to the labor share (which is one minus the capital share) times the growth rate of technical change. So if labor-saving technological change were growing at 3 percent, then we would say technological change accounted for two percentage points of the 3 percent growth.

Alwyn Young of the Chicago Business School did this kind of calculation for the fast-growing East Asian economies—the so-called gang of four (Korea, Taiwan, Singapore, and Hong Kong). He reached the conclusion that most of the fast growth of East Asia was due to capital accumulation and a relatively small part due to technological progress. His most startling finding was for Singapore; there, technological progress occurred at a rate of only 0.2 percent per year. Paul Krugman later popularized this finding in *Foreign Affairs.* He drew an analogy between capital-intensive Singaporean growth and capital-intensive Soviet growth, setting off a cyclone of protest. Singapore's prime minister denounced Krugman publicly and announced that Singapore would henceforth have a goal of 2 percent per year technological progress.[18]

Scholars as well as prime ministers have criticized the Young-Krugman finding (justly in my view) on several grounds. First, it doesn't take into account our official motto: people respond to incentives. Robert Barro of Harvard and Xavier Sala-i-Martin of Columbia pointed out in their textbook on growth that capital accumulation itself responds to technological change. If technology is improving, then the rate of return of capital is improving. If the rate of return on capital is improving, then more capital will be accumulated. In the long run, capital per worker, labor-saving technology, and output per worker will all grow at the same rate (as they did in the example). But we would say that the cause of growth is the growth in technology, to which both capital accumulation and output growth respond. When Peter Klenow and Andrés Rodríguez-Clare redid the Young calculations, taking into account the response of capital to technological change, they found that technological change accounted for a much higher share of output growth than Young had found for the gang of four.

Second, the finding that capital accumulation accounts for East Asian growth, even if it were true, does not address whether that experience can be replicated elsewhere. To address the latter question, we need to see how much the variation in capital growth rates across countries accounts for the variation of growth per worker across countries. The answer is not much. Klenow and Rodríguez-Clare attribute only 3 percent of the variation of growth per worker across countries to variations in capital growth per worker, while variations in technological progress accounted for 91 percent (human capital accounted for the puny remaining 6 percent).[19] Another study finds that variations in the growth of physical capital explain only 25 percent of the variations in growth performance across countries.[20]

To make things concrete, consider some East Asia and non–East Asia country examples. Both Nigeria and Hong Kong increased their physical capital stock per worker by over 250 percent over the 1960 to 1985 time frame. The results of this massive investment were different: Nigeria's output per worker rose by 12 percent from 1960 to 1985, while Hong Kong's rose by 328 percent. And consider another even more capital-intensive pair: the Gambia and Japan both increased their capital stocks per worker by over 500 percent between 1960 and 1985. The result in the Gambia was that output per worker rose 2 percent from 1960 to 1985, while in Japan it rose 260 percent.[21] These are among the worst comparisons that one can make, but the result holds for the whole sample: variations in capital growth do not explain much of the variations in output growth. (It may be that capital investment is measured incorrectly because not all of the measured "investment" really went into productive machines. I still would conclude that measured investment is not the key to growth.)

To give another example of failure of capital led growth, capital per worker in Tanzania's manufacturing sector grew at 8 percent per annum over the period 1976 to 1990, but manufacturing output per worker fell at 3.4 percent per annum over the same period. This is particularly striking because one would expect that manufacturing equipment and technological expertise could be purchased on the international market, and so the relationship between inputs and outputs in manufacturing should not differ much among countries.[22]

Third, the rates of return in East Asia did not behave the way they were supposed to if capital accumulation was the main source of growth. As we saw, the rate of return to capital must be high at the beginning if transitional capital accumulation is the main source of growth. Capital accumulation should lead to diminishing returns; the rate of return to capital should fall. A study in 1997 found that the rate of return to capital in Singapore actually increased over time.[23] This 1997 study concludes that technological progress was central to Singapore's high growth of output per worker. He reached similar conclusions for the other three members of the gang of four.

Conclusion

The World Bank helped finance the Morogoro Shoe Factory in Tanzania in the 1970s. This shoe factory had labor, machines, and the latest in shoe-making technology. It had everything except—shoes. It never produced more than 4 percent of its installed capacity. The factory, which had planned to supply the entire Tanzanian shoe market and then export three-quarters of its planned production of 4 million shoes to Europe, never exported a single shoe. The plant was not well designed for Tanzania's climate; it had aluminum walls and no ventilation system. Production finally ceased in 1990.[24]

Why machines in many developing countries are no more pro-ductive than tail fins on a Chevy has little to do with the machines themselves and everything to do with the environment in which producers used the machines. Morogoro Shoe Factory was owned by the government of Tanzania, a government that had failed at every big and small development initiative since independence.

Multiplying machines when incentives for growth were lacking was useless. Maybe the machines would produce things nobody wanted. Or maybe the machines were there but other crucial inputs were unavailable (a common problem in Tanzania and elsewhere was that imported raw materials and spare parts were often un-available because of government controls on selling dollars to producers). Not only could machines not be a permanent source of growth, even their genuine productive potential often went to waste because governments messed up the market incentives to use machines efficiently.

Even when machines were used efficiently, Solow's original insight that capital could not be the ultimate source of growth was right on target. There is more capital in richer economies, but that is because technological progress offsets diminishing returns.

The facts contradict the capital fundamentalists. The imams of capital fundamentalism who applied the Solow model to the tropics turned this insight on its head. If transitional capital accumulation were the main source of growth differences, then countries should have very high rates of return to capital at the beginning. They do not. If transitional capital accumulation were the main source of growth differences, we would expect the poor capital-scarce countries to grow faster than the rich as they respond to these high returns to capital. They do not. If transitional capital accumulation were the main source of growth differences, we would expect financial capital to flow from rich to poor countries in response to the high returns to capital. It does not. If transitional capital accumulation were the main source of growth differences, we would expect capital accumulation to explain a lot of the cross-country differences in growth. It does not. Trying to grow by physical capital alone was another useless panacea.

That's not the end of the story, because there would be a determined effort to revive the application of the Solow model to poor countries by augmenting it with education of workers—human capital. A new group of scholars would claim that controlling for education and saving, poor countries did tend to grow faster than rich countries. To see if education proved to be the panacea for growth, let's turn to the next chapter.

Intermezzo: Dry Cornstalks

Albert and Mercegrace Barthelemy and their children Detanie, Mercenise, Amors, Indianise, and Alfese live in La Brousse, Haiti. For twenty years they have lived in the same house, whose dry mud wall is now crumbling. The house has a dirt floor, and its only room is divided into sections by a curtain. The thatched roof will likely be destroyed by the next heavy rain.

Last year, a daughter "got sick in the chest" and died. Mercegrace, age forty-nine, doesn't know what disease killed her daughter, just as she does not know that the disease that has handicapped Alfese, age eight, is called polio. Indianise, fourteen, is a deaf mute.

Albert, fifty years old, goes out to his job of building a road connecting their village to another. Albert is in debt from paying for the burial of his daughter last year. The interest rate from the moneylender is 50 percent. Mercenise, age twenty, is waiting to marry her fiancé, but there is no money for the trousseau or the wedding.

Amors, age seventeen, goes out in the morning to examine the dried-out cornstalks in the garden, the family's food supply, looking for edible ears.[1] Today he finds an edible ear and a piece of sugarcane. Mercenise lights the fire, grills the corn, and divides it into six portions. Afterward each person sucks on a piece of cane.

Amors goes off to receive his year-end report card from the school, an hour's walk over the mountain. Indianise goes to fetch water from the spring with two jerry cans and a donkey.

As darkness falls, the family goes to bed. Albert reads his son's report card with the light of a bit of kerosene burning in a milk bottle. Amors needs another two years to graduate from primary school. At seventeen, he can hardly read and write. Albert may not be able to pay for Amors's school fee for the coming years. Still, he dreams of Amors's finishing his education and leaving for the city, where he could earn money to lift them out of poverty.

4   Educated for What?

To be sure of hitting the target, shoot first, and call whatever you hit the target.
Ashleigh Brilliant

Having devoted twenty-two out of the first twenty-eight years of my life to getting an education, I have a natural bias toward thinking education is important. So do many other well-educated experts.

In 1996, the UNESCO Commission on Education for the Twenty-first Century published *Learning: The Treasure Within*. The chairman of the commission, former European Commission president Jacques Delors, wrote in the introduction that the commission did not see education as a "miracle cure." Rather the members saw it as "one of the principal means available to foster a deeper and more harmonious form of human development and thereby to reduce poverty, exclusion, ignorance, oppression and war."

The Commission on Education for the Twenty-first Century was made up of a distinguished collection of unemployed statesmen and stateswomen. Another member was Michael Manley, the former prime minister of Jamaica, apparently not disqualified as a development expert by his having bankrupted the Jamaican economy from 1972 to 1980.

Delors, in the introduction to *Learning: The Treasure Within*, quoted some poetry from La Fontaine:

Be sure (the ploughman said), not to sell the inheritance
Our forebears left to us:
A treasure lies concealed therein.

Then Delors drew on his own poetic muse to add:

But the old man was wise
To show them before he died
That learning is the treasure.

Others have echoed the sentiment that education is "one of the principal means" to "human development." UNESCO, UNICEF, the World Bank, and the United Nations Development Program convened a previous global body, the World Conference on Education for All, held in Jomtien near Bangkok, Thailand, from March 5 to 9, 1990. In their official World Declaration on Education for All, they noted that education accomplishes such tasks as ensuring "a safer, healthier, more prosperous and environmentally sound world, while simultaneously contributing to social, economic, and cultural progress, tolerance, and international cooperation."[1] The World Conference on Education for All set a goal of universal primary education in every country by the year 2000. (They didn't make it, apparently as ineffectual as they were well meaning.)

The secretary general to UNESCO, Federico Mayor, chimed in with rather less poetic language: "The level of education of the overall population of a particular country ... determine that country's ability to share in world development, ... to benefit from the advancement of knowledge and to make progress itself while contributing to the education of others. This is a self-evident truth that is no longer in dispute."[2]

Other statements of this self-evident truth don't go quite that far but still stress education as one of the secrets to success on the quest for growth. The Inter-American Development Bank (IADB) noted "that investment in human capital [education] promotes economic growth is well recognized." The 1997 *World Development Report* of the World Bank notes that "many attribute a good part of the East Asian countries' economic success to their unwavering commitment to public funding for basic education as the cornerstone of economic development."[3] A World Bank economist summarizes the conventional wisdom: "The education and training of men and—although often neglected—of women contributes directly to economic growth through its effects on productivity, earnings, job mobility, entrepreneurial skills, and technological innovation."[4]

In the light of these affirmations of faith in education, it may come as a surprise—as it did to me—to learn that the growth response to the dramatic educational expansion of the last four decades has been distinctly disappointing. The failure of government-sponsored educational growth is once again due to our motto: people respond to incentives. If the incentives to invest in the future are not there, expanding education is worth little. Having the government force you to go to school does not change your incentives to invest in the future. Creating people with high skill in countries where the only profitable activity is lobbying the government for favors is not a formula for success. Creating skills where there exists no technology to use them is not going to foster economic growth.

The Education Explosion

From 1960 to 1990, reflecting the paeans to education in government policy circles, there was a remarkable expansion of schooling. Fueled by the emphasis of the World Bank and other donors on basic education, primary enrollment had reached 100 percent in half of the world's countries by 1990. In 1960, only 28 percent of the world's nations had had 100 percent primary enrollment. The median primary enrollment increased from 80 percent in 1960 to 99 percent in 1990. Behind these figures lie educational miracles like Nepal, going from 10 percent primary enrollment in 1960 to 80 percent in 1990.

In 1960, there were such secondary education disasters as Niger, which had only 1 in 200 of children of secondary school age in school. Since 1960 the median rate of secondary enrollment in the countries of the world has more than quadrupled, from 13 percent of secondary school age children in 1960 to 45 percent in 1990.

We see similar explosions in university enrollment. In 1960, twenty-nine countries had no college students whatsoever. By 1990, only three countries (the Comoros, the Gambia, and Guinea-Bissau) had none. From 1960 to 1990, the median college enrollment rate of the countries of the world increased more than seven times, from 1 percent to 7.5 percent.

Where Has All the Education Gone?

What has been the response of economic growth to the educational explosion? Alas, the answer is: little or none. The lack of association between growth in schooling and GDP growth has been noted in several studies. The lack of African growth despite an educational explosion, caused one study to ask, "Where has all the education gone?"[5] This study constructed a series on the growth in human capital (education) and could find no positive association between growth in education and growth of output per worker. (It actually found a negative and significant relationship in some statistical exercises.)[6] Figure 4.1 compares East Asia and Africa with numbers from this study.

African countries with rapid growth in human capital over the 1960 to 1987 period—countries like Angola, Mozambique, Ghana, Zambia, Madagascar, Sudan, and Senegal—were nevertheless growth disasters. Countries like Japan, with modest growth in human capital, were growth miracles. Other East Asian miracles like Singapore, Korea, China, and Indonesia did have rapid growth in human capital, but equal to or less than that of the African growth disasters. To take one comparison, Zambia had slightly faster expansion in human capital than Korea, but Zambia's growth rate was seven percentage points lower.

This study also pointed out that Eastern Europe and the former Soviet Union compare favorably with Western Europe and North America in years of schooling attained. Yet we now know their GDP per worker was only a small fraction of Western European and North American levels. For example, the 97 percent secondary enrollment ratio of the United States is only slightly higher than Ukraine's 92 percent, but the United States has nine times the per capita income of Ukraine.

Another fact about the world also reflects poorly on education's contribution to growth. The median growth rate of poor countries has fallen over time. The growth of output per worker was 3 percent in the 1960s, 2.5 percent in the 1970s, −0.5 percent in the 1980s, and 0 percent in the 1990s. This study noted that the decline in growth happened at the same time as the massive educational expansion in the poor countries.

Because this study's findings are so surprising, it's worth checking if they are replicated in other studies.[7] Another set of economists did a similar study of how growth responds to the percentage change in the labor force's average years of schooling from 1965 to 1985.[8] They also found that there is no relationship between growth in years of schooling and per capita GDP growth, a nonrelationship that holds even when they controlled for other determinants of growth. (They did find a positive relationship between initial level of education and subsequent productivity growth.)

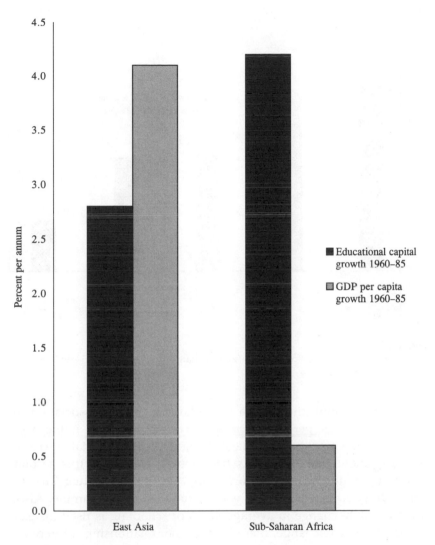

Figure 4.1
Where has all the education gone? *Source:* Pritchett 1999

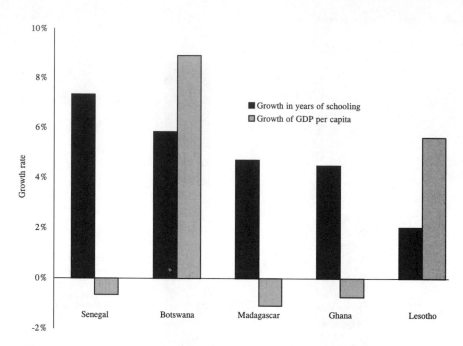

Figure 4.2
Diverse growth outcomes from educational expansion in Africa, 1965–1985. *Source:* Benhabib and Spiegel 1994

You might think that Africa is explaining the nonassociation in these two studies, perhaps because starting from a low initial base may have blown up the percentage change in human capital in Africa. And we know that Africa has had poor growth. But this second study still found a lack of correlation between schooling growth and GDP growth when Africa was excluded from the sample. Also, if the absolute change in average years of schooling is used instead of the percentage change, there is still a nonrelationship. Moreover, the educational expansion had very different effects within Africa (Figure 4.2).

This study did find that the level of initial schooling is positively correlated with subsequent productivity growth. Thus, a country with high initial human capital will grow fast through the indirect effect of human capital on growth through productivity. Other economists have similarly found the growth of output to depend positively on initial schooling.[9] This relationship is usually thought to be temporary. When there is a high level of human capital relative to physical capital, the return to investing in physical capital will be high and thus growth will be higher until physical and human capital come back into balance.[10]

The relationship has to be temporary, because the set-up of growth depending on initial schooling doesn't make much sense in the long run. As the first study noted, growth tends to fluctuate around a constant average while schooling trends upward. The growth–initial schooling relationship would imply that growth should trend upward, but this didn't happen. For example, world average growth decreased from the 1960s to the 1990s despite the increase in education levels. However well the initial schooling might drive growth for short periods like decades or twenty-year averages, it doesn't make much sense as a long-run determinant of growth.

A third set of economists also found that variations in growth across nations have very little to do with variations in human capital growth. If a country's per capita growth rate is 1 percentage point faster than average, they attribute only 0.06 percentage point of this to human capital growth being faster than average, while growth in productivity accounts for 0.91 percentage point of the output growth being 1.0 percentage points faster. (The other factor that is also supposed to be a key to development, physical capital, contributes only 0.03 percentage point to the 1 percentage point faster growth.)[11]

Yet a fourth study pointed out a more subtle problem with the idea that growth in human capital is a major force behind growth. If human capital growth is driving GDP growth, then rapidly growing economies will have rapidly growing human capital. This means that young workers will have considerably more human capital than those who were educated during a time of much lower human capital. This factor would tend to give the young workers higher wages than the old workers. But everywhere we see wages increasing with years of experience; the older workers always earn significantly more than the young, even in rapidly growing economies. Even if years of experience count for something, we would have expected fast-growing countries to have less of a wage increase with experience, because of the human capital advantage of the young. We do not find this. So the growth of human capital cannot be that rapid in a fast-growing economy, and cannot account for its rapid growth.[12]

This study pointed out an even more serious flaw in the level of schooling to subsequent growth relationship. The causality between initial schooling and subsequent growth could be the reverse. If you can forecast growth to some extent, then higher growth in the future will raise the rate of return to today's education. Education is worth more where the skilled wage is rapidly growing than where the skilled wage is stagnant. The magnitude of the relationship between initial schooling and subsequent growth is more consistent with the story of growth causing schooling rather than schooling causing growth.[13]

The bottom line is that education is another magic formula that has failed to live up to expectations.

Education and Income

The finding that education doesn't matter much for growth is intensely controversial. Despite the failure of physical capital and human capital growth to explain variations in growth, a number of economists aver that physical capital and human capital can explain the large international variations in income. These economists, like Gregory Mankiw of Harvard, point out that income in the long run in the Solow model is determined by saving in the form of physical capital and by saving in the form of human capital. Mankiw uses the percentage of children enrolled in secondary school as his measure of human capital saving. There is indeed a strong association between income levels and secondary enrollment ratios. Mankiw shows that his measures of saving in physical capital and human capital can explain as much as 78 percent of the per capita income differences among nations.[14] How can this finding be reconciled with the finding that growth in output is not related to growth in human capital?

Before getting to this question, however, notice how neatly Mankiw ties up some of the loose ends in the Solow framework (as applied to poor countries) by adding human capital. Physical capital accumulation could not be a source of growth in the Solow model because it had severe diminishing returns, a consequence of the low share (about a quarter to a third) of physical capital in output. Once we add human capital, however, the share of all types of capital in output goes all the way up to 80 percent. Diminishing returns to human and physical capital together are much less severe. It's as if we are expanding the flour and milk together in the pancake example. These two ingredients are such an important part of the recipe that we can increase pancake production quite a bit by increasing them even if all the other ingredients stay unchanged. In the same way, there is significant scope for increasing output by expanding physical and human capital together. This meant that countries with the same technology could have very different incomes because of human and physical capital accumulation. Supporting Mankiw's view, several studies gave evidence that high rates of physical and human capital accumulation explained most of the high growth in East Asia.[15]

Second, Mankiw tied up the loose end of the slow growth of poor countries. Remember that poor countries were supposed to grow faster but didn't. Mankiw finds that once capital accumulation and education are controlled for, poor countries did tend to grow faster. The idea in the Solow model that all countries were moving toward the same destination did not have to hold. Countries with different rates of capital accumulation and education were headed to different destinations. The ones who were saving a lot (both in the form of human and physical capital) were moving toward being rich; the ones who were saving little were moving toward being poor. But being poor relative to your own final destination meant you would move faster toward that destination. Another widely cited study also found that poor countries grew faster, conditional on different control variables than Mankiw's.[16]

Third, Mankiw tied up the loose end of the lack of capital flows to poor countries. He supposed that human capital (people with skills) could not move across countries but physical capital could. If poor countries' poverty is explained by their low human capital, then international investors will not want to invest in these countries because skilled labor is necessary to get a good return on machines. If the skilled labor is absent, then the return on machinery is low. This could explain why capital flows went more to rich countries than to poor ones.

Alas, nice theoretical packages don't always bear close scrutiny. There are three problems with Mankiw's relationship between secondary enrollment and income.

The first problem is that secondary education is a very narrow measure of educational accumulation. What about primary education? The relationship between per capita income and primary enrollment is considerably less satisfying. There appears to be no strong relationship as one goes from primary enrollment of 0.2 to 0.9. All of these countries are poor. The many countries with universal primary enrollment have a higher average income than this group but also have an incredible range of incomes, from very poor to very rich. In short, primary education varies much less across countries than secondary education and explains much less of the variation in income. Concentrating on secondary education alone, Mankiw exaggerated the variation of education in general.[17]

The second problem is with human capital's earnings under the Mankiw assumptions. Mankiw assumed that capital flows would equalize rates of return to physical capital. That leaves only human capital to have different rates of return across countries. Explaining income differences with human capital alone is like explaining income differences with physical capital alone. You are back to explaining big differences in income with a relatively minor ingredient. If a poor country is poor because of lack of skills, as Stanford's Paul Romer pointed out in his comment on Mankiw's work, the few skilled workers must be earning very high salaries.

Let's compare the United States and India again. The United States has fourteen times the per capita income of India in 1992. This is also the ratio of unskilled wages in the United States to unskilled wages in India. Unskilled labor is abundant in India while skilled labor is scarce. Mankiw's assumptions implied the wage for skilled labor should be three times larger in India than in the United States.[18] Such wage differentials should induce skilled labor to try to move from the United States to India. Instead, we see the reverse: skilled Indians coming to the United States. What's more, if the predictions of Mankiw's approach had come true, we would expect that the unskilled Indians would be the ones who want to move to the United States while skilled Indians would stay put. That didn't happen: educated Indians were 14.4 times more likely to move to the United States than uneducated Indians.

This propensity of skilled Indians to migrate to the United States is part of the general brain drain phenomenon. A recent study of sixty-one poor countries found that people with secondary education and above were more likely to move to the United States than those with primary education and below in all of the sixty-one countries. Those with university education were more likely to migrate than those with secondary education in fifty-one of the countries. Some countries are losing most of their skilled workforce to the United States. In Guyana, for example, a conservative estimate is that 77 percent of those with university education have moved to the United States.[19]

We see the reverse of Mankiw's prediction that the skilled would want to move to poor countries, because the skilled wage differential is actually in favor of the rich countries. An engineer in Bombay earns $2,300 per year; an engineer in New York earns $55,000 a year.[20] Instead of skilled wages being three times higher in India than in the United States, as the Mankiw framework predicted, skilled wages are twenty-four times higher in the United States than in India. Mankiw's framework predicts a negative association between skilled wages and per capita income; instead, the association is strongly positive.

The Mankiw framework also implies a nonsensically high ratio of skilled to unskilled wages in India. The United States has fourteen times the unskilled wage of India, according to Mankiw's assumptions. Mankiw predicted that the skilled wage in India would be three times higher. If the ratio of skilled to unskilled wages is two in the United States (as Mankiw suggested), then the skilled wage in India should be eighty-four times the unskilled wage. If people respond to incentives, then there should a massive movement into education in India to acquire skills to earn the skilled wage. The rate of return to education should be forty-two times higher in India than in the United States. But no such mammoth skill differential exists in India (or any other poor countries). The wage of engineers in India is only about three times the wage of building laborers. And studies find that returns to education in poor countries range no higher than twice that of rich countries—not forty-two times higher and even then, the rate of return to education is only higher because the cost of the investment—foregone earnings—is lower in poor countries.[21]

The third problem is causality (again). What if high school education is a luxury in which you indulge yourself as you get richer? Then naturally demand for high schools would go up as per capita income rises, but that would not prove anything how much high schools make anyone more productive.

This brings me to a more fundamental problem I have with Mankiw's explanation of income differences across nations. Even if we accepted his argument that income differences are explained by differences in saving, then what explains differences in saving? This solution only shifts the problem of explaining growth differences to one of explaining savings differences across nations. I find it unappealing to say that poor nations are poor because they're not naturally thrifty. This is too close to blaming the poor for their own poverty.

Education and Incentives

One clue as to why education is worth little more than hula hoops to a society that wants to grow comes from what the educated people are doing with their skills. In an economy with extensive government intervention, the activity with the highest returns to skills might be lobbying the government for favors. The government creates profit opportunities by its interventions. For example, a government that fixes the exchange rate, prohibits trading of foreign currency, and creates high inflation has created the opportunity for profitable trading in dollars. Skilled people will want to lobby the government for access to foreign exchange at the low fixed rate and then resell it on the black market for a fat profit. This activity does not contribute to higher GDP; it just redistributes income from the poor exporter who was forced to turn over his dollars at the official exchange rate to the black market trader. In an economy with many government interventions, skilled people opt for activities that redistribute income rather than activities that create growth. (One somewhat whimsical piece of evidence that supports this story is that economies with lots of lawyers grow more slowly than economies with lots of engineers.)[22] For example, economies with a high black market premium on foreign exchange have low growth regardless of whether they have high or low schooling. Economies with a low black market premium have more growth with higher schooling than with lower schooling. Schooling pays off only when government actions create incentives for growth rather than redistribution.

Another clue is that the state largely drove the educational expansion by providing free public schooling and requiring that children attend school. Administrative targets for universal primary education do not in themselves create the incentives for investing in the future that matter for growth. The quality of education will be different in an economy with incentives to invest in the future versus an economy where there are none. In an economy with incentives to invest in the future, students will apply themselves to their studies, parents will monitor the quality of education, and teachers will face pressure to teach. In a stagnant economy without incentives to invest in the future, students will goof off in the classroom or sometimes not show up at all, parents will often pull their children away to work on the farm, and teachers will while the time away as overqualified babysitters.

Corruption, low salaries for teachers, and inadequate spending on textbooks, paper, and pencils are all problems that wreck incentives for quality education.

In Vila Junqueira, Brazil, people told interviewers that the "state school is falling apart, there are whole weeks without a teacher, no director or efficient teachers, no safety, no hygiene." In Malawi, respondents said:

We hear the government introduced free primary education and provides for all essential requirements, note books, pens and pencils. The pupils have never received these items. We still have to provide them ourselves. We strongly believe it is not the government's fault but it is sheer malpractice on the part of the school's management. We have seen several teachers going around selling notebooks and pens. In addition the teachers are not dedicated to their duty. Often pupils go back home without attending even a single lesson. We hear they [the teachers] are unmotivated by poor working conditions. Their salaries are particularly inadequate. It is not surprising that they divert free primary education resources to supplement their miserable salaries. This has adversely affected the standards of education at school. Only ten pupils have been selected to secondary schools in the last six years.[23]

In Pakistan, politicians dispense teaching positions as patronage. There is large-scale cheating at examinations, supervised by unscrupulous or intimidated teachers. Three-quarters of the teachers could not pass the exams they administer to their students. The medium of instruction in the public schools is Urdu, although the working language in this multilingual society is English. Some of the publicly supported schools are Islamic schools, where the students mainly learn the Koran. The other public schools are of such poor quality that anyone who can afford to do so sends their children to expensive private schools. High school students from rival religious factions have fought each other in the schools with AK-47s.[24] Not much good is going to happen when there are more guns than textbooks in the schools.[25]

Although teachers are often underpaid, there are sometimes too many of them. A common pattern is that much more is spent on teacher salaries (a convenient vehicle for political patronage) than on textbooks, paper, and pencils. Filmer and Pritchett find that spending on school materials has a rate of return ten to one hundred times larger than additional spending on teachers, which means that school materials are very scarce relative to teachers.[26]

A third clue comes from what is going on with other investments in the economy. High skills are productive if they go together with high-tech machinery, adaptation of advanced technology, and other investments that happen in an economy with incentives to grow. Without incentive to grow, there is no high-tech machinery or advanced technology to complement the skills. You have created a supply of skills where there is no demand for skills. And so the skills go to waste—with, say, highly educated taxi drivers—or the skilled people emigrate to rich countries where they can match with high-tech machines and advanced technology.

It is true that the creation of skills itself could lead to incentives for investing in high-tech machinery and adapting advanced technology. However, if government policy has destroyed the incentive to grow, this will more than offset the incentives to make other investments that the high skills could have otherwise created.

Conclusion

Despite all the lofty sentiments about education, the return to the educational explosion of the past four decades has been disappointing. I think that learning under the right circumstances is a very good thing, but administrative targets for enrollment rates and overwrought rhetoric from international commissions do not in themselves create the incentive to grow. Education is another magic formula that failed us on the quest for growth.

The creation of skills in people will respond to incentives to invest in the future. No country has become rich with a universally unskilled population. Enrollment in formal schooling may be a poor measure of creation of skills.

Belatedly realizing that lack of incentives for growth might be responsible for the disappointing response to accumulation of machines and schooling, the international community turned next to another idea: controlling population growth so as to economize on machines and schools.

Intermezzo: Without a Refuge

Sudan has been at war for seventeen years, a civil war between the north and the south. The civil war is the second since independence; the first also lasted for seventeen years. More than that, the war of north versus south is a continuation of ethnic tensions that have existed for centuries. (To oversimplify, the ethnic split is roughly Arabic-Islamic north versus African-Christian south). The civil war began again when President Numayri of the northern-dominated government in Khartoum promulgated Islamic law, the Shari'a, in September 1983.[1]

Around 20,000 boys between the ages of seven and seventeen in southern Sudan fled their villages at the beginning of the war, fearing that the government would draft them as soldiers for the north. Some of them set out for refugee camps in Ethiopia, a journey of six to ten weeks. They had to cross a large wilderness. Some boys lost their blankets, shoes, clothes, and pots to bandits en route. Some were killed by epidemics or by starvation. The survivors found a temporary peace in Ethiopia.

In May 1991, a new Ethiopian government asked them to leave, and they had to return to Sudan. It was the rainy season, and some of the boys drowned trying to cross the rivers. The remnant made it to a refugee camp back in Sudan run by the Red Cross. But fighting broke out around them again in late 1991, and they fled to refugee camps in Kenya. Since 1992, UNICEF has reunited about 1,200 boys with their families. The rest are still in the camps in Kenya. As fourteen-year-old Simon Majok said, "We children of the Sudan, we were not lucky."[2]

In 1999, there were fresh reports of Sudanese children fleeing into Kenya, this time to escape intertribal warfare in the South.[3] In March 2000, the organization Christian Solidarity International (CSI) alleged that pro-government forces enslaved 188 southern Sudanese women and children during raids on three villages in northern Bahr al Ghazal.[4]

5   Cash for Condoms?

The only thing more dangerous than an economist is an amateur economist.
Bentley's Second Law of Economics

The most unprepossessing candidate for the Holy Grail of prosperity is seven inches of latex: a condom. In the view of many of us development experts, population control is the elixir that would avoid catastrophic starvation and enable poor nations to become rich. Foreign aid to finance population control—cash for condoms—is the panacea that would bring prosperity to poor countries.

If there is a single thing that has scared observers of the Third World, it is population growth. To many, population growth catastrophically imperils the prosperity of poor nations, if not the very lives of their inhabitants. Conversely, control of population through family planning—using condoms during sex to be explicit—will promote the prosperity of poor nations.

Population is an old concern in economics. Thomas Malthus in the early nineteenth century famously saw exponential population growth outracing food production, which he said would lead to a major population correction in the form of widespread famines. The latter-day incarnation of Thomas Malthus is Stanford biologist Paul Ehrlich. Ehrlich in his famous *cri de coeur* of 1968, *The Population Bomb*, foresaw that within a decade after his writing, famines would sweep "repeatedly across Asia, Africa, and South America," killing perhaps as many as one-fifth of the world's population.[1] Worldwide disease epidemics among the crowded poor, possibly including a resurgence of bubonic plague, would add to the death rates.

The great population scare is mainly notable for what didn't happen: widespread deaths from famine. In the 1960s, when Ehrlich penned his eloquent alert, about one out of every ten nations was having a famine at least once per decade. By the 1990s, just one country out of the two-hundred in the world had a famine. Global population did about double from 1960 to 1998, but food production tripled over the same period in both rich and poor nations.[2] Far from us seeing increasing food shortages, food prices have fallen by nearly half over the past two decades.[3]

In Pakistan, for example, one of the many places where Ehrlich anticipated famine and food riots "possibly in the early 70s, certainly by the early 1980s," food production has doubled over the past decade and a half.[4] Food production in the entire developing world rose 87 percent over the same time period. Perhaps this is why Ehrlich confessed recently that it takes him "constant effort to realize that the habitability of earth is rapidly decaying."[5]

Ehrlich was concerned in 1968 about population growth. The rate of annual world population growth peaked about when *The Population Bomb* was published, at about 2.1 percent. Since then the population growth rate has declined, with the World Bank now projecting world population growth of 1.1 percent per year out to 2015.[6] Population growth has fallen despite the fall in death rates, because birthrates have fallen even more.[7]

Still, the population scare is very much alive. A contemporary heir to the throne of population alarmism is Lester Brown of the World Watch Institute. According to the press release for his 1999 book, modestly entitled *Beyond Malthus*, "The world is now starting to reap the consequences of its past neglect of the population issue." "After nearly half a century of continuous population growth," the news release dolefully continues, "the demand in many countries for food, water, and forest products is simply outrunning the capacity of local life support systems."[8] *State of the World 2000* from the World Watch Institute warns that population growth "may more directly affect economic progress than any other single trend, exacerbating nearly all other environmental and social problems."[9] And Pakistan is imperiled again: "Pakistan's projected growth from 146 million today to 345 million by 2050 will shrink its grainland per person from 0.08 hectares at present to 0.03 hectares, an area scarcely the size of a tennis court."[10]

The organization Population Action International notes that "the capacity of farmers to feed the world's future population is also in jeopardy."[11] The Population Institute warns bluntly of "The Four

Horsemen of the 21st Century Apocalypse: Overpopulation. Defores-
tation. Water Scarcity. Famine." As a a result, "Developed countries
will be looking at staggering disaster relief budgets as a result ... and
only a few years from now."[12]

Not only that but, according to Lester Brown, population grows
faster than jobs: "In the absence of an accelerated effort to slow
population growth in the years ahead, unemployment could soar to
unmanageable levels." As for Pakistan, its "work force is projected
to grow from 72 million in 1999 to 199 million by 2050."[13]

The alarmists' response to the population scare is to call for more
family planning (more condoms). Another one of those conclaves of
do-gooders, the U.N.-sponsored International Conference on Population and Development in Cairo in 1994 adopted a program of
action that "advocates making family planning universally available
by 2015 ... provides estimates of the levels of national resources and
international assistance that will be required, and calls on Governments to make these resources available." The Cairo conference
urged "the international community to move, on an immediate basis,
to establish an efficient coordination system and global, regional and
subregional facilities for the procurement of contraceptives and other
commodities essential to reproductive health programmes of developing countries and countries with economies in transition."[14]

Lester Brown concurs that the answer is cash for condoms:
"Enhanced domestic and international support for family planning
services ... will yield the dual benefits of better living conditions and
brighter job prospects in the next century."[15]

A review of the Cairo Resolutions in 1999 noted hopefully that "as
the demand for smaller families has increased and the access to safe
and accessible contraception has improved, fertility levels have declined." However, "over 150 million couples still have an unmet
need for contraception."[16] At a U.N. review in 1999 of the implementation of the 1994 Cairo Conference Resolutions, the secretary-
general of the U.N., Kofi Annan, wistfully noted, "We cannot do it
without funds." He recognized other budgetary priorities faced by
rich and poor countries, but asked rhetorically, "What could be more
important than the chance to help the world's people control their
numbers?"[17]

The self-explanatory advocacy group Zero Population Growth
warns Americans that they will "also be affected by political conflicts
that arise from environmental refugees fleeing overpopulated and

environmentally degraded areas in search of more benign conditions, or from concerns over the rights to finite natural resources like oil fields, water resources, or land."[18]

So the elixir for promoting growth and avoiding population disaster, to oversimplify, comically is: cash for condoms. UNICEF states the creed with characteristic restraint: "Family planning could bring more benefits to more people at less cost than any other single technology now available to the human race."[19]

The U.S. aid agency USAID plays an important role in promoting family planning: "USAID manages a global system for the delivery of contraceptive supplies. Numerous countries and donors rely on USAID's contraceptive supply forecasting system, designed to ensure availability and choice of contraceptives year-round."[20] So devoted to contraceptive provision is USAID that it floods the market with condoms. In USAID recipients like El Salvador and Egypt, there are so many condoms given away that people blow them up as balloons to festoon soccer matches.

The Myth of Unwanted Births

The unlikely elixir of cash for condoms is inconsistent with the principle that people respond to incentives. All of this focus on aid for contraceptives implies that the free market left to itself would not supply enough contraceptives to meet demand. The "150 million couples" who "still have an unmet need for contraception" would stop having babies if only aid-financed condoms were available to them. But a condom is just like any other good that the free market can supply, like a can of Coca-Cola. We don't have any aid programs to 150 million couples who have an unmet need for Coca-Cola.

Defenders of cash for condoms might say that poor families cannot afford condoms, a splendid bit of illogic, since an unwanted child is far more expensive than a condom. Condoms can be purchased internationally for about thirty-three cents apiece.[21] The price of a condom is really a minor factor compared to the other incentives and disincentives to have a child.

The contraceptive aid advocates will reply that people in poor countries don't have access to condoms at any price. This answer, though, begs the question of how free markets fail to supply a cheap good that should be in hot demand if 150 million couples have an unmet need for contraception. Free markets don't have any trouble supplying Coca-Cola to poor countries around the world.

It turns out that we can do even better than just apply elementary economic logic to the alleged unmet contraceptive demand. There have been systematic household surveys of desired number of children for many different countries. Lant Pritchett compared the desired number of children to the actual number of children in different countries. He found that in countries with a large number of actual births per woman, women also had a high number of desired births. About 90 percent of the differences across countries in actual fertility were explained by desired fertility. So much for the alleged unmet demand for contraception.[22]

Checking for Population Disasters

If population growth causes famine, water shortages, massive unemployment, and other disasters, we would expect to see it show up in overall economic performance. Countries that have rapid population growth should have low or negative GDP growth per capita. The population growth is, according to the alarmists, overwhelming the existing productive capacity's ability to generate jobs and outstripping food production, so GDP per capita should fall when population growth gets "too high."

This prediction can be—and has been—easily tested. The relationship between per capita economic growth and population growth is one of the most intensively studied in all of the statistical literature. This literature has grown so extensive that we now have surveys of surveys. One survey concludes that "most economists who have specialized in population issues" have a "distinctly non-alarmist" view. The general wisdom among economists from these studies is that there is no evidence one way or the other that population growth affects per capita growth.[23] The most well-known statistical relationship between growth and its most fundamental determinants finds no significant effect of population growth on per capita growth.[24] When the effect of population growth on economic growth is allowed to vary for plausible reasons like level of development or resource scarcity, population growth still does not matter for economic growth.[25] When I control for government policy determinants of growth in the 1960s through the 1990s, I find a positive but insignificant relationship between population growth and per capita GDP growth.[26]

There are some facts about the world that make the lack of a relationship between population growth and per capita economic growth unsurprising.[27] First, we know that both population growth and per capita economic growth have accelerated over the very long run. Both population and income growth were slow until the nineteenth century for today's industrial nations; then both accelerated at the same time. Over the past few decades, both population growth and per capita economic growth slowed in industrial nations. It's hard to reconcile this fact with the idea that population growth is disastrous and that population control is a panacea for growth.

The second fact about the world is that population growth does not vary enough across countries to explain variations in per capita growth. GDP per capita growth varies between -2 and $+7$ percent for all countries for the period 1960 to 1992. Population growth varies only between 1 and 4 percent. Even if population growth lowered per capita growth one for one (the general view of the population alarmists), this would explain only about one-third of the variation in per capita growth. We have countries like Argentina with slow population growth and slow per capita economic growth, and countries like Botswana with rapid population growth and rapid per capita economic growth. East Asia grew much more rapidly than industrial nations, although it had higher population growth than industrial nations. Even much-maligned high-fertility Africa has not had the kind of general famine that the alarmists predicted.

Third, population growth has slowed down by about 0.5 percentage point from the 60s to the 90s in the Third World. But, as we have seen, Third World per capita growth slowed down over the same period. Moreover, there is *no* association across countries between success at slowing population growth and success at raising per capita growth (figure 5.1). Virtually all countries had a per capita growth slowdown, and the degree of the slowdown is not related to changes in population growth.

Obviously economic growth depends on a number of factors that have nothing to do with population growth. In fact, we have seen that once we control for those other factors, there is no evidence that population growth has any effect on per capita growth.

The view that increased population would lower per capita income and increase unemployment implicitly assumes that an additional

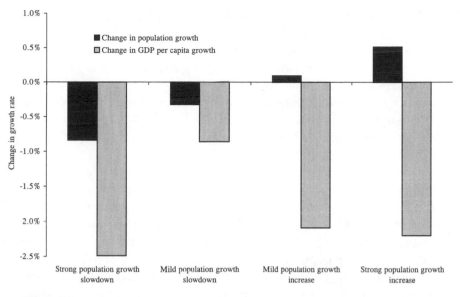

Figure 5.1
Change in population growth and per capita growth from 1961–1979 to 1980–1998. Each group is one-fourth of sample, ordered from strongest population growth slowdown to strongest population growth increase.

person has zero productivity, and so the only effect of increased population is to spread the existing GDP around more thinly. Again, besides being a rather insulting view of human potential in poor countries, this is incompatible with the principle that people respond to incentives. An additional person is a potential profit opportunity to an employer that hires him or her. An additional person has the incentive to find productive employment so as to subsist. The real wage will adjust until the demand for workers equals their supply.

Higher Population Good or Bad?

Having said all this, there still could be an argument for subsidizing population control. Parents deciding to have children do not take into account all of the effects of their decision on society. A higher population may harm the natural environment. For example, it may lead to more crowding of the land area, to the displeasure of the current inhabitants. Parents do not take these possible costs to the rest of society into account when having children.

But there also could be positive effects of additional children on society that parents do not take into account. One more baby is one more future taxpayer who can help pay for existing government programs. The main reason that social security is financially troubled in most rich countries is that population growth has slowed, lowering the proportion of tax-paying workers to benefit-receiving retirees. The better state of social security in the United States, compared to other rich countries, is that our population is growing faster (thanks to immigration, not to fertility, as it turns out).

A more ethereal reason that there could be positive effects of higher population is the genius principle. The more babies there are, the greater is the likelihood that one of them will grow up to be Mozart, Einstein, or Bill Gates. This effect, first pointed out by Simon Kuznets and Julian Simon, raises the stock of ideas that can then be used by any size population to better itself.

Since ideas can be shared with additional persons at zero cost—an unlimited number of people can listen to a Mozart aria—new ideas are used more effectively in large than in small populations. The one-time cost of implementing a new idea can be spread across more people, all of whom can use the idea at zero cost. The one-time cost of setting up the Internet will be less burdensome the more people there are to share it, and the benefit of the Internet increases the more people there are. More traditional innovations, like the conversion from hunter-gathering to farming and the conversion from farming to industry, will be more beneficial the more people there are to share the costs and amplify the benefits.

Population growth may also spur technological innovation precisely because it increases stress on available resources. As the ratio of people to land rises, for example, people are forced to come up with new ideas to get more food out of existing land. This "population pressure" principle was first stated by Ester Boserup.

Harvard University economist Michael Kremer did a simple test of the Kuznets-Simon-Boserup principle of beneficent population growth in a provocative article entitled "Population Growth Since 1 Million BC." He noted that this principle suggests a positive relationship between initial population and subsequent population growth.[28] A higher initial population means more idea creation, more people to use the idea, and more people to share the fixed cost of implementing the idea. The benefits to society then should make possible the support of more new babies, and so population growth should increase. This prediction is in stark contrast to the Thomas Malthus–Paul Ehrlich–Lester Brown principle that higher initial population will lead to a population crash as famine sets in. So who is right: Boserup or Malthus?

Kremer pointed out that the evidence of the very long run is in favor of Boserup. World population has been growing steadily over time, from 125,000 in 1 million B.C., to 4 million in 10,000 B.C., to 170 million at the time of the Christ, to about 1 billion at the time of Mozart, to 2 billion at the time of the Great Depression, to 4 billion at the time of Watergate, to 6 billion today.[29] And population growth has been accelerating, not falling. There is a positive relationship over the very long run between initial population and subsequent population growth, as Boserup-Kuznets-Simon predicted, not a negative relationship, as Malthus-Ehrlich-Brown predicted.

If we step back from the eons of time into the recent present, this positive relationship no longer holds. Population has continued to increase since the 1960s, while population growth has started to fall. But even this does not support Malthus. Population growth is falling because of falling birthrates, not because of increasing death rates due to famine—as the Malthusians would have it.

So what is the answer on whether we should subsidize population control? First, even if desirable, it is clear that subsidizing contraceptives is not the way to go, because the price of contraceptives is a very minor factor in the decision to have a child. Second, the net benefits and costs of a larger population are very unclear. Probably each country has to decide on its own whether increased population is putting an intolerable strain on natural resources, or whether an increased population is a fertile breeding ground for new tax revenues and new ideas.

Development, the Best Contraceptive

Suppose a country does want to lower population growth, for whatever reason. There is one statistical regularity that everyone agrees on, and this is the negative relationship between per capita income and population growth. Parents in rich countries have fewer babies than parents in poor countries. The poorest fifth of countries have on average 6.5 births per woman, while the richest fifth of countries have on average 1.7 births per woman.[30] In a phrase that some might find repugnant, parents are deciding on quality versus quantity of

children. Parents in rich countries have fewer children than do parents
in poor countries, but invest much more in each child in the form of
schooling, nutrition, and ballet lessons.

Why is this so? Again, people responding to incentives is at work.
Nobel Prize winner Gary Becker pioneered the insight of incentives
as applied to family life, even if to a degree that some might find
cold-hearted. He pointed out that as people become richer, their time
becomes more valuable. Any time not spent on the high-paying job is
income lost. Caring for children is time-consuming, as I can cheer-
fully attest. Richer parents choose to spend more time on the job
and less on parenting, in other words, having fewer offspring. Poorer
parents get less reward from working and so spend more time
parenting, having more offspring.

Although the rich are having fewer children than the poor, they
are investing more in each one of them. It is plausible that the payoff
from investing in skill increases with the initial skill level. The return
to learning geometry is higher for those who already know arithmetic. The high skill level of the rich parents is transmitted to their
children partly through natural at-home learning. Investing in high-
quality schooling then carries a higher return for the rich parents and
children than it does for the poor parents and children. So the rich
invest in more skill acquisition for their children than do the poor.
For a country as a whole, depending on the average initial skill
level of parents, the society can wind up with high fertility and low
income—or low fertility and high income.

Both conditions are self-perpetuating. The poor society has low
returns to skill, so it's not worth investing in skill acquisition. Because
of the lack of investment in skills, it stays poor. Because the average
parent is poorly paid, he or she spends less time working and more
time rearing children—having more offspring. The rich society has
high returns to skills, so it keeps investing in skill acquisition, getting
perpetually richer. Because the average parent is well paid, he or she
spends less time rearing children, because of having a smaller family.
Jump-starting development will shift a society from high-fertility
poverty to low-fertility prosperity.[31] Development itself is a far more
powerful contraceptive than cash for condoms.

The Two Revolutions

Our age has benefited from two revolutions: the industrial revolution (to use somewhat out-of-date terminology) and the demographic

revolution. In the industrial revolution, there was a leap in how much production could be gotten from a given amount of natural resources. In the demographic revolution, population growth first accelerated and then decelerated again.

The interesting question is how these two revolutions are related. As already discussed, technological advance and population growth were positively associated in the initial phases of the industrial revolution. More population meant more genius inventors and a larger scale of the market, improving technology. The advance in technology in turn made feeding a larger population feasible. Both the technological frontier and the level of population have grown together for centuries, with the rate of growth of both accelerating until recently. This phase of growth is often called extensive growth because the extent of labor inputs and production expands without an increase in living standards. Extensive growth has now spread to every region of the world, which is what has scared the alarmists, but so far without the disasters that the alarmists predicted.

In the next phase of the two revolutions, the rate of growth of per capita income accelerated in the richest countries while population growth went down in those countries. This phase of growth is usually called intensive growth, because each worker is producing more output to raise living standards; industry uses each worker more intensively. Intensive growth has not yet spread to all regions, but it has taken hold in the Western industrial countries and East Asia.

Nobel Prize winner Robert Lucas argues that an increase in the rate of return to knowledge and skills, or "human capital," explains the switch from extensive to intensive growth.[32] The technological advance got to the point where it raised the rate of return to human capital higher than the rate at which we discount the future. This makes it worthwhile for us to invest in human capital that has payoff in the future. This implies two things. First, production per person will increase because each person can produce more at a higher skill level. Second, parents who care about their children's welfare will take advantage of this higher return to skill by investing more education in each child and decreasing the number of children they have (trading off quantity of children for quality of children, to use again the cold-hearted expression of economists). Thus, we will get intensive growth with rising living standards and falling population growth.

There are two caveats to make about intensive growth. First, the investment in human capital should not be taken as necessarily formal schooling, which does a poor job of explaining growth. Human capital is much broader, including knowledge gained from friends, family, and coworkers, skill learned on the job, and worker training. We have a hard time measuring this broader definition of human capital but do know how to increase it: create incentives to invest in the future.

This brings me to my next caveat, which is why intensive growth hasn't taken hold everywhere. If the return to human capital increased as a result of worldwide technological progress, why haven't all countries taken advantage of these high returns to knowledge and skills? We will see in part III that some governments interfered with the returns to skill by not letting their citizens keep all their income. Countries with such governments remained stuck in extensive growth. Governments that safeguarded property rights and let free markets work (most of the time) did move to intensive growth (Western Europe and its offshoots, East Asia). We will see also that starting off at too low a level of skill may prevent realizing the high returns to skill available in the global marketplace.

The answer for those worried about population growth is to raise the incentive to invest in people. Parents will then want to reduce the number of children they have, without the international do-gooders having to hand out cash for condoms.

To try to create the right incentives, international institutions started making loans conditional on policy reforms. To see if that worked, turn to the next chapter.

Intermezzo: Tomb Paintings

Shahhat, age twenty-nine in 1981, lives in Berat on the Egyptian Nile 450 miles south of Cairo. Berat, with a population of 7,000, is divided into eleven hamlets, each near its ancestral fields. Local farmers still use the same hoes, forks, well sweeps, and threshing sledges pictured in ancient tomb paintings. Shahhat heads a family of seven and feeds a steady stream of visiting nieces and nephews as well. He owns a buffalo, a donkey, and eight sheep and about two acres of land.

Shahhat is one of twenty children born to his mother, Ommohamed, but fourteen of the children died in infancy or childhood. Ommohamed and other village women lived in terror of trachoma and other endemic diseases; they often bought amulets from the village sorceress to try to ward them off.[1] Fever and diarrhea seemed to sweep through the village every summer at the time of the khamsin, *the dust-carrying southerly wind.[2] Neither Shahhat nor his mother Ommohamed has ever been to school.*

Berat has strong traditions of male domination and violence. A father murdered his unmarried daughter, to preserve the family honor, after she became pregnant. He waited until she was washing clothes in a well, then held her head under water until she drowned. Violent threats were part of daily life in Berat; most men carried a heavy stave, a knife, or a gun. Violence would break out suddenly over questions of family honor, sexual passion, or quarrels over money, affecting a dozen lives at once. Jail sentences for murder in a feud or unpremeditated quarrel were light. But a day after a quarrel, it is common to make up and be laughing and joking as if nothing had happened.

Eleven years later, in 1992, Shahhat had left farming to become a foreman at one of the archaeological sites along the Nile. He earned about a hundred dollars a month. Now forty, he lived in a one-room mud brick house on his ancestral land. He had sold a small clover field in front of his house to take a seventeen-year-old second wife, much to the first wife's outrage, and now had six surviving children. After Shahhat started drinking more heavily, both of his wives took him to court for nonsupport of the children.[3]

6   The Loans That Were, the Growth That Wasn't

One more such victory and we are lost.

Pyrrhus

On August 18, 1982, Mexican finance minister Jesus Silva Herzog announced that Mexico could no longer service its external debt to international commercial banks. Mexico, and many other middle-income countries, had overborrowed from commercial banks, and now banks were unwilling to make further loans. Without new loans, Mexico could not service the old loans.

Silva Herzog's seismic announcement began the debt crisis for middle-income countries in Latin America and Africa as new commercial lending was abruptly cut off. The debt crisis for low-income countries in Africa worsened at the same time, as they had over-borrowed from official lenders. The Middle East and North Africa went into crisis as well, with some overborrowing and then the decline of oil prices in the 1980s.

Like passengers on the deck of the *Titanic*, we development experts did not comprehend at first what we were in for. The 1983 *World Development Report* of the World Bank optimistically projected a "central case" of 3.3 annual percent per capita growth in the developing countries from 1982 to 1995. The most pessimistic scenario was a "low case" annual per capita growth rate of 2.7 percent over the period 1982 to 1995. (The actual per capita growth would turn out to be close to zero.)[1]

To avert a growth collapse, we thought we had a good solution: aid and lending to developing countries conditional on their making policy reforms. Instead of aid financing investment, it was now aid financing reform.

Previously World Bank loans had been for projects and carried conditions only about those projects. But in 1980, the World Bank began to make general loans that carried conditions on economic policies to countries in crisis. This *adjustment lending* would meet the debt crisis by inducing the recipients to adjust their policies to promote growth, while providing needed money in the absence of commercial lending.

The IMF had always had conditions on its loans, but after 1982 it expanded the number and lengthened the maturity of the loans it was making. Aid donors and official creditors (like export promotion agencies) now also made their grants and loans more conditional by coordinating their lending with the IMF and World Bank.

Adjustment loans were supposed to offset the blow from the commercial cutoff of lending, while facilitating changes in policies that would keep growth going. (A similar strategy would be tried thirteen years later with the second Mexican debt crisis of 1994–1995 and then again two years after that in the East Asia crisis of 1997–1998.)

"Adjustment with growth" was the popular slogan of the time. When I searched the World Bank–IMF library for titles that are some variation on "adjustment with growth," I turned up 192 entries. In June 1983, for example, the World Bank and IMF published excerpts of speeches by their respective heads under the overall heading: "Adjustment and Growth: How the Fund and the Bank Are Responding to Current Difficulties."[2] In 1986, World Bank president A. W. Clausen gave a speech entitled "Adjustment with Growth in the Developing World: A Challenge for the International Community."[3] In 1987, the World Bank and IMF published a volume entitled *Growth-Oriented Adjustment Programs*, with an introduction discussing the "fundamental complementarity" of "adjustment and economic growth."[4]

The World Bank and IMF pursued the ambitious hope of achieving "adjustment with growth" through intensive involvement with tropical recipients. In the 1980s, the World Bank and IMF gave an average of six adjustment loans to each country in Africa, an average of five adjustment loans to each country in Latin America, an average of four adjustment loans to each country in Asia, and an average of three adjustment loans to each country in Eastern Europe, North Africa, and the Middle East.

The operation was a success for everyone except the patient. There was much lending, little adjustment, and little growth in the

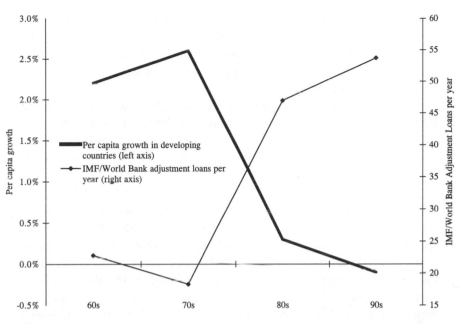

Figure 6.1
IMF/World Bank adjustment lending failed to ignite third world growth.

1980s and 1990s. A later study showed that World Bank predictions overestimated long-run growth in adjustment lending recipients by 3.5 percentage points.[5] The per capita growth rate of the typical developing country between 1980 and 1998 was zero.[6] The lending was there, but the growth wasn't (figure 6.1).

Growth in Africa, Latin America, Eastern Europe, the Middle East, and North Africa went into reverse in the 1980s and 1990s. Only Asia escaped the general pall over the tropical economies (until 1997, when Asia began its own crisis). The record on adjustment lending was unfortunately mixed. We will see that adjustment lending was incompatible with "people respond to incentives." Adjustment lending did not create the right incentives—for either the lenders or the recipients—to restore growth.

Some Successes

There were some success stories of adjustment lending, which shows its potential under the right conditions.

In October 1985, I went on my first trip for the World Bank, to Ghana. Reformist Ghana was a test case of adjustment lending. Donor involvement in Ghana was so intense that there were no rooms available at the decent hotel where all the donor representatives stayed. I stayed at a rather substandard hotel, where among other hardships the roof above my bed gave way during a rainstorm and my air conditioner exploded.

Notwithstanding my sufferings, the World Bank and IMF gave Ghana nineteen adjustment loans between 1980 and 1994. After serious reforms in 1983, Ghana grew at 1.4 percent per capita over the 1984 to 1994 period, a big improvement over negative 1.6 percent per capita growth between 1961 and 1983.

There were other successful cases. The World Bank and IMF gave Mauritius seven adjustment loans between 1980 and 1994. Mauritius had a stellar per capita growth rate of 4.3 percent per year during that time. The World Bank and IMF gave Thailand five adjustment loans over this same time period. Thailand grew at an even more stellar 5.3 percent per capita per year. And finally the Bank and the Fund gave most stellar Korea seven adjustment loans, mainly concentrated at the beginning of the period from 1980 to 1994. Korea managed to muster per capita growth of 6.7 percent per year during that time. (Thailand and Korea would need new adjustment loans in 1997–1998 after a new crisis; the results are not yet in on these loans.)

And in Latin America, adjustment lending was eventually successful in the 1990s, after initial disappointment in the 1980s. The World Bank and IMF gave Argentina fifteen adjustment loans between 1980 and 1994. Argentina made several failed (and disastrous) attempts at reform but eventually was successful at reform in the 1990s. Growth responded to reform: after per capita growth of −1.9 percent per year between 1980 and 1990, per capita growth was 4.7 percent per year between 1990 and 1994. (Growth then declined again, unfortunately.)

Peru shows another turnaround. The World Bank and IMF gave Peru eight adjustment loans between 1980 and 1994. Peru at first did not reform (again disastrously), but it also eventually reformed in the 1990s. Per capita growth turned around as well, from −2.6 percent per year between 1980 and 1990 to +2.6 percent per year between 1990 and 1994.

Lending Without Adjustment

Why didn't adjustment lending work that well for all countries? Why did it take so long in Argentina, Peru, (and even now success remains tenuous) and other Latin countries that we had a lost decade of Latin growth? The key clue comes from which countries the donors were financing and what those countries were doing in response to this financing. The loans were there, but too often the adjustment was not. This indiscriminate lending created poor incentives for making the reforms necessary for growth.

Zambia received twelve adjustment loans from the World Bank and IMF between 1980 and 1994. During that time, the flow of resources from official lending and aid reached one-quarter of Zambian GDP. Yet at the end of that period, Zambia had inflation above 40 percent every year except two from 1985 to 1996.

Everyone agreed that high inflation created bad incentives for growth, and conditions on adjustment lending generally required action to reduce inflation. So why did donors keep lending to Zambia despite the high inflation?

What happened in Zambia is a typical pattern. Countries with triple-digit inflation received as much official lending as countries with single-digit inflation. This lending could be justified if the loans went to a country with initially high inflation in order to help bring the inflation down. But in Zambia (and a number of other countries), lending continued and even increased as inflation remained high or went even higher. The IMF noted in 1995 that the "record of achieving ... low inflation" under its programs in low-income economies "was at best mixed." In fact, half of those with IMF programs had inflation go down, and half had it go up.[7] This is about as impressive as calling a coin flip correctly half of the time.

Trouble in Transition

Another case of failing to bring inflation under control with adjustment loans was in the critical years from 1992 to 1995 in Russia after it introduced a free market on January 1, 1992. In line with what we'll see later as a tendency to react to crises after they happen rather than trying to prevent them, the World Bank and IMF failed to have adjustment loans ready on the critical date on which Russia introduced the free market. In between Yeltsin's triumph after the failed coup in August 1991 and the freeing of prices on January 1, 1992, the IMF and World Bank failed to act with sufficient vigor to support the economic reformers putting in place their shock therapy program. After inflation was already ignited into the thousands of percent with the freeing of prices, and the Russian central bank was printing money helter-skelter to finance credits to state enterprises, only then did the IMF and World Bank give adjustment loans to Russia. By then the reformers had lost much credibility and political support from the population who saw their savings and pensions eaten away by high inflation. And as with many adjustment loans elsewhere, inflation was still not brought under control. It would not be until 1995 and another IMF adjustment loan that inflation was finally stabilized. Meanwhile, critical years were lost in which the Russian public became disenchanted with free markets, the political consequences of which continue to haunt Russia today.

Russia is only one example of one of adjustment lending's (and economists') most notorious misadventures: the failure to facilitate a smooth transition from Communism to capitalism. Mistakes made in the tropics were reenacted in the northern countries impoverished by the legacy of central planning. The 24 former Communist economies were the recipients of 143 adjustment loans and much advice from Western economists in the 1990s. The outcome wasn't pretty: a cumulative output decline in the 1990s of 41 percent for the typical ex-Communist economy in eastern Europe, with the percent of population living on less than $2/day increasing from 1.7% to 20.8%. Although transition was a complex process, we couldn't even get the basics right—inflation stayed high and volatile in the ex-Communist economies to whom we were lending, poisoning their initial experience with "free markets". By 1998, cumulative inflation of the average ex-Communist economy since 1990 was 64 thousand percent, despite all the adjustment loans (figure 6.2).[8]

Other Policies

The same phenomenon of aid going to countries with bad policies is true of other policies besides inflation. Mauritania had an average black market premium of above 100 percent for every year over the 1982 to 1989 period. The black market premium is the percentage amount by which the exchange rate of the currency in the black market is above the official exchange rate. It reflects a tax on exporters, since they usually purchase inputs at the black market exchange rate and are forced to sell products at the official exchange rate. Adjustment loans would usually carry the condition that the official exchange rate be one at which exporters can be competitive. Yet despite Mauritania's high black market premium, the World

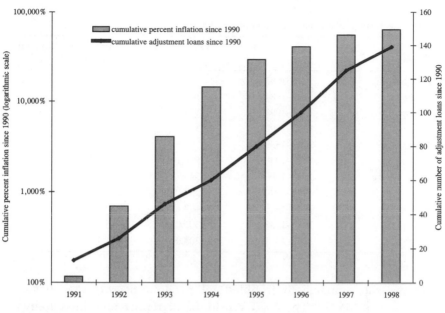

Figure 6.2
Inflation and adjustment lending in the ex-Communist countries

Bank and the IMF gave Mauritania six adjustment loans between 1982 and 1989. Other donors followed the Bank-Fund example, so Mauritania received an average of 23 percent of GDP per year in grants and official lending over this period. There are other examples of us donors giving high aid to countries with black market premiums above 100 percent, as shown in table 6.1.

We reach the same conclusion of unmet conditions by examining the average aid receipts at each level of the black market premium. Aid donors seem remarkably oblivious to how high the black market premium is when they give aid. Aid remains steady at black market premiums that are below 10 to those that are above 100 percent.

Another type of condition that Bank and Fund loans often include is the restructuring or shutting down of loss-making government enterprises. Here too conditions are observed about as often as the Ten Commandments.

Let me give one example: government-owned Kenya Railways. The World Bank and IMF gave Kenya nineteen adjustment loans between 1979 and 1996, loans that included conditions on solving the problems of sick state enterprises. Observers had identified Kenya

Table 6.1
Examples of high black market premiums and high aid

Country	Years	Black market premium (%)	Official development finance/GDP (%)
Bangladesh	1985–1992	198.9	7.4
Costa Rica	1981–1984	179.2	6.0
Ethiopia	1984–1993	176.8	10.4
Guyana	1980–1990	344.4	14.3
Mauritania	1982–1989	156.8	23.0
Nicaragua	1981–1988	2116.1	17.7
Sierra Leone	1987–1990	545.7	7.0
Sudan	1984–1990	269.0	6.5
Syria	1984–1991	403.6	10.1
Uganda	1980–1988	301.0	5.7
Zambia	1987–1991	308.0	14.0

Railways as a financially troubled enterprise in need of remedies as long ago as 1972.[9] The 1983 World Bank report identified Kenya Railways as having "severe financial difficulties," although it hoped the recently announced policy intentions to "examine and streamline the parastatals" would improve the situation.[10] The 1989 Public Expenditure Review noted that the government had prepared a corporate plan for Kenya Railways, for which the authors had high hopes—except that there were "considerable delays in implementing the Plan," noted the 1989 report, resulting in a still "poor financial condition of Kenya Railways."[11] Once again in 1995, according to the IMF, Kenya Railways "continued to have liquidity problems and accumulate arrears on its servicing of government-guaranteed external debt. The implementation of ... staff cuts and divestiture of peripheral activities was also delayed."[12] A 1996 Bank report noted the "poor financial performance" of Kenya Railways, its "substandard" technical performance, and the urgent need for "maintenance and upgrading." At last report, at the dawn of the new millennium, Kenya Railways was still losing money and unreformed. Apparently reforming this embodiment of government patronage and inefficiency will continue to be delayed.

We donors are also seemingly mindless about unmet conditions on budget deficits. The Bank and the Fund gave Côte d'Ivoire eighteen adjustment loans between 1980 and 1994. Yet, it ran an average budget deficit of 14 percent of GDP from 1989 to 1993. Everyone agreed that high budget deficits created bad incentives for growth. As a 1988 World Bank report on Côte d'Ivoire put it, "The present large deficits and the expectations of even larger deficits in the future create an environment of uncertainty which is not conducive to private investment."[13] And conditions on loans generally required reducing the budget deficit. So how could Côte d'Ivoire have a double-digit budget deficit to GDP ratio after eighteen adjustment loans?

Côte d'Ivoire is not an isolated case. The IMF and World Bank made twenty-two adjustment loans to Pakistan between 1970 and 1997. All of these loans had as a condition that Pakistan reduce its budget deficit. Yet the deficit remained stuck at 7 percent of GDP throughout this period. In the new millennium, the IMF and World Bank are giving new adjustment loans to Pakistan, conditional on its reducing its budget deficit.

To be fair, part of the high deficit with aid is intentional. Donor projects that have a high rate of return and are financed by aid are included in the budget deficit; the more such projects there are, the higher are both aid and the deficit. But the intention of the donors is also that countries would gradually wean themselves from reliance on donor aid to finance good projects themselves. The Côte d'Ivoire and Pakistan examples seem to show continuous feeding, not weaning. Côte d'Ivoire is also representative of a more general pattern. There is a pattern of high deficits going together with high official development financing.

Another policy mistake that slips by us heedless donors is one of severely negative real interest rates. The real interest rate (the interest rate minus the inflation) typically gets highly negative when the government fixes the interest rate and simultaneously prints money to create high inflation. This is a tax on bank depositors. This tax goes far toward destroying the banking system, since no one wants to hold on to bank deposits that are losing value. And a well-functioning banking system is crucial for economic growth. Yet the pattern is that countries with severely negative real interest rates get more aid than countries with positive real interest rates. Table 6.2 gives some examples that lie behind the pattern.

Perhaps most alarming of all, adjustment lending did not discriminate very much between more corrupt and less corrupt governments. Not much good is going to happen by disbursing aid loans to a corrupt government, as I will examine more in a later chapter.

Table 6.2
Examples of severely negative real interest rates and high aid

Country	Years	Real interest rate (%)	Official development finance/GDP (%)
Bolivia	1979–1985	−49.4	5.6
Guinea-Bissau	1989–1992	−15.9	38.3
Nicaragua	1989–1991	−86.7	54.5
Sierra Leone	1983–1991	−34.4	6.3
Sudan	1979–1984	−15.6	10.7
Somalia	1979–1988	−24.9	40.4
Uganda	1981–1988	−41.8	5.7
Zambia	1985–1991	−33.6	17.0

According to the International Credit Risk Guide ratings, the most corrupt developing countries in the world in the 80s and early 90s were Congo/Zaire, Bangladesh, Liberia, Haiti, Paraguay, Guyana, and Indonesia. Nevertheless, together these countries received 46 adjustment loans from the World Bank and IMF in the 80s and early 90s. It's hard to understand how Mobutu Sese Seko of Zaire, whose loot was measured in billions of dollars, received nine adjustment loans from the World Bank and IMF.

These stories and tables are part of a more general problem. A recent World Bank study found that aid does not influence countries' choice of policies. Nor do donor experts consider the worthiness of countries' policies in determining which ones are given aid. Aid appears to be determined by the strategic interests of donors, not by policy choices of the recipients. For example the United States gives large amounts of aid to Egypt as a reward for the Camp David peace agreement. France gives large amounts of aid to its former colonies. (Multilateral institutions like the World Bank do tend to give more aid to good-policy countries, but the reward for better policies is small. Moving from the worst policies to the best policies results in only a quarter of a percentage point of GDP more aid.)[14]

How to Pretend to Adjust

Max Escher has a famous print called *Ascending and Descending*. Through his mastery of illusion, Escher shows people ascending and descending a quadrangular staircase until they come back to where they started. So too did many countries seem to be adjusting and adjusting as they received adjustment loans, only to end up where they started.

A government that was irresponsible before the adjustment loan has unchanged incentives to be irresponsible after the adjustment loan. Only a change from a bad government to a good government will truly change policies. An unchanged irresponsible government will create the illusion of adjustment without doing the real thing. Even when donors enforce the reductions in the budget deficit, for example, the irresponsible government has every incentive to do creative fiscal accounting to avoid real adjustment.

Today's deficit is a way to borrow against the future. The deficit is financed with new debt that makes possible higher government receipts today at the cost of having to make higher payoffs of the debt tomorrow. But public debt is not the only way a government that doesn't value the future can borrow against it. There are many ways the government can free up money today in return for higher outlays tomorrow. For example, it can cut current spending on maintenance of roads, yielding extra money it can use for patronage and consumption. Unfortunately, the lost maintenance will cause later road reconstruction costs many times higher than the savings on maintenance. The World Bank's *World Development 1994* estimated that "timely maintenance of $12 billion would have saved road reconstruction costs of $45 billion in Africa in the past decade."

Although donors are aware of these techniques for pretending to adjust, it is difficult to enforce the conditions anyway. The conditions on the deficit, as weak as they are, are still stronger than the conditions on operations and maintenance spending. Consider the example of trying to preserve operations and maintenance spending during deficit cutting. To return to Kenya again, with its nineteen adjustment loans from the World Bank and IMF between 1979 and 1996, the World Bank did several public expenditure reviews in Kenya over this period. These reviews were designed to induce the country to cut wasteful spending and preserve good spending like road maintenance during adjustment, but the public expenditure reviews in Kenya were little heeded.

The World Bank country economist for Kenya in 2000 complained about woefully inadequate spending on operations and maintenance, echoing the World Bank's 1996 Public Expenditure Review, which noted "an abysmal record on maintaining equipment and facilities that is widely observed across ministries."[15] The 1994

Public Expenditure Review pointed out "the severe inadequacy of resources for operations and maintenance."[16] The 1989 review noted that operations and maintenance expenditure is "substantially underprovided in all of the sectors reviewed by the mission." The 1983 Country Economic Memorandum noted that insufficient funding for intermediate inputs "resulted in projects operating at activity levels below those planned and facilities remaining unused for a time after completion of physical assets."[17] The 1979 Country Economic Memorandum noted "a serious problem of insufficient recurrent funds to maintain existing projects at full capacity." The memorandum detected a particularly serious shortfall of funds for routine maintenance of roads (although it noted with hope that "the Government has already initiated measures to substantially improve road maintenance").[18]

Eating the Future

The fundamental principle remains the same: a government that eats away at the future by incurring debt will also eat away at the future in other ways. For example, the government can cut investment in infrastructure that would have brought future revenue, thus lowering today's deficit while increasing tomorrow's. African state telephone companies have cut new telecommunications investment so much that customers wait an average of more than eight years for new telephone service, yet revenue per line in Africa is exceptionally high by world standards.[19]

The government can also get revenue today by selling off profitable state enterprises, at the cost of forgone future revenue. Nigeria between 1989 and 1993 had two IMF standby agreements and two World Bank adjustment loans that placed constraints on its budget deficit and public debt. During that period, it sold government equity shares in upstream oil ventures for $2.5 billion—during a period in which $12 billion in oil revenues disappeared from the official accounts, possibly into the pockets of Nigerian government officials. This is a general pattern: countries that receive adjustment loans get more revenue from selling off state companies than do countries without adjustment programs.

Countries with adjustment programs also pumped oil out of the reserves in the ground faster than during periods without adjustment programs. They thus got more revenue today at the cost of making less oil revenue available for sale in the future.[20]

Governments can also simply shift other expenditures and revenues across time to meet today's cash deficit targets.[21] Brazil in 1998 issued zero coupon government bonds whose principal and interest were not due until the next year, thus lowering this year's interest expenditure. Many governments resort to the expedient of delaying payments to government workers or suppliers. These arrears lower this year's cash deficit and explicit public debt, while increasing next year's cash deficit and the implicit public debt.[22]

Tropical nations may have learned some of these tricks from the industrial nations. During the Gramm-Rudman bill's effort to contain deficits, the U.S. Congress in 1987 postponed a $3 billion payday for military personnel into the following fiscal year. Defense Secretary Caspar Weinberger also stretched out procurement of new weapons systems so as to lower the current expenditure, although the stretch-out increased per unit costs.[23] The U.S. government also liked the idea of selling off state assets. Congress had stalled on privatization of the railway company Conrail for a while until Gramm-Rudman came along. When Gramm-Rudman created incentives for getting privatization revenues to meet budget targets, the Congress suddenly sold Conrail.

Governments can also shift taxes over time. There are many anecdotes of developing countries' getting advance payments of taxes to meet IMF program deficit targets.[24] The U.S. Congress moved about $1 billion in excise tax collections forward to meet the Gramm-Rudman deficit ceiling in 1987.[25]

Another sleight of hand is to reduce current expenditure today in return for a future liability. For example, the government could switch from granting subsidies to state enterprises to guaranteeing the bank loans made to these enterprises to cover their losses, creating the appearance of a deficit reduction. When the enterprises eventually default on their debt, the government pays off the debt and so winds up paying for state enterprise losses just as it had when subsidies were explicit. Egypt, for example, phased out budgetary support to state enterprises in 1991, but allowed loss-making enterprises to continue to operate on bank overdrafts and foreign loans. The Egyptian government periodically has to cover for loan defaults by these enterprises.[26]

Creative governments can make state enterprise losses disappear by having public financial institutions (whose balances deficit definitions seldom include) subsidize the state-owned firms. For example in Uganda in 1987–1988, the central bank gave the state-owned breweries and tobacco companies foreign exchange at an artificially low exchange rate, reducing their imported input costs. In Argentina before 1990, the central bank gave a subsidized interest rate on loans to loss-making public enterprises, reducing their interest costs and their losses.[27] In China, state banks make loans to state enterprises at negative real interest rates.

Governments also can help themselves to subsidies from their pension funds. For example, many countries required their pension funds that accumulated surpluses early in the life cycle of the plan to lend to the government at negative real interest rates. Examples include Costa Rica, Ecuador, Egypt, Jamaica, Peru, Trinidad and Tobago, Turkey, and Venezuela. In the worst case, Peru, the real return on the pension fund was −37.4 percent—not a reassuring figure to Peruvian retirees. Lower interest rates on government debt reduce the budget deficit but also reduce the reserves available when the pension plan begins to run deficits later in its life cycle.[28] The government will have to honor the net pension liabilities, so the negative real interest rate scheme just redistributes spending from today to tomorrow.[29]

There are similar tricks the government can perform on other reform conditions. To meet an inflation target, the government can keep the budget deficit unchanged but substitute debt financing for money creation. It can keep doing this until the debt burden becomes too great and lenders are no longer willing to lend. Then the government is forced to resort to printing money and inflation all over again. But this time money creation and inflation proceed at a higher rate, because the government now needs to service the debt that accumulated in the meantime.[30] All the government has accomplished is to lower inflation today at the cost of higher inflation tomorrow. (Argentina's failed inflation reductions before 1990 follow this story line to the letter.)

All of these stories show that countries can improve in the short run and appear to be meeting the loan conditions, when in fact they are only postponing the problem. So in the future, they get new adjustment loans to deal with the now larger problem of adjustment. This may give some insight into countries that received a remarkably high number of adjustment loans.

Consider first the short-term crisis loans of the IMF (called *stand-by loans* in IMF jargon). These loans are meant to address a situation of acute crisis, such as a country running out of international reserves.

Ideally, the IMF and other international agencies would help a country to resolve its crisis in a way so as to prevent future crises. But this does not happen. Countries get stuck on a merry-go-round of crisis-IMF bailout-crisis-IMF bailout, and so on ad infinitum. Haiti went through this merry-go-round 22 times, Liberia 18 times, Ecuador 16 times, and Argentina 15 times. The motto of the IMF, World Bank, and the recipient governments sometimes seems to have been "millions to resolve a crisis, not a dollar to prevent one."

Twelve countries received fifteen or more World Bank and IMF adjustment loans over the fifteen-year period 1980 to 1994: Argentina, Bangladesh, Côte d'Ivoire, Ghana, Jamaica, Kenya, Morocco, Mexico, Pakistan, Philippines, Senegal, and Uganda. The median per capita growth rate for those twelve countries over that period was zero. This is perhaps the most important failing of adjustment lending: the failure to put in place policies that would promote growth. Higher growth expands tax revenues and export proceeds faster, enabling debts to be serviced more easily in the future, eliminating the need for future adjustment loans. The IMF, World Bank, and other donors worried so much about the debts (the liabilities) of these economies that they paid insufficient attention to incentives to expand the assets of those same economies—namely, their ability to generate future income through economic growth. A recent study by Przeworski and Vreeland (2000) found a *negative* effect of IMF programs on growth. A long inconclusive literature within the World Bank and IMF has tried to estimate the effects of their programs on growth controlling for other factors, with positive growth effects maddeningly hard to detect. What is clear is that the hopes for "adjustment with growth" did not work out. There was too little adjustment, too little growth, and too little scrutiny of the results of adjustment lending.

Incentives for Donors and Recipients

So why had our adjustment lending by the late 1980s become too often the heedless giving to the hopeless? Why wasn't adjustment lending the magic formula that would have prevented two decades of lost growth? Why weren't we enforcing the reform conditions? Once again, our official motto—people respond to incentives—gives the answer. Incentives are not checked at the door of the international organizations. Lenders face incentives that cause them to give loans even when the conditions of the loans are not met. Recipients face incentives that cause them not to make reforms even when they get conditional loans. Many different kinds of incentives cause these problems.

First, the donors wouldn't be donors if they didn't care for the poor in the recipient country. But this solicitude for the poor makes their threat of cutting off lending if conditions go unmet not very credible. After the fact, even if the conditions are not met, the donors want to alleviate the lot of the poor, and so they give the aid anyway. The recipients can anticipate this behavior of donors and thus sit tight without doing reforms or helping the poor, expecting to get the loans anyway. As we saw with deficit cutting, they may create the appearance of reforms.

The donors' concern for the poor creates even more perverse incentives for the recipients. Since countries with larger poverty problems get more aid, those countries have little incentive to alleviate their poverty problem. The poor are held hostage to extract aid from the donors.[31]

How could one correct this problem of perverse incentives? Paradoxically, the poor in the recipient country will be better off if the aid disbursement decision is delegated to a hard-hearted agency that doesn't care about the poor. This Scrooge agency can credibly threaten to withhold aid if the recipient does not meet the conditions and alleviate poverty. The recipient will then meet the conditions, and the poor will benefit.

Donors also face the wrong incentives for disbursing aid for a less magnanimous reason. Most donor institutions are set up with a separate country department for each country or group of countries. The budget of this department is determined by the amount of resources it disburses to recipients. A department that does not disburse its loan budget will likely receive a smaller budget the following year. Larger budgets are associated with more prestige and more career advancement, so the people in the country departments feel the incentive to disburse even when loan conditions are not met.

Lenders create another perverse incentive for loan recipients by making loans respond to the change in policies. This creates a kind of zigzagging adjustment in which countries continually adjust and then go back on adjustment. When they adjust, they get the new loans because of the favorable change in policies. When they backslide, they get no further new loans. Then they adjust again, setting off a new round of adjustment lending by the World Bank and IMF and other donors. The *Economist* magazine describes the process in Kenya:

Over the past few years Kenya has performed a curious mating ritual with its aid donors. The steps are: one, Kenya receives its yearly pledges of foreign aid. Two, the government begins to misbehave, backtracking on economic reform.... Three, a new meeting of donor countries looms with exasperated foreign governments preparing their sharp rebukes. Four, Kenya pulls a placatory rabbit out of the hat. Five, the donors are mollified and the aid is pledged. The whole dance then starts again.[32]

There is sometimes a fourth reason that official lenders give new loans to nonreforming countries. Often these countries have already borrowed a lot from official lenders and are having some difficulty paying them back. The official lenders don't want to declare publicly that the loans are nonperforming, because that would be a political embarrassment that might threaten the official lender's budget allocation at home. So official lenders sometimes give new loans to enable the old loans to be paid back.

Recipients are aware of the donors' incentives. Surprisingly enough, the impoverished recipients are in the driver's seat during negotiations over disbursement of aid loans. The threat that the country department will not disburse the loan if conditions go unmet is not very credible. The borrowers know that the aid lenders care about the poor and that aid lenders' budgets depend on the lenders' new lending. The borrowers can also threaten not to service their old debt unless they get new loans, so disbursements are made anyway.

What Could Have Been

A sage once said that the definition of tragedy is *what might have been*. A recent World Bank study found that aid *would have had* a positive impact on growth if the recipients had had good policies. It found too that aid does not have a significant impact on growth on average. However, when policies such as the budget balance and inflation are good, aid does have a positive impact. Among low-income countries with good policies, one more percentage point of GDP worth of aid is associated with 0.6 percentage point of GDP faster growth.

There is now a trend among the low-income countries toward better policies. Fifteen out of forty low-income economies had reached the level of good policy by 1994 at which the effect of aid on growth was significantly positive. There are also signs that the lenders and donors are becoming more selective about recipients of their money. The World Bank, for example, is pursuing reforms to become more selective about where its loans go.

Unfortunately, in 1994, industrial nations gave the smallest share of their GDP as aid in twenty years. The irony is that aid went up as policies were getting worse, and now aid is going down as policies are finally getting better.

If at times adjustment lending in the 1980s and 1990s seemed to be no more constructive than shipping sand to the Kalahari, it's because there were poor incentives for both lender and recipient. Adjustment lending conditional on reform was another failed formula on the quest for growth.

Looking Forward

We should tie aid to past country performance, not promises, giving the country's government an incentive to pursue growth-creating policies. The better a country's policies are for creating growth, the more aid per capita it gets. We should rank all poor countries according to their policy performance and then give more aid to a country the higher it is up the list. The exact formula is not important; all that is important is that aid increases with policy performance, so that governments have an incentive to pursue good policies.

We will see in later chapters that we know something about what policies are associated with growth. For now, let's say that a country that has a high black market exchange rate relative to its official exchange rate, a high inflation rate, a controlled interest rate well below the inflation rate, a high budget deficit, and widespread corruption should not be getting aid. A poor country that has no black market premium on foreign exchange, low inflation, free market interest rates, a reasonably low budget deficit, institutions to protect private property and the sanctity of contracts, and strict anticorruption policies should get a lot of aid.

Giving aid according to policy performance would drastically change aid allocation. I looked at a country's ranking in official development financing per capita received in the 1980s. I then examined a country's policy performance ranking in the 1980s (policy performance is an index-averaging performance on the government deficit, corruption, inflation, financial development, and the black market premium on foreign exchange). I found that in the 1980s, policy performance and development financing were virtually independent. Therefore, having aid depend on policy would have drastically increased official financing in the 1980s in some countries (like India, Thailand, and Malaysia). Having aid depend on policy would have drastically reduced official financing in others (like Nicaragua, Jamaica, and Ecuador).

To enforce the conditions on policy performance for receiving aid, countries should enter into "aid contests," whereby they would submit proposals for growth-promoting use of the aid money. In their proposals, they would document policy performance achieved thus far and announce plans for future progress on policy performance.

However, aid should respond mainly to the level of policy performance already achieved and not as much on proposed changes in policy. This reverses the current system, under which promised changes in policy are enough for donors to disburse aid. Under the current system, countries have successfully played a game under which they start with bad policies, switch to good policies long enough to get the aid, then revert to the bad policies. The result is that many countries with bad policy on average have nevertheless received aid.

As countries' incomes rise because of their favorable policies for economic growth, aid should increase in matching fashion. This is the opposite of what happens in actuality. A country with destructive policies and declining income gets more concessional terms on aid. For example, Kenya used to be rich enough that it was eligible only for market interest rates on World Bank loans until bad policies and a decline in income made it eligible for low-interest loans. Conversely, countries that prosper actually "graduate" from eligibility for low-interest concessional loans. The change in aid should always be positive as income increases, not negative. (Granted, at the beginning of a new aid regime, the poor countries should be the ones designated to be eligible for aid. I am not recommending foreign aid for Austria. Since this designation is done only at the beginning it does not create perverse incentives to remain poor.) This is a drastic change from conventional wisdom, which decreases aid as income rises, thus giving a negative incentive against getting richer. This negative incentive could be offset by other positive incentives to get richer, but it certainly does not help matters. If aid were given to the most deserving countries (those with the best policies), we could at last get donors' and governments' incentives aligned for growth.

The ultimate sign of failure of adjustment lending is to admit that the debts cannot be repaid because it shows that the money was not used productively. The international institutions indeed came to such an admission, as the next chapter discusses.

Intermezzo: Leila's Story

My friend Leila (I've changed her name to protect her privacy) is a Bangladeshi-American woman who always seems to wear a sympathetic smile. She has bright, shining eyes that transmit life and joy. She's a professional woman of some accomplishment. But there is a darker edge to Leila that I've often wondered about. One day she told me her story.

She was ten in 1971 and living in Bangladesh when the war for independence broke out. After agitation by Bengali nationalists for a measure of regional autonomy for what was then East Pakistan, West Pakistani troops launched a campaign of terror in Bangladesh on March 25. The Pakistani army compiled a hit list of Bengali professionals to exterminate the leadership of the autonomy movement. Leila's father, a prominent Bengali economist, was on the list. He disguised himself as a peasant and walked all the way to safety at the border with India. Leila, her brother, and her mother escaped by air out of Bangladesh soon afterward, to find safety with friends in Paris. With the help of India, Bangladesh won its independence. The story could have had a happy ending for Leila and her family, but it didn't.

Two of Leila's aunts came out from their nine-months' refuge in the cellar where they had hid while the war thundered overhead. They thought it was safe now that the fighting had stopped. They drove their car with their sons, Leila's cousins, aged eight and eleven, sitting in the back seat. But the Pakistani soldiers, who had already surrendered, had not yet been disarmed and were randomly firing their weapons at Bangladeshi civilians in rage and frustration. A single bullet from a Pakistani rifle entered the car of Leila's aunts and went through the heads of her two cousins, killing them instantly. Leila's family had not escaped the war after all.

Forgive Us Our Debts

Concessionary finance used unproductively leads to indebtedness which is then used as an argument for further concessionary finance.

Lord P. T. Bauer, 1972

Haiti, a poor country, has a high foreign debt and is not growing. The ratio of foreign debt service to exports has reached 40 percent, well above the 20 to 25 percent thought to be "sustainable."[1] Unfortunately, the debt was incurred not to expand economic production capacity, but to finance the government's patronage employment and large military and police forces. Corruption has been endemic, so there is the strong suspicion that some of the proceeds of foreign loans found their way into the pockets of the rulers. This is a description of Haiti's experience in the nineties. However, the decade to which these facts refer is not the 1990s but the 1890s.[2]

The problem of poor countries with high foreign debts is not a new one. Its history stretches from the two Greek city-states that defaulted on loans from the Delos Temple in the fourth century B.C., to Mexico's default on its first foreign loan after independence in 1827, to Haiti's 1997 ratio of foreign debt to exports of 484 percent.[3]

But the problems of poor countries with high foreign debts are very much in the news today. Many aid advocates call for a forgiveness of all debt of poor countries on the occasion of the turning of the millennium. This campaign to forgive the debt is called Jubilee 2000. Support for Jubilee 2000 has been expressed by such diverse figures as Bono from the rock group U2, the economist Jeffrey Sachs, the Dalai Lama, and the pope. I saw a webcast of unlikely companions Bono and Sachs consulting the pope about Third World debt on September 23, 1999. In April 2000, thousands gathered on the Mall in Washington, D.C., to demonstrate for "dumping the debt." Even Hollywood has taken notice. In the recent hit movie *Notting Hill*, Hugh Grant mentions "cancellation of Third World debt" to woo Julia Roberts.

The World Bank and IMF already have a program, the HIPC (Highly Indebted Poor Countries) Initiative, to provide debt forgiveness for poor countries with good policies. This program includes, for the first time, partial forgiveness of IMF and World Bank debts. The summit of the seven largest industrial countries (the G-7) in Cologne in June 1999 called for an expansion of the HIPC program, speeding up the process of receiving relief and increasing the amount of debt relief provided for each country. The membership of the World Bank and IMF—about every country's government in the world—approved the expansion in September 1999. The expansion will increase the total cost (in terms of today's money) of the HIPC Initiative from $12.5 billion to $27 billion.[4] So debt forgiveness is the latest panacea for relieving poverty of poor countries. As the official web site for the Jubilee 2000 campaign puts it, "Millions of people around the world are living in poverty because of Third World debt and its consequences." If only the Jubilee 2000 debt forgiveness plan goes through, "the year 2000 could signal the beginning of dramatic improvements in healthcare, education, employment and development for countries crippled by debt."[5]

There is just one problem: the little recognition among the Jubilee 2000 campaigners, such as Bono, Sachs, the Dalai Lama, and the pope, that debt relief is not a new policy. Just as high debt is not new, efforts to forgive debtors their debts are not new. We have already been trying debt forgiveness for two decades, with little of the salutory results that are promised by Jubilee 2000.

Two Decades' History of Debt Forgiveness

Although there were intimations as long ago as 1967 that "debt-service payments have risen to the point at which a number of countries face critical situations," the current wave of debt relief for poor countries really got underway in 1979.[6] The 1979 World Debt Tables of the World Bank noted "lagging debt payment" on official loans to poor countries, although "debt or debt service forgiveness has eased the problems for some." The 1977–1979 UNCTAD meetings led to official creditors' forgiving $6 billion in debt to forty-five poor countries. The measures by official creditors included "the elimination of interest payments, the rescheduling of debt service, local cost assistance, untied compensatory aid, and new grants to reimburse old debts."[7]

The 1981 Africa report by the World Bank noted that Liberia, Sierra Leone, Sudan, Zaire, and Zambia (all of which would become HIPCs) had already experienced "severe debt-servicing difficulties" in the 1970s and "are likely to continue to do so in the 1980s." The report hinted of debt relief: "longer-term solutions for debt crises should be sought" and "the present practice of [donors'] separating aid and debt decisions may be counterproductive."[8] The 1984 World Bank Africa report was more forthright, at least as forthright as bureau-speak can get: "Where monitorable programs exist, multi-year debt relief and longer grace periods should be part of the package of financial support to the program."[9] The wording got even stronger in the World Bank's 1986 Africa report: low-income Africa's financing needs will "have to be filled by additional bilateral aid and debt relief."[10] The World Bank noted in 1988 that "the past year has brought increasing recognition of the urgency of the debt problems of the low-income countries of Sub-Saharan Africa."[11] The Bank's 1991 Africa report continued escalating the rhetoric: "Africa cannot escape its present economic crisis without reducing its debt burden sizably."[12]

The G-7 All World Tour

The rich countries were responding to World Bank calls for debt forgiveness for poor countries. The June 1987 summit of the G-7 in Venice called for interest rate relief on debt of low-income countries. The G-7 agreed on a program of partial debt forgiveness that became known as the Venice terms (beginning an onslaught of technocrat-speak that would name the latest debt relief program after the site of the most recent G-7 summit). One year later, the June 1988 G-7 summit in Toronto agreed on a menu of options, including partial forgiveness, longer maturities, and lower interest rates. These became known as the Toronto terms.[13]

Meanwhile, in order to help African countries service their official debt, the World Bank in December 1987 initiated a Special Program of Assistance (SPA) to low-income Africa. The IMF complemented the SPA with the Enhanced Structural Adjustment Facility (ESAF).

Both programs sought to provide "substantially increased, quick-disbursing, highly concessional assistance to adjusting countries."[14]

The 1990 Houston G-7 summit considered "more concessional reschedulings for the poorest debtor countries." The United Kingdom and the Netherlands proposed "Trinidad terms" that would increase the grant element of debt reduction to 67 percent, from 20 percent under the Toronto terms.[15] The 1991 London G-7 summit agreed "on the need for additional debt relief measures ... going well beyond the relief already granted under Toronto terms."[16] Through November 1993, the Paris Club (the club of official lenders) applied Enhanced Toronto Terms that were even more concessional.[17] In December 1994, the Paris Club announced "Naples terms" under which eligible countries would receive yet additional debt relief.[18]

Then, in September 1996, the IMF and World Bank announced the HIPC Debt Initiative, which was to allow the poor countries to "exit, once and for all, from the rescheduling process" and to resume "normal relations with the international financial community, characterized by spontaneous financial flows and the full honoring of commitments." The multilateral lenders for the first time would "take action to reduce the burden of their claims on a given country," albeit conditional on good policies in the recipient countries.

The Paris Club at the same time agreed to go beyond the Naples terms and provide an 80 percent debt reduction.[19] By September 1999 and the time of the meeting of Bono, Sachs, the Dalai Lama, and the pope, debt relief packages had been agreed for seven poor countries, totaling more than $3.4 billion in debt relief in today's money.[20] Then, there were renewed calls in 1999 for expansion of this program, an expansion that Jubilee 2000 said did not go far enough. As of October 2000, the World Bank said that twenty poor countries will receive "meaningful debt relief" by the end of the year.

Besides explicit debt relief, there also has been an implicit form of debt relief going on throughout the period, which is the substitution of concessional debt (debt with interest rates well below the market rate) for nonconcessional (market interest rate) debt. It's remarkable that the burden of debt service for HIPCs rose throughout the period despite the large net transfers of resources from concessional lenders like the International Development Association of the World Bank and the concessional arms of bilateral and other multilateral agencies.

The necessity to provide continuing waves of debt relief one after another, all the while substituting concessional for nonconcessional debt, all the while having Jubilee 2000 call for even more debt relief, all the while having Bono, Sachs, the Dalai Lama and the pope wring their hands in dismay, may suggest something is wrong with debt relief as a panacea for development. There is the paradox that a large group of countries came to be defined as highly indebted at the end of two decades of debt relief and increasingly concessional financing.

The rest of this chapter reviews possible explanations for what went wrong over the past two decades of attempted debt relief. The revealed preference of debtors for high debt may simply lead to new borrowing to replace old canceled debts. The granting of progressively more favorable terms for debt relief may also have perverse incentive effects, as countries borrow in anticipation of debt forgiveness. High debt may remain a persistent problem simply because it reflects "irresponsible governments" that remain "irresponsible" after debt relief is granted.

Selling Off the Future

The Jubilee 2000 debt campaigners treat debt as a natural disaster that just happened to strike poor countries. The truth may be less charitable. It may be that countries that borrowed heavily did so because they were willing to mortgage the welfare of future generations to finance this generation's (mainly the government clientele's) standard of living.

This is a hypothesis that we can test. If it is true, it has explosive implications. If "people respond to incentives," then some surprising things will happen in response to debt relief. Any debt forgiveness granted will result in new borrowing by irresponsible governments until they have mortgaged the future to the same degree as before. Debt forgiveness will be a futile panacea in that case; it will not only fail to spur development, it won't even succeed in lowering debt burdens.

There are more subtle signs of mortgaging the future that we can check to see if the "irresponsible borrowing" hypothesis holds. We can see if in addition to incurring high debt, the poor countries also sold off national assets at a disproportionately high rate, another way of expropriating future generations. Just as a profligate heir in Victorian novels turns from running up debts to selling off the family silver, we should expect to see "irresponsible governments" both incurring new debt and depleting assets.

To examine the response of new debt and assets to debt relief,
I examine the forty-one HIPCs as so classified by the IMF and World
Bank: Angola, Benin, Bolivia, Burkina Faso, Burundi, Cameroon,
Central African Republic, Chad, Congo (Democratic Republic),
Congo (Republic), Côte d'Ivoire, Equatorial Guinea, Ethiopia, Ghana,
Guinea, Guinea-Bissau, Guyana, Honduras, Kenya, Laos, Liberia,
Madagascar, Malawi, Mali, Mauritania, Mozambique, Myanmar,
Nicaragua, Niger, Rwanda, São Tomé and Príncipe, Senegal, Sierra
Leone, Somalia, Sudan, Tanzania, Togo, Uganda, Vietnam, Yemen,
and Zambia.

The data on debt relief from the World Bank's World Debt Tables
go back only to 1989. The relationship between debt relief and new
borrowing over this period is interesting: total debt forgiveness for
forty-one highly indebted poor countries from 1989 to 1997 totaled
$33 billion, while their new borrowing was $41 billion. This seems to
confirm the prediction that debt relief will be met with an equivalent
amount of new borrowing.

New borrowing was the highest in the countries that got the most
debt relief. There is a statistically significant association between
average debt relief as a percentage of GDP and new net borrowing
as percentage of GDP. Consistent with the mortgaging-the-future
hypothesis, governments replaced forgiven debt with new debt.

Another bit of evidence that debt forgiveness did not lower
debt significantly is to look at the burden of the debt over the period
1979 to 1997. Debt relief over this period should have lowered debt
burdens, unless governments were replacing forgiven debt with
new debt. For the burden of the debt, I use the present value of debt
service as a ratio to exports. The present value of debt service is
simply the amount that the government would have to have in the
bank today (earning a market interest rate) to be able to meet all their
future debt service. That doesn't mean that it should have such an
amount in the bank; it's just an illustrative calculation that allows us
to summarize in one number the whole stream of future interest and
debt repayments.

I again use 1979 as a base year because it was the year the
UNCTAD summit inaugurated the current wave of debt relief. I have
data for twenty-eight to thirty-seven highly indebted poor countries
over the period 1979 to 1997. Despite the ongoing debt relief, the
typical present value debt to export ratio rose strongly from 1979 to
1997. We can see three distinct periods: (1) 1979 to 1987, when debt

ratios rose strongly; (2) 1988 to 1994, when debt ratios remained constant; and (3) 1995 to 1997, in which debt ratios fell. The behavior in periods 1 and 2 is consistent with failed debt relief, while the fall in the last period may indicate that the 1996 HIPC debt relief program has been more successful than earlier efforts.

Despite the fall in the last period, however, the typical debt to export ratio was significantly higher in 1997 than it was in 1979. This suggests that for the forty-one highly indebted countries, new borrowing (more than) kept pace with the amount of debt relief, as would have been predicted by the mortgaging-the-future view of how high debt came about.

I next turn to data on selling off assets, a more subtle sign of mortgaging the future. One type of asset important for some HIPCs is oil reserves. Pumping out and selling oil is a form of running down assets, since it leaves less oil in the ground for future generations. There are ten HIPCs that are oil producers, for which we have data for 1987 to 1996. Did HIPCs have higher oil production growth over this period of debt relief than did the non-HIPC oil producers? Yes. The average growth in oil production is 6.6 percentage points higher in the HIPCs than in the non-HIPCs, which is a statistically significant difference. The average log growth in oil production in HIPCs was 5.3 percent; in non-HIPCs, it was −1.3 percent.

Another form of selling off assets taking place at this time was sales of state enterprises to private foreign purchasers ("privatization"). We have data on privatization revenues for 1988 through 1997. Over this period, total sales of state enterprises in the HIPCs amounted to $4 billion. This is an underestimate, because not all privatization revenues are recorded in the official statistics. Even using these flawed data, there is a positive and significant association across the forty-one HIPCs between the amount of debt forgiveness and the amount of privatization of foreign exchange revenues. Privatization may have been done for efficiency reasons or even as a condition for debt relief, but it also may suggest a profligate government running down its assets.

The most general sign of running down assets is also the most worrisome. The per capita income of the typical HIPC declined between 1979 and 1998. This is worrisome first of all because two decades of debt relief failed to prevent negative growth in HIPCs. This is not good news for Jubilee 2000 campaigners who claim that debt relief will bring growth.

Second, the decline in income is an indirect sign of the governments' running down their economies' productive capacity. The governments' policies may have favored present consumption over future investment. The decline in income may have been an indirect sign that governments were running down public infrastructure like roads, schools, and health clinics, lowering returns to private investment, and contributing to the general depression in the HIPCs.

High Debt from Bad Policy or Bad Luck?

Another sign of irresponsible governments that we would expect to see—in particular with high-debt countries—are high external and budget deficits. Indeed, the average levels of external deficits and budget deficits (with or without grants) between 1980 and 1997 were worse for HIPCs than for non-HIPCs, controlling for per capita income.

Nor are these the only signs of irresponsible behavior by high-debt governments. They are also more likely to follow shortsighted policies that create subsidies for favored supporters while penalizing future growth. For example, they may control interest rates below the rate of inflation, granting subsidized credits to government favorites. However, the poor depositors, seeing that inflation is eroding their deposits in real terms, will take their money out of the financial system and put it into real estate or foreign currency. This shrinks the size of the total financial sector, which is too bad since a large and healthy financial sector is one of the prerequisites for growth. Indeed, we find that HIPCs have smaller financial systems than do other economies, controlling for per capita income.

Irresponsible governments will also tend to subsidize imports to their favored clients. They can do this by keeping the exchange rate artificially low (that is, keeping their currency at an artificially high value), making imports cheap. Unfortunately, an exchange rate that keeps imports cheap will also depress the domestic currency price that exporters receive for their exports, lowering their incentive to export their products. Since exports are an important engine of growth, an artificially overvalued currency will tend to depress growth. Private investors will not invest in what would have been profitable export activities but for the misaligned exchange rate. I indeed find that HIPCs tend to have a more overvalued currency relative to non-HIPCs, controlling for income. This is another way that HIPCs mortgage the future in favor of the present: subsidizing consumption of imported goods at the cost of future growth.

But what if HIPCs suffered worse luck than other countries? Could that explain why they became highly indebted, instead of the "irresponsible governments" hypothesis? We can test this alternative hypothesis directly. One form of bad luck is to have import prices climb faster than export prices (terms of trade deterioration, in technocrat jargon). Did HIPCs see their terms of trade deteriorate more than did non-HIPCs? No.

Another form of bad luck is war. Many poor countries had war over the period in which HIPCs became HIPCs. Did HIPCs suffer from the collapse of output that often accompanies war, making their debts more burdensome? No. HIPCs were not any more likely than non-HIPCs to be at war over this period. The "irresponsible governments" hypothesis explains much more how the poor countries' high debt came about than does the "bad luck" hypothesis.

Showdown at Financing Gap

So far I have been looking at irresponsible behavior from the viewpoint of the borrower. However, someone had to be willing to lend to these irresponsible borrowers. Was there irresponsible lending as well as irresponsible borrowing? I think you can guess the answer.

Let us examine the composition of financing the irresponsibly high external deficits in HIPCs. There are some intriguing patterns First, HIPCs received less foreign direct investment (FDI) than other less developed countries (LDCs), controlling for income. This may be an indirect indicator of the bad policies found on the other indicators: investors don't want to invest in an economy with high budget deficits and high overvaluation. Investors may also have worried what debt relief may have meant for other external liabilities like the stock of direct foreign investment.

Second, despite their poor policies, HIPCs received more in World Bank and IMF financing than other LDCs. The result on World Bank financing is controlling for initial income (negatively related to World Bank financing). The additional amount of World Bank financing for HIPCs (0.96 percent of GDP) is small relative to the size of the current account deficit but large relative to the average amount of

World Bank financing in all LDCs (1.1 percent of GDP). The share of World Bank financing in new external loans also was significantly higher (by 7.2 percentage points) in HIPCs than in non-HIPCs.

The results are similar for the IMF. The IMF did lend more to HIPCs than to non-HIPCs, controlling for initial income. Like the World Bank HIPC effect, the effect is small relative to current account deficits (0.73 percent of GDP) but large relative to the non-HIPCs' average IMF financing (0.5 percent of GDP). The HIPC effect for the IMF's share of new external loans is of the same sign and significant: the IMF had 4.4 percentage points higher share of new external loans to HIPCs than to non-HIPCs, controlling for income. The HIPCs got to be HIPCs in part by borrowing from the World Bank and IMF.

Third, the results are similar examining the trends in composition of new lending to HIPCs over 1979 to 1997. Private credit disappears and multilateral financing assumes an increased share. World Bank low-interest-rate loans, termed International Development Association (IDA) loans, alone more than tripled their share in new lending. The share of private credit in new lending began the period 3.6 times higher than the IDA share; by the end of the period, the share of IDA was 8.6 times higher than that of private financing.

Fourth, we can examine the net flow of resources to the HIPCs, that is, the new loans minus debt repayments and interest. During the period in which the debt burden increased (1979–1987), the bulk of the net transfer of resources was from concessional sources (IDA, other multilaterals, and the bilateral donors like USAID), although there were also positive transfers of resources from private lenders. Concessional sources made total net transfers to the HIPCs of $33 billion. This huge concessional transfer makes it all the more striking that these countries became increasingly indebted in net present value terms over this period.

There was then a huge shift in net transfers from 1979–1987 to 1988–1997, a period in which debt ratios stabilized. Large positive net transfers from IDA and bilateral donors offset negative net transfers for IBRD (nonconcessional World Bank loans), bilateral nonconcessional, and private sources. This was another form of debt relief, since it exchanged low-interest-rate, long-maturity debt—debt that has a large grant element—for nonconcessional debt. However, remarkably, the net present value of debt remained roughly unchanged over this period, at least until the past few years. IDA and bilateral donors were bailing out all the nonconcessional lenders, piling on new debt fast enough that the debt burden remained constant even though the nonconcessional lenders were getting their money out.

The bottom line is that the debt burden of the poor countries came about because of lending by the IMF, World Bank (IDA), and bilateral donors, in the face of withdrawal by private and nonconcessional lenders. How did this happen?

The lending methodology of the donor community (the IMF, the World Bank, and the bilateral donors) encouraged granting of new loans to irresponsible governments, a methodology known as *filling the financing gap*. We have already seen the financing gap make its ill-starred appearance in chapter 2, where it was the gap between "required investment" and domestic saving. Here the financing gap is defined as the gap between the "financing requirement" in the external balance of payments and the available private financing. The financing requirement is equal to the sum of the trade deficit, the interest payment on the old debt, and the repayment of maturing old debt. "Filling the financing gap" implies giving more concessional aid to countries with higher trade deficits, higher current debt, and lower private lending. This perversely rewards the "irresponsible governments," whose policies scare away private lenders and lead to higher trade deficits and higher debt. Filling the financing gap pours good money after bad, creating an official debt spiral in which the inability of countries to service their existing debt is the reason that they are granted new official loans.

Then in the ultimate folly, the donor community calculates the amount of "necessary" debt relief to "close the financing gap." The reward for having a large financing gap is to have the debt wiped off the books, erasing the memory of irresponsible behavior of both borrowers and lenders.

By 1997, with the coming of the new multilateral debt relief initiative, HIPCs received 63 percent of the flow of resources devoted to poor countries despite accounting for only 32 percent of the population of those countries.

The Curious Case of Côte d'Ivoire

Including debt reduction as aid, Côte d'Ivoire received 1,276 times more per capita aid net flow than India in 1997. It would be interesting to explain to the poor in India why Côte d'Ivoire, whose government has twice created lavish new national capitals in the hometowns of successive leaders, should receive over a thousand times more aid per capita than they do.

This explanation grows all the more difficult when we examine how Côte d'Ivoire got into trouble. From 1979 to 1997, it ran a deficit on the current account of the balance of payments that averaged over 8 percent of GDP. That is, on average, it spent more on imports and interest on debt than it received on exports, by 8 percent of GDP. The most likely suspect for this excess spending is the government, which ran a budget deficit over this period of over 10 percent of GDP.

How did this big government budget deficit come about? The government benefited from a rise in international coffee and cocoa prices in the 1970s, since it required all domestic coffee and cocoa producers to deliver their products to its "marketing board" at a fixed price. This "marketing board" price to producers did not increase with international prices, leading to a huge windfall for the government, which was buying low and selling high. (Between 1976 and 1980, cocoa farmers got only 60 percent and coffee producers only 50 percent of the world price.)[21] The government used these extra revenues to go on a spending spree that continued even after the windfall revenues from cocoa and coffee vanished as international cocoa and coffee prices dropped sharply in 1979.[22] With unchanged spending and sharply diminished revenue, the Ivorian government began to run large budget deficits.

The government's excess spending on such things as new national capitals caused domestic inflation to be faster than foreign inflation, which caused the currency to appreciate in real terms since the exchange rate was fixed. The average overvaluation of the currency over this period was 75 percent, which made for cheap imports for consumers but strong disincentives for exporters—reinforcing the large external deficit. The profligate government caused the burden of the external debt to double over this period, from 60 percent of GDP in 1979 to 127 percent of GDP in 1994, when debt forgiveness began.

We can tell that the loans were not used for anything very productive, because the income of the average Ivorian fell in half between 1979 and 1994. Ivorians in poverty—in whose name the loans would be made and the loans forgiven—rose from 11 percent of the population in 1985 (the earliest date for which we have data) to 37 percent in 1995.[23] There was some output recovery after the currency was devalued in 1994, but it was a long road back after the steep economic decline.

And who was doing the lending to Côte d'Ivoire over the period of irresponsible policies in which its debt burden doubled? As a 1988 World Bank report put it, "On the questionable assumption that sufficient foreign financing could be secured, the ratio of public foreign debt to GDP would rise to around 130 percent by 1995."[24] Note how close this prediction is to the actual outcome, so the "questionable" financing was indeed found. On average, the World Bank and IMF accounted for 58 percent of new lending to Côte d'Ivoire between 1979 and 1997. The IMF alone made eight adjustment loans to the Ivorian government over this period, and the World Bank made twelve adjustment loans. The share of the World Bank and IMF trended up over time from 10 percent in 1979 to 76 percent in 1997.

Within the World Bank lending to Côte d'Ivoire, there was an important shift away from nonconcessional lending (known as IBRD lending) to concessional lending (known as IDA lending). One of the perverse incentives in the foreign assistance business is that the more irresponsible governments become eligible for more favorable lending terms.

Most of the rest of the lending was from rich country governments, with a key role for France (whose government must also bear some of the blame for postponing Côte d'Ivoire's necessary devaluation). Meanwhile, private foreign loans plummeted from 75 percent of all new lending in 1979 to near zero from 1989 on. The private lenders did indeed consider lending to Côte d'Ivoire questionable by the time of the 1988 World Bank report. The official lenders did not have the same common sense as private ones.

So it was only fitting that in March 1998, the World Bank and IMF announced a new debt forgiveness program for Côte d'Ivoire that forgave some of their own past loans. The debt forgiveness was subject to Côte d'Ivoire's fulfilling a few conditions like reining in its budget deficit and cleaning up its act on cocoa and coffee pricing. The IMF gave a new three-year loan to Côte d'Ivoire in March 1998, again subject to these conditions. World Bank lending continued as well, with about $600 million in new loan commitments in 1999.[25]

For awhile, the Ivorian government met key conditions. Then things began to go wrong. The IMF noted in July 1999, "Performance under the 1998 program was mixed, and there were some difficulties in its implementation."[26] The currency was still overvalued by 35 percent in 1998. In 1998, Côte d'Ivoire was rated as being in the most corrupt third of countries in the world. The European Union suspended aid to Côte d'Ivoire in 1999 after its previous aid was embezzled. The embezzlement was so imaginative as to perform "vast over-billing of basic medical equipment purchased, such as a stethoscope costing about $15 billed at $318, and $2,445 for a baby scale costing about $40."[27] The IMF suspended disbursements of its program in 1999. The army finally put the latest corrupt government out of its misery with a coup just before Christmas 1999.

Conclusion

We should do everything in our power to improve the lives of the poor, in both high-debt and low-debt nations. It seems to make sense that high debt could be diverting resources away from health and education spending that benefits the poor. Those who tell us to forgive the debt are on the side of the angels, or at least on the side of Bono, Sachs, the Dalai Lama, and the pope. Our heart tells us to forgive debts to help the poor.

Alas, the head contradicts the heart. Debt forgiveness grants aid to those recipients that have best proven their ability to misuse that aid. Debt relief is futile for countries with unchanged government behavior. The same mismanagement of funds that caused the high debt will prevent the aid sent through debt relief from reaching the truly poor.

A debt relief program could make sense if it meets two conditions: (1) it is granted where there has been a proven change from an irresponsible government to a government with good policies; (2) it is a once-for-all measure that will never be repeated. Let's look at the case for these two conditions.

It could be that the high debt is inherited from a bad government by a good government that truly will try to help the poor. We could see wiping out the debt in this case. This tells us that only governments that display a fundamental shift in their behavior should be eligible for debt relief. To assess whether countries have made such a fundamental shift, the international community should see a long and convincing record of good behavior prior to granting debt relief. There were important steps in this direction in the 1996 HIPC initiative, which unfortunately may have been weakened by subsequent proposals such as the 2000 World Bank IMF annual meetings proposals that speeded up the process of debt relief and made more countries eligible.

In the absence of a change in government behavior, official lenders should not keep filling the financing gap. The concept of financing gap should be abolished, now and for all time, since it has created perverse incentives to keep borrowing. Although loans are made and loans are forgiven all in the name of the poor, the poor are not helped if the international community creates incentives simply to borrow more.

To avoid the incentive to borrow more, the debt relief program has to attempt to establish a credible policy that debt forgiveness will never again be offered in the future. If this is problematic, then the whole idea of debt relief is problematic. Governments will have too strong an incentive to keep borrowing in the expectation that their debt will be forgiven.

A debt relief program that fails either of these two conditions results in more resources going to countries with bad policies than poor countries with good policies. Why should the HIPCs receive four times the aid per capita of less indebted poor countries, as happened in 1997? If there is any expectation that donors will continue to favor the irresponsible governments in the future, then debt relief will run afoul of peoples' (governments') response to incentives. Debt forgiveness will then be one more disappointing elixir on the quest for growth.

Intermezzo: Cardboard House

Julia was born in 1925 near Guadalajara, Mexico. Her parents were not married. Her father grew maize, chickpeas, and wheat.

When Julia was ten, she entered school. It did not go well, as she repeated the first year three times. That was all of her education, leaving her almost illiterate. In fact, Julia had already started working before entering school, at the age of eight, as a domestic servant. Her father's agricultural output was so scanty that all members of the family had to participate in the desperate search for money.

Julia's mother left her father and married another man, but then her mother died when Julia was eleven. The family sent Julia to live with an aunt and uncle in Guadalajara. She continued her domestic servant's job as well as doing domestic chores for her aunt and uncle.

Julia married Juan when she was eighteen. Juan brought in a decent income as a fitter, so Julia stopped working. But in 1947, Juan was injured in a work accident. He was unemployed while he recovered, so Julia again started working as a domestic servant and as a tortilla maker. In 1949, Juan again got a job as a fitter at a construction site. His earnings now were irregular, however, because he was drinking heavily and sometimes not sober enough to work. In 1958, he had another work accident, falling 17 meters to a factory floor. Since that time, Julia has been the main income earner for the household, while Juan has kept drinking and occasionally working. His alcoholism peaked in 1965, according to Julia, when "he was drunk for the whole year."

Julia gave birth in 1965 to her tenth child. All of them except for the first three died in infancy. Her oldest daughter, Rosa, emulated her mother's example by starting work as a domestic servant at eight years of age. Julia's and Rosa's earnings made it possible for them to buy a plot of land, on which they built their own house. However, Julia soon after developed pneumonia, and Juan had to sell the land plot to pay the medical bills.

They moved in 1973 to Rancho Nuevo, where they still live today. Rancho Nuevo is a slum in Guadalajara where there is no drinking water, no sewerage, and no public lighting. It stands next to a huge, foul-smelling garbage dump where clandestine workshops illegally dump their industrial waste. The inhabitants of Rancho Nuevo also use the dump to put their trash, since there is no public trash collection.

Julia and Juan lived rent free in a house that belonged to Juan's niece. The niece finally grew tired of this arrangement and evicted them in 1982.

They then "invaded" a plot of land and constructed a house of cardboard with a dirt floor. Nobody knew who was the owner of the land they and thirty other families "invaded." With their title to the land uncertain, Julia and Juan have no incentive to build a sturdier house. The cardboard house is very hot in spring, floods during the summer rains, and is cold in winter, when the ground temperature falls to 4 degrees centigrade. The police periodically harass them for bribes to avoid eviction from the illegally occupied land.[1]

III

People Respond to Incentives

In part II, we saw that the search for a magic formula to turn poverty into prosperity failed. Neither aid nor investment nor education nor population control nor adjustment lending nor debt forgiveness proved to be the panacea for growth. Growth failed to respond to any of these formulas because the formulas did not take heed of the basic principle of economics: people respond to incentives. In part III, we will see that poor people often don't have good incentives to grow out of poverty even when government is not subverting free markets. Overcoming the bad luck and initial poverty that trap the poor often requires direct government-created incentives to grow out of poverty. We will see that sometimes bad luck rather than bad policy is to blame. We will also see how governments do subvert free markets and create incentives that kill growth. One of the ways that governments destroy economies is through corruption. Creating incentives to combat corruption and to foster free markets often requires fundamental institutional reforms that make governments accountable to the laws and to their citizens. Even when government policies or corruption are the problem, they are hard to change because government officials themselves often have incentives to create policies that destroy their own economies. High inequality and ethnic polarization make it more likely that governments will choose destructive policies, because they act in the interest of a particular class or ethnic group and not in the interest of the nation. Making sure that growth happens often requires conscious government effort to supply health, education, and infrastructure services. Growth fails when we, through our governments, either "have done what we ought not to have done" or "have not done what we ought to have done" (to use the words of the Book of Common Prayer).

Getting incentives right is not itself another new panacea for development. It is a principle that has to be implemented bit by bit, stripping away the encrusted layers of vested interests with the wrong incentives, giving entry to new people with the right incentives. It is like cutting away the brambles that block our path to development, fighting hard for every inch of cleared space—sometimes finding it difficult or impossible to make headway. The interwoven webs of incentives between government, the donors, and the people are hard to get right. Of course, the new incentive-based views of growth could turn out to be as badly misguided as the panaceas that failed. It's easy with the benefit of hindsight to point to what failed; it's harder to come up with ideas that might work. We are in a better position than our predecessors for doing this for two reasons: we now have four decades of experience to draw on to see what worked and what didn't, and the economics profession has made some progress in developing analytical tools that give insights into growth.

8 Tales of Increasing Returns: Leaks, Matches, and Traps

Them what's got shall get
And them what's not shall lose
So the Bible says
And it still is news

Billie Holiday, "God Bless the Child"

The potential for future high income is a potent incentive to do whatever it takes to get there. What could mess up incentives for poor individuals? If technology was the most important determinant of income and growth differences across nations, why didn't all poor countries respond to the high incentives to implement advanced technology? The answer to all of these questions is: increasing returns. The answer is: leaks of knowledge, matches of skills, and traps of poverty.

Stories of leaks, matches, and traps took economists down some strange byways. How did a small investment in a shirt factory by a Bangladeshi enterpreneur named Noorul Quader scare the U.S. textile industry? What did the defective O-ring that caused the space shuttle *Challenger* to blow up have to do with the underdevelopment of Zambia? What does the formation of urban ghettos have to do with the poverty of Ethiopia? How do leaks and matches cause the poor to be trapped in poverty?

Let's think more about incentives for growth. Growth is the process of becoming rich. Becoming rich is a choice between today's consumption and tomorrow's. If I cut my consumption sharply and save a large proportion of my wage income, then in a few years I will be richer because I will have both wage income and the interest earnings on my savings. If I consume all of my wage earnings, then I will have just my wage earnings forever onward.

Under the old view of growth, however, savings economy-wide did not affect long-run growth. Growth was determined by a fixed rate of technological progress. Diminishing returns meant that increased economy-wide savings would lower interest rates to the point that the economy was saving just enough to keep up with technological progress. So long-run growth would be at the rate of technological progress no matter what the incentives to save.

But are there really diminishing returns to capital? New theories of growth argued that the answer was no.[1] How could it be no, when trying to have more machines for the same number of workers would clearly show diminishing returns to machines? The answer is that people could accumulate technological capital: knowledge of new technologies that economize on labor.[2]

If this is sounding a lot like the technological progress that made growth possible in the Solow vision, it should. The change in the Solow vision was to make technology, and all the other things that make a given amount of labor go further, *respond to incentives*.

The core idea is simple. Diminishing returns requires one ingredient of production to be in fixed supply, like the labor force. But profit-seeking entrepreneurs will seek out ways to get around the constraint of fixed labor. They will seek out new technologies that economize on labor.

This effect of incentives on growth is a big change from the Solow framework in which the technological progress that occurred for noneconomic reasons always determined growth in the long run. Now changes in incentives would permanently change the rate of economic growth.

But technology has some strange features. Technological knowledge is likely to *leak* from one person to another. Technology reaches its potential when high-skilled individuals *match* with each other. And low-skilled people can get left out of the whole process and stuck in a *trap*.

Leaks

Noorul Quader watched in April 1980 as his brand-new factory, Desh Garments Ltd. in Bangladesh, produced its first shirts. Bangladesh did not have a large garment industry to speak of before

Quader started Desh Garments Ltd. Bangladeshi garment workers in 1979 were a lonely group, because there were only forty of them.[3]

Quader's machines kept humming the rest of 1980, producing 43,000 shirts in his first year of operation.[4] A factory that produced this many shirts, exported for $1.28 each to yield total sales of $55,500, was still not much even by Bangladeshi standards: $55,050 was less than one-ten-thousandth of Bangladeshi exports in 1980.[5]

More impressive was what happened next, a story of leaks, unintended consequences, and increasing returns. As a direct result of Noorul Quader's Desh factory and its $55,050 in sales, Bangladesh today produces and exports nearly $2 billion worth of shirts and other ready-made garments—54 percent of all Bangladeshi exports.[6]

To see how Quader's $55,050 turned into $2 billion, we have to go back a step, before his factory got started. Quader, a former government official with a lot of international connections, had an ally in his quest to start a shirt factory in previously shirtless Bangladesh. The ally was the Daewoo Corporation of South Korea, a major world textile producer. Daewoo was looking for a new base to evade garment import quotas that the Americans and Europeans had imposed on the Koreans. These quotas did not cover Bangladesh, so a Daewoo-supported venture in Bangladesh would be a way to get shirts into forbidden markets.

Daewoo and Quader's company, Desh Garment Ltd., signed a collaborative agreement in 1979. Its key feature was that Daewoo would bring 130 Desh workers to Korea for training at Daewoo's Pusan plant. Desh would pay royalties and sales commissions to Daewoo in return, amounting to 8 percent of sales value.[7]

The collaboration was a great success—too much of a success, from Daewoo's point of view. Desh Ltd. managers and workers learned too fast. Quader canceled the collaborative agreement on June 30, 1981, after little more than a year of production and watched production soar from 43,000 shirts in 1980 to 2.3 million in 1987. Although Daewoo did not do badly from the collaboration, the benefits of its initial investment in knowledge had leaked well beyond what Daewoo intended.

But not even Desh Ltd. could control the shirt mania from leaking to others. Of the 130 Desh workers trained by Daewoo, 115 of them left Desh during the 1980s to set up their own garment export firms.[8] They diversified into gloves, coats, and trousers. This explosion of garment companies started by ex-Desh workers brought Bangladesh its $2 billion in garment sales today.

The Bangladeshi garment explosion soon was noticed on the world stage. Astonished U.S. garment manufacturers begged for protection from the Bangladeshis, who in some product lines had surpassed such traditional bugaboos of the protectionist lobby as Korea, Taiwan, and China.[9] The U.S. government, led by that ardent believer in free enterprise Ronald Reagan, slapped garment import quotas on Bangladesh as early as 1985. Unfazed, the Bangladeshis diversified into Europe and successfully lobbied for relaxing their U.S. quotas. Although still vulnerable to world trade policies, the industry is going strong today.

I don't mean this story to be a morality play for how nations can succeed. I don't even mean it to be a morality play for how Bangladesh can succeed, since the Bangladeshi economy as a whole is less than a clear success story. I want instead to use this story to illustrate why there might be increasing returns.

The story of the birth of the Bangladeshi garment industry illustrates the principle that investment in knowledge does not remain with the original investor. Knowledge leaks.

Investment in Knowledge

Economist Paul Romer argued that knowledge grows through conscious investment in knowledge. Solow had taken technological knowledge as a given, independent of investment level. To Solow, knowledge came from things that were independent of economics, like basic science. But if knowledge has a big economic payoff, then people will respond to this incentive by accumulating knowledge.

Investment in knowledge is all over the Desh Ltd. example. Why was Daewoo's participation in the collaborative venture so valuable? Why hadn't Bangladeshis already been making shirts on their own, before Daewoo volunteered its services? The answer is that Daewoo had learned something about how to make shirts and how to sell them on the world market. Since Daewoo was founded in 1967, Daewoo managers and workers had created new knowledge about garment production that would one day be valuable to others, like Noorul Quader of Desh Ltd., and transmitted this knowledge to Desh workers. They had the Desh workers do the cutting, sewing, finishing, and machining in Daewoo's factory in Pusan, Korea, from

April 1 to November 30, 1979. Daewoo's investment in 1967 created knowledge that could be sold to Desh in 1979.

Creating knowledge does not necessarily mean inventing new technologies from scratch. Some aspects of garment manufacturing technology were probably several centuries old. The relevant technological ideas might be floating out there in the ether, but only those who apply them can really learn them and can teach them to others.

Back in Bangladesh, investment in knowledge continued as Daewoo and Desh adapted Daewoo's methods to local conditions. One obstacle to surmount was Bangladesh's heavily protectionist trading system. It would be hard to be competitive on world markets if they had to pay several times world prices for their fabric because of the government's tariffs and quotas. The Bangladeshi government was willing to do a deal, known as the special bonded warehouse system, to give duty-free imports to exporters like Desh. Daewoo knew well the ins and outs of special bonded warehouse systems, because there was such a scheme in Korea. Daewoo explained to Desh how to use the system and advised the Bangladeshi government how to administer the scheme efficiently.

Daewoo and Desh also explained to local Bangladeshi banks how to open back-to-back import letters of credit. They figured out how to get the government to go along with such back-to-back import letters of credit under the government's strict foreign exchange controls.

A financing firm called Empire Capital Group Inc. from California gives the following simple explanation of back-to-back import letters of credit:

We can arrange back-to-back letters of credit when the intermediary desires the producer and the buyer be kept apart for competitive reasons and at the same time insuring payment to the respective parties. The instruments operate in a very simple manner. The incoming (primary L/C) letter of credit is opened to our designated lender as Beneficiary. This is the primary source of repayment and typically the only source. The lender opens an outgoing (secondary L/C) to a Beneficiary identified by you. The terms and conditions of payment under this outgoing L/C normally are identical to those found in the incoming L/C. However, use of back-to-back L/Cs accommodate "difference of conditions" where a minimum performance risk is present. For example, a primary L/C states payment for assembled furniture. Cost efficiency requires knock down in order to fill container. Solution is a back-to-back L/C. As a general rule Lenders will not accept any degree of performance risk.[10]

You can see why some technical assistance was required for the Bangladeshis!

The key principle again is: *knowledge leaks*. Useful knowledge about how to produce things at low cost—that is, how to get rich—is hard to keep a secret. People have a high incentive to observe what you are doing. People who work with you have a high incentive to leave and do what you were doing to get rich.

Knowledge has one special property that makes it prone to leak and generally beneficial to society when it does leak. Unlike a piece of machinery, a piece of knowledge can be used by more than one person at a time. It gets crowded around one of Desh's sewing machines if one hundred Desh workers are trying to use the same machine. It's not all that feasible for one hundred workers to use the same machine at the same time. It *is* feasible for one hundred different Bangladeshi manufacturers to use simultaneously the abstract idea of the back-to-back import letters of credit. An idea itself imposes no limits on how many people can use it.

Complementary Knowledge

A second property of knowledge is important for the leaks story: new knowledge is complementary to existing knowledge. In other words, a new idea is worth more to the society the more the society already knows. This property of knowledge means that there are increasing returns to investment in knowledge. This is very plausible since most knowledge gains are incremental. Right now I am writing this using the knowledge embodied in Microsoft Office 97, which offers a leap in productivity without requiring much investment in a society widely familiar with the old Microsoft Office and personal computers in general. But think of the state of knowledge in the 1970s, before the personal computer revolution started. The payoff of Office 97 would have been nonexistent in the PC-less and clueless 1970s.

Increasing returns has a very important implication. As the name implies, it means that returns to capital (including knowledge capital) increase as capital increases. Returns to capital are high where capital is already abundant; returns to capital are low where capital is scarce. This is the opposite of diminishing returns, where returns to capital were high when capital was scarce.

How did we overcome diminishing returns to get increasing returns? As a society gets more and more machines for a given number of workers, it is still true that each additional machine contributes less and less additional production, as we discussed in chapter 3. It would be absurd to think of an Alice in Wonderland world where an additional sewing machine's value goes up the more sewing machines there already are. Just how many sewing machines can one person operate?

But knowledge is different. As a society gets more and more productive ideas, each additional idea contributes more and more additional production. If this investment in knowledge leaks to everyone, then this new knowledge raises the productivity of all existing knowledge and machines throughout the economy. If this knowledge creation and leaking are strong enough, they overwhelm the normal process of diminishing returns to machines. The more existing knowledge there is, the higher is the return to each new bit of knowledge. The higher the return to each new bit of knowledge, the stronger is the incentive to invest in yet more knowledge.

We have seen that both physical capital and human capital tend to flow toward the richest economies. If different levels of knowledge across nations explain income differences, then it is obvious why physical capital and human capital want to go to the high-knowledge economy, where rates of return to physical and human capital will be higher.

Increasing returns seems to be what happened in the Bangladeshi garment industry. The Desh workers watched Daewoo and Noorul Quader create useful knowledge about making shirts, selling shirts abroad, using special bonded warehouse systems, and using back-to-back import letters of credit in Bangladesh. They took that knowledge with them when they left Desh and started their own garment firms. By 1985, there were over seven hundred Bangladeshi garment companies. Knowledge leaks.

To take one example, in January 1985, Mohammadi Apparels Ltd. began operations, making shirts on 134 Japanese-made sewing machines. Mohammadi Ltd. had to buy its own machines, which no one else could use at the same time. But it could use the same ideas that seven hundred other firms were using—ideas that originated at Desh. The production manager at Mohammadi was a former production manager at Desh; the marketing manager at Mohammadi was a former marketing manager at Desh; ten other former Desh workers worked at Mohammadi, providing training to the Mohammadi workers. Within thirty-one months of beginning operations, Mohammadi had already exported $5 million worth of shirts, with Norway the single biggest customer.

Noorul Quader's Desh was not suffering too much from all the competitors. Desh saw production increase fifty-one-fold by 1987. The world garment market, where the Bangladeshis were operating, was a big ocean.

Still Noorul Quader did not get fully rewarded for the benefits he brought to Bangladesh by inadvertently creating the Bangladeshi garment industry. The return to his initial investment was mostly a return for society, not a private return to him. The distinction between society-wide returns and private returns is important, as I will discuss in a moment.

Since we have seen that physical capital investment is not a highly important determinant of growth, it seems plausible that direct investments in knowledge are fairly important. Noorul Quader acquired knowledge by paying royalties to Daewoo; this knowledge then leaked to other Bangladeshi producers.

Before Noorul Quader's breakthrough, the return to an investment in a Bangladeshi garment factory was low. Once Noorul Quader got the industry rolling with his Daewoo-supported knowledge creation, the return to an investment in a garment factory was high.

The leak part is critical to make the story workable. Suppose that any knowledge created did not leak and the investor in knowledge was the only one to benefit. As the investor gets more and more personal knowledge, his returns will be higher than anyone else's, and they will keep getting higher the more he invests. He will reinvest his vast profits in his own enterprise. He will even attract investment from others, since he offers higher returns than anyone else. This highly successful and canny investor will grow, but nobody else will. That one investor will take over the economy—first the industry, then the nation, eventually the world ...

A theory of growth in which one company takes over the world is not appealing, and it just hasn't happened, despite the best efforts of some people. Something more is needed to make the theory reasonable. The something more is: *knowledge leaks*. The leaks create a distinction between social and private returns. With leaks, there are social increasing returns, not private increasing returns. A society benefits from a lot of investment in knowledge by that society; an individual does not fully benefit from a lot of knowledge creation by that individual. This means that market incentives to create knowledge will not be strong enough, even when that knowledge is socially beneficial. The free market will not lead to the best possible outcome, because there are differences between the private and the social return to knowledge investments.

Circles

The principle that knowledge leaks sets up the potential for virtuous and vicious circles. Think of an economy in which a lot of investment by a few individuals has created some knowledge. That knowledge has leaked to others, giving them high returns to their own knowledge investments. Liking high returns when they see them, the others invest. Knowledge increases further, leaking to yet others. The additional others invest in knowledge, increasing knowledge further and leaking to yet others, and so on.

The initial wave of investment sparked a virtuous circle of further investment and growth. The Desh case seems to fit, at least for purposes of illustration. Noorul Quader got things going. Others invested in creating even more knowledge, raising the return to even more investment in knowledge.

But virtuous circles do not always happen, and some suffering countries get stuck with vicious circles instead. To complete the story, we need one more element—a minimum rate of return that investors require for investments. It is eminently plausible that there is such a required rate of return, also known as the discount rate.

If there is such a discount rate for, say, Bangladeshi investors, they are going to need a minimum rate of return to give up some of today's consumption and invest in a Bangladeshi garment factory instead. So what happens to a country that starts out with a low level of both machines and knowledge?

The rate of return to new knowledge depends on how much knowledge there already is; how much knowledge there is depends on the incentives to invest in knowledge. If at the beginning there is little knowledge, then there is a low rate of return. If this low rate of return falls below the minimum required rate of return, that is, the discount rate, then there will be no investment in new knowledge. If there is no investment today, there will be still be low knowledge tomorrow, so there will still be a low rate of return tomorrow—and so no investment tomorrow either. The day after tomorrow, there will still be low knowledge. Rather than a virtuous circle, this country is stuck in a vicious circle. A poor country in a vicious circle is in a *trap* from which there is no easy escape.

It doesn't matter why knowledge was too low at the beginning—a recent stroke of bad luck perhaps, or the accumulation of past bad luck. Perhaps Bangladeshi knowledge about garment production was lost in the disastrous war of independence at the beginning of the 1970s. Maybe the initial wave of socialism by the independent government killed off the industry. Maybe there never was a garment industry.

Nor does it matter what provides an initial wave of investment in knowledge that gets one out of the vicious circle and over the threshold into the virtuous circle. It was pure luck from Desh's point of view that Daewoo was shut out of U.S. shirt markets and needed to find a base in a previously shirt-free country. The Bangladeshi government cooperated by permitting duty-free imports for exporters, which we can think of as raising the feasible rate of return to the new investments. We can speculate that the initial wave of investment and the change in government policy got the rate of return up over the minimum, and then the industry just fed on itself.

There's still the big question: if virtuous circles are so wonderful, why don't they always happen? Surely everybody would like to get into a virtuous circle, so why doesn't everybody act like Noorul Quader of Desh Ltd.? This is where the distinction between private and social returns to investment again is crucial. A single individual, even a Noorul Quader, cannot make his own luck. He cannot start a virtuous circle by himself.

Part of the problem is that the individual is not rewarded for the social contributions he makes when he invests. When he invests in knowledge, he increases the stock of knowledge available to everyone. He gets no reward for doing that, and so is less likely to make such contributions to social knowledge.

The other side of the problem is that returns to the individual's investment depend on everyone's investments in knowledge and not just his. The rate of return to new investment in knowledge depends on the total stock of knowledge in the economy. If the rate of return is falling well short of the minimum, then a single individual's investment is too small to move the whole industry or the whole economy above the threshold. All the individual is going to see is that he is making investments that carry a below-minimum rate of return, so he doesn't invest in knowledge, nobody else invests, and everybody remains facing below-minimum returns.

Noorul Quader was entrepreneurial and lucky enough to benefit from the big injection of knowledge from Daewoo that made it worthwhile to start investing in Bangladeshi garment production. Even he did not get rewarded fully for the benefits he brought to everyone else, and Daewoo got rewarded even less. The fortuitous combination of loopholes in international trade restrictions and local government duty exemptions made it worthwhile for Daewoo and Quader at the beginning nevertheless. The sheer luck involved in getting the Bangladeshi garment industry started illustrates how hard it is for a poor country to find those virtuous circles where knowledge leaks.

This story about knowledge leaks also makes clear that the market left to itself will not necessarily create growth. Laissez-faire policy by the government may well leave the economy, or some parts of the it, in a vicious circle. Getting into the virtuous circle may require conscious government intervention in knowledge creation. The principle that knowledge leaks fundamentally changes our view of how markets work for good or ill. Markets will often need an injection of government subsidies to start the knowledge ball rolling.

Matches

What did the explosion of the space shuttle *Challenger* on January 28, 1986, have to do with the poverty of Zambia? *Nothing* would be a good first guess, but both events turn out to be metaphors for increasing returns, metaphors that illustrate essentially the same principle: the principle of matches.

The explosion seventy-three seconds after the *Challenger*'s liftoff was caused by the failure of a single component, a rubber seal known as an O-ring, in the right-hand-side solid rocket booster.[11] When the people in charge of the O-ring on the *Challenger* made fatal errors, all of the billions of dollars of well-functioning parts in the rest of the spacecraft turned lethal.

The metaphor applies to many products besides a space shuttle. Production is often a series of tasks. Think of an assembly line in which each worker successively works on a product. The value of each worker's efforts depends on the quality of all the other workers' efforts. In the extreme, if one worker makes a disastrous error, all of the other tasks go for naught. This creates strong incentives for the best workers to match up with each other on the same assembly line. Very good workers want to be on an assembly line with other very good workers, so that they get the payoff from their high-quality skills.

Complements

With the O-ring story, one highly skilled worker complements another. My productivity as a worker is higher, the higher is the skill level of my coworkers. If this reminds you of the basic increasing returns principle—returns to skills for the individual go up with the existing skill average in the society—it should. The matching story features increasing returns to skills.

Diminishing returns would have said the opposite. With diminishing returns, one highly skilled worker substitutes for another. If I am a highly skilled worker, then the availability of another highly skilled worker makes my kind of skills more abundant—and therefore less valuable.

Diminishing versus increasing returns accounts for the ambivalence you feel when a person with skills similar to yours joins your office. On one hand, everyone else in the office might value you less because now there's somebody else similar who is available as a substitute. That's diminishing returns. On the other hand, your productivity might be higher because you can now talk shop with your similar coworker. That's increasing returns. Whether you lose or win depends on whether you and the new coworker, on balance, substitute for each other or complement each other. I prefer having coworkers who are similar to me in skills, which suggests that workers in my office complement each other, and we have increasing returns to skills.

This has something to do with why the most skilled lawyers live in New York and not in New Mexico. If skilled workers can freely move wherever they want, then they will tend to congregate in places where they can match with lots of other skilled workers. The economy will exhibit strong concentrations of high skill in a few places, surrounded by large swathes of low skill.

Evidence for Complements

This story is one explanation of the still powerful pull of the big cities, despite their well-documented disadvantages of crowds, crime, and Calvin Klein billboards. Cities are where high-skilled people match up. In the United States, counties that belong to metropolitan areas have income per person that is 32 percent higher than that of rural counties. It also explains why property values are higher in big cities than in rural areas. The richest urban county—New York,

New York—has a median housing value twenty-two times higher than the poorest rural county—Starr County, Texas.[12] As Robert Lucas at the University of Chicago said, "What can people be paying Manhattan or downtown Chicago rents *for*, if not for being near other people?"[13]

Another study found evidence for this story when it examined wages and rents across cities in the United States. It found that the wage of an individual with the same skill and education characteristics was higher in cities whose populations had higher average skills. In other words, a person who moved from a low-human-capital city to a high-human-capital city would earn higher wages. This study's interpretation is that an individual with given schooling is more productive—and so gets paid more—when he or she lives and works with more highly skilled people.

Cities with more skilled populations also had higher average housing rents for the same types of housing and local amenities. This study's interpretation of the higher rents is that people will pay more for the opportunity to live and work near the highly skilled.[14]

A World Bank study found something similar when it studied provinces in Bangladesh. Households in the Tangail/Jamalpur district of Bangladesh have 47 percent lower real consumption than households with identical skills in Dhaka. A Bangladeshi woman who moved from the Tangail/Jamalpur district to Dhaka would have a higher standard of living.

Another study found a related result with U.S. immigrant groups. One characteristic of immigrant groups is that they are more likely to match with another member of the group than someone outside the group. An individual belonging to an immigrant group that had a high average wage was more likely to have a high wage than an individual belonging to an immigrant group having a low average wage. If you think I'm saying something tautological, I'm not. The individual is too small to affect the average of the immigrant group. If there were no benefits from matching, we would expect to see individual wages determined solely by the individual's skills. Instead we see the individual's wage influenced by the wage of the group to which he or she belongs. The patterns found by these studies suggest that an individual's opportunity for matching with other skilled individuals is as important as the individual's own skills.

What if skilled workers can move across national boundaries? The matching story helps explain the brain drain of some skilled workers from the poor countries to the rich countries. A star chef in Morocco knows that he can match with more highly skilled restaurant people in France than in Morocco, and thus will be paid more in France. A surgeon from India will be paid more when she can match up with highly skilled nurses, anesthesiologists, radiologists, medical technicians, bookkeepers, and receptionists. The highly skilled surgeon from India would prefer to move to the United States, where other highly skilled workers can be found.

Under diminishing returns, unskilled labor should want to migrate to capital-abundant rich countries. Skilled labor should want to stay in poor countries where it's scarce. With the matching story, skilled labor from the poor country will want to move to the rich country to match up with the skilled labor there. In fact, as we have seen, an educated Indian is fourteen times more likely to emigrate to the United States than an uneducated Indian.[15]

(The same incentives imply that financial capital will also flow toward the richest countries. Increasing returns means the rate of return to capital is higher where it is already abundant. We saw in chapter 3 that the richest—and therefore most capital abundant— 20 percent of the world population received 88 percent of private capital gross inflows; the poorest 20 percent received 1 percent of private capital gross inflows.)

Of course, there are immigration restrictions on movements between countries. It might be more informative to check how the many skilled people who cannot move are doing in countries that have a lot of skills and those that don't. The large differences in skilled wages between countries also fit with the matching story. Recall from chapter 4 that engineers in 1994 earned $55,000 a year in New York and $6,000 a year in Bombay.[16]

This story so far begs an average question. How come workers in the poor country are less skilled than those in the rich country in the first place?

How Not to Get Rich in Real Estate

Increasing returns stories usually have higher returns to individual investment, when there is higher average knowledge capital in the society. Is that a feature of this matching game? Absolutely.

A clear example from everyday life of the matching game, one that lends itself to analyzing individual investment, is real estate. Beautiful mansions do not get built in urban ghettos, where land is cheap.

And someone who becomes rich usually moves out of the ghetto rather than stays behind and renovates. The real estate game creates powerful incentives for matching. The value of a beautiful mansion would be pulled down by the low housing values of its poor neighbors, which may reflect negative neighborhood effects like higher crime and lower school quality. These neighborhood spillovers create powerful incentives for matching. A new house built in a neighborhood is usually of about the same kind and value as the existing houses.

You can see the incentives or disincentives for self-improvement. Suppose my neighbors have little interest in keeping up appearances. They leave rusting old Fords in the front yard and opt for the natural look of peeling paint and bare gray wood. Since most home buyers don't find my neighbors' tastes appealing, the neighboring houses lower my house's value. That weakens my incentive to maintain my own house.

There are vicious and virtuous circles in real estate. Neighborhoods that are dilapidated stay dilapidated, because it's not worth it for any individual to make home improvements. Neighborhoods that are high priced stay high priced, because it would be costly for anyone to let their own housing value slip (and costly for their neighbors, who might apply a little peer pressure).

Skill Improvement and Matching

Let's get back to the more serious issue of skills in nations. People upgrading their skills in the national matching game are like homeowners upgrading their houses in the neighborhood real estate game. It's worth it if the neighbors (fellow workers) have high home quality (high skill quality).

Suppose a country starts out poor, with everyone having low skills. Ms. X is deciding whether to make the sacrifices necessary to get trained as a doctor. If she gets a medical education, she will have to forgo working at an unskilled job that she could get immediately. She will not be able to support her aged parents or her young siblings for the duration of her medical training. But after she becomes a highly skilled physician, she can earn more. She will be able to support her parents and siblings even better after a few years of privation. But how much will her earnings increase after she becomes a doctor?

We are back to where we were before. How much her earnings increase depends on how successful she is at matching up with other skilled workers—say, nurses, pharmacists, and bookkeepers. The likelihood of a profitable match depends on how much education everyone else is getting. Her problem after getting skilled is going to be to find other people of comparable skill.

She could try to coordinate with a bunch of others in advance, to match up after graduation with other people getting trained. But this is asking her to know a lot more about many other individuals than she could realistically know and to make binding agreements that are impossible to enforce. Probably the best she can do is to check how much people on average are getting educated in her future sphere of operations. At best, she will have some aggregated information like the national average of educational attainment. If a lot of people are highly educated, then the chances of her matching with other skilled people are much greater. She knows that going to medical school is worthwhile in a country where there are already plenty of skilled nurses, pharmacists, and bookkeepers. It's not worthwhile when such skilled workers are rare.

This is her bottom line: go to school if average nationwide skills are already high; don't go to school if average nationwide skills are still low. Her decision rule is sensible for her—but disastrous for the nation. The nation with low average skill is going to be stuck with low average skill because no single individual is going to find it worthwhile to go to school.

The situation is even worse if skills are complementary to the general state of knowledge in that nation. People who get educated in a society with little knowledge don't benefit as much as those in a knowledge-abundant society. Even if knowledge leaks, the value of being educated is much less if there is not much knowledge to leak. Even if the workers do go to school in a low-knowledge society, the nation will stay impoverished (remember how surprisingly worthless was the educational explosion discussed in chapter 4).

Like the other tales of increasing returns, the matching story raises the possibility that a poor country is poor just because it started poor. There are vicious circles in education. If a nation starts out skilled, it gets more skilled. If it starts out unskilled, it stays unskilled. There is nothing natural about who is skilled and unskilled in this worldview. It does not reflect virtues or vices of individuals. It just reflects where the nation started. Once again we have a nation stuck in a vicious circle.

Hewers of Wood, Drawers of Water

There is also nothing natural about the international pattern of specialization in this worldview. The poor unskilled nation will produce raw materials. The rich skilled nation will produce secondary- or tertiary-stage goods like manufactured consumer goods.

Suppose you are a businessman with an unskilled labor pool and you are deciding what to produce. One characteristic of unskilled workers is that they are more likely to make a mistake, and so to ruin the product they are working on. Is it more profitable to have them work on a product that has already gone through a lot of costly processing—high-quality linen made from flax—or is it better to have them work on a product that has had little processing—like growing the flax? If they have equal probability of ruining the product in either case, it is better to risk ruining a low-value product with no processing (the flax) rather than a high-value product already embodying a lot of processing (the linen).

So in practice, the poorest countries, with the lowest skills, produce relatively more raw materials; the richest countries, with the highest skills, produce relatively more manufactured goods. Economists used to think that producing agriculture versus manufactures just reflected comparative advantage—that is, who had the better agricultural land, who had the better sites for manufacturing, and so forth. The skill acquisition story fits reality much better.

The United States, whose agricultural advantages are legendary, devotes 2 percent of its economy to agriculture.[17] Ethiopia, whose frequent droughts, mountainous land, and cattle killing tsetse fly make it about as ideal for agriculture as the lunar surface, devotes 57 percent of its economy to agriculture.[18] Americans have high skills, with less than 5 percent of the population illiterate. Ethiopians on average have low skills, with 65 percent of the population illiterate.[19] Comparative advantage in agriculture and manufactures is itself manufactured.

Traps

The matching story offers an explanation for income differences between countries. A country in which all the workers are skilled will display much higher average salaries than one in which all the workers are unskilled. The income difference will be much greater than the skill difference of individual workers. In the rich country, the skilled workers raise each other's productivity; in the poor country, the unskilled workers lower each other's productivity. To make it even worse, anyone who does happen to get skilled in the poor country will try to move to the rich country. The matching story provides a possible explanation of the forty-fold difference in incomes between countries, even when the difference in education per worker is much less than forty-fold. It could help explain why the income differences between nations are so persistent: individuals in poor nations face weak incentives, while individuals in rich nations face strong incentives.

The matching story could also apply to the ethnic differences in education and income. Suppose that there are two ethnic groups, purples and greens. The purples start out with high education. The greens start out with low education, for some obscure historical reason (perhaps the purples enslaved the greens back in the bad old days). Suppose that there is legal segregation between the two ethnic groups so that by law purples work only with other purples, and greens work only with other greens. Then greens do not have much incentive to get educated for the same reason as in the story for nations: the chances of an educated green's finding another of comparable skill are low. If there is nobody of comparable skill with whom to match, the return to acquiring skills is low. Each green does this calculation and refrains from acquiring new skills, and so the expectation that there will not be many greens with skills is fulfilled.

But even if there is no legal segregation, the greens could still be trapped in low education. Employers, who are almost entirely purple since they are the highly skilled ones, know that greens historically have low skills. Suppose that employers have trouble discerning each individual's skill level. In the absence of other information, lazy purple employers could just assume that greens are low skilled and purples are high skilled. So purple high-skilled employers looking for high-skilled workers will always hire purples. If an individual green gets an education, it will not do him any good because the employers will assume he is poorly educated anyway. So the greens will not get educated, fulfilling employers' expectations.[20]

Of course, what I really have in mind with the purple and green story is the ethnic income differentials in the United States between blacks and whites. Blacks earn 41 percent less than whites. These are not the only ethnic differentials in the United States. Native Americans earn 36 percent less than whites, Hispanics earn 31 percent less, and Asians earn 16 percent more.[21] There are even more subtle ethnic differences in prosperity in the United States. George Borjas found that individuals whose grandparents immigrated from Austria earn 25 percent more than people whose grandparents immigrated from Belgium. The initial differences in income have percolated across two generations. Similarly, there are ethnic differentials even between the largely poor native Americans. The Iroquois earn almost twice the median household income of the Sioux.

Other ethnic differentials in the United States appear by religion. Episcopalians earn 31 percent more income than Methodists.[22] Forty percent of the 160 richest Americans are Jewish, although only 2 percent of the U.S. population is Jewish.[23]

There are clear examples of ethnic-geographic poverty traps within many countries. Almost every country has its persistently poor regions, like the south of Italy, the northeast of Brazil, Baluchistan in Pakistan, or Chiapas in Mexico. Most of these regions have deep historical roots for their poverty. Brazilian economic historian Celso Furtado traces the plight of northeast Brazil back to the collapse of sugar prices in the sixteenth century.

Within the United States, there are five well-defined poverty clusters: (1) inner-city blacks, (2) rural blacks in the Mississippi delta, (3) native Americans in the West, (4) Hispanics in the Southwest, and (5) whites in southeastern Kentucky (Figure 8.1 shows the rural poverty traps; the inner city ones are too small in land area to show up.) The southeastern Kentucky cluster is interesting because it

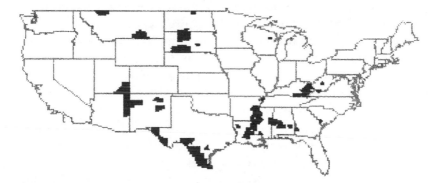

Figure 8.1
Poverty traps in the United States (counties with poverty rate above 35 percent)

shows the poverty trap to be more localized than the cliché that Appalachian whites are poor. In fact, eighteen of the twenty poorest all-white counties in the United States are in southeastern Kentucky. All of these poverty traps have been in existence for some time.

Other nations also have ethnically defined poverty traps. Mexican indigenous people have a poverty rate of 81 percent, while white or mestizo Mexicans have a poverty rate of 18 percent.[24] Guatemalan indigenous people are twice as likely to be illiterate (80 percent of the indigenous are illiterate) as other Guatemalans.[25] There are differences even among the indigenous. Quiche-speaking indigenous people in Guatemala have 22 percent less income than Kekchi-speaking indigenous people.[26]

In Brazil, residents of poor *favelas* complained that employers would not hire anyone who has an address in *favelas* with a reputation for violence. Those *favela* residents would give false addresses and even get fake electricity bills borrowed from friends in other locations.[27]

In South Africa, there is the well-known difference between whites and blacks: whites earn 9.5 times more. The large differentials among blacks by ethnic group are less well known. Among all-black traditional authorities (an administrative unit something like a village) in the state of KwaZulu-Natal, with its many diverse ethnic groups, the ratio of the richest traditional authority to the poorest is 54.

Ethnic differentials are also common in other countries. The ethnic dimension of rich business elites is not a big secret: the Jews in the United States, the Lebanese in West Africa, the Indians in East Africa, the overseas Chinese in Southeast Asia. Virtually every country has its own ethnographic group noted for their success. For example, in the Gambia, a tiny indigenous ethnic group called the Serahule is reported to dominate business out of all proportion to their numbers; they are often called "Gambian Jews." In Zaire, Kasaians have been dominant in managerial and technical jobs since the days of colonial rule; they are often called "the Jews of Zaire."[28]

And then, as we have seen, there is evidence of poverty traps at the national level. India was near the bottom in 1820 of the twenty-eight nations on which we have data from 1820 to 1992. India was still near the bottom of these twenty-eight nations in 1992. Northern Europe and its overseas offshoots were at the top in 1820; they are still at the top today.

The Rich Are Trapped Too

The matching story that predicts poverty traps also predicts wealth traps. There will be some areas where valuable skills are concentrated that will be much richer than everybody else. Casual observation reveals such concentrations: cities. And there is strong concentration even among cities: metropolitan counties in the Boston-Washington corridor are 80 percent richer per person than other metropolitan counties.[29] Since the Boston-Washington corridor roughly corresponds to the zone of initial settlement of the United States, I suspect that having a head start in the distant past has a lot to do with this income difference.

It's also obvious that there are neighborhood poverty traps and wealth traps within each metropolitan area. The rich and the poor are not randomly mixed across the metropolitan area but are concentrated within certain neighborhoods, confirming the prediction of the real estate matching game. More generally, if knowledge leaks, rich people will want to be around other knowledge-rich people to benefit from the leaks. If the benefit of a knowledge leak is increasing in the amount of knowledge you already have, a knowledge-rich person can outbid a poor person for a house in the rich neighborhood.

In the metro area of Washington, D.C., for example, you can draw a vertical north-south line down the middle dividing rich and poor (the line roughly coincides with Rock Creek Park). The richest fourth of zip codes in the city and suburbs lie to the west of this line, and the poorest fourth of zip codes lie to the east. The richest zip code (Bethesda, Maryland 20816) is about five times richer than the poorest zip code (College Heights in Anacostia, D.C.). This has a strong ethnic dimension, as usual, since Bethesda 20816 is 96 percent white and College Heights is 96 percent black.[30]

Economic geography shows spatial concentration worldwide. This concentration has a fractal-like quality in that it recurs at each level of aggregation. Using national data, we can calculate that 54 percent of world GDP is produced on 10 percent of its land area. Even this calculation vastly understates concentration, because it assumes that economic activity is evenly spread across the map within each nation. This is obviously not true; within the United States, for example, 2 percent of the land area produces 50 percent of the GDP. This obviously reflects the dominant contribution of cities to production. But even within cities there is concentration.

Complements and Traps

It's important to keep in mind what special features the "traps" story has—that determine whether its predictions will come true. Stories are interesting only if they might conceivably be false. The key assumption of the matching story, which might be false, is that skills strongly complement each other. A key assumption of the leaks story is that new knowledge strongly complements existing knowledge. We need both *strongly* and *complement* for this story to work. Workers' skills have to complement each other, and they have to complement each other so strongly as to overwhelm the normal diminishing returns to skills as skills get more and more abundant. New knowledge has to complement existing knowledge and machines strongly to overcome the diminishing returns to machines. Strongly complementary skills and knowledge create traps.

The matches story, like the leaks story, has a tension between the individual and the society. What matters more for my economic productivity: what I do or what the society does? Loosely speaking, if it's what I do, as it is under diminishing returns, then I don't have to worry about virtuous and vicious circles. I will get what is coming to me for my own efforts. This is the view of the Mankiw application of the Solow model I discussed earlier. If what matters more is what the society does, then vicious circles can form. My efforts go for naught because the rest of the society is not putting out similar efforts. So I don't make the effort. Everyone else does this calculation and nobody makes the effort, confirming each of us in the wisdom of not making an effort.

I have talked about poverty traps at different levels of aggregation: the neighborhood, the ethnic group, the province, the nation. Perhaps even the world was one big poverty trap prior to the industrial revolution. At the other extreme, even the household or extended family could be the relevant "society." The level at which poverty traps form depends on what is the relevant society over which leaks and matches happen. If neighborhood (or household) members associate only with each other (for noneconomic reasons), then the neighborhood (household) is the "society" for the individual. At the other extreme, if the global economy is wide open to at least some individuals and companies, then the world is the relevant society for those individuals and companies. Unfortunately, it is the poor who tend to have a constricted society because they don't have the training, the personal computers, and the contacts that would give them access to global knowledge.

In Malawi, there is a saying, *Wagalimoto ndi wagalimoto, wa wilibala ndi wa wilibala* (Those who possess vehicles chat among themselves, while those who possess wheelbarrows chat among themselves also). In Kok Yangak, Kyrgyz Republic, people reported in interviews, "The rich and the poor [do] not like each other and would not associate with each other." And in Foua, Egypt, people were "compartmentalized along socio-economic divides ... the rich engage in social activities together, and the poor stay together."[31]

Leaks, matches, and traps explain how abject poverty is consistent with people responding to incentives. Income differences are explained not by the individuals' effort to accumulate physical and human capital, but by differences in knowledge and matching opportunities across nations, across regions within a nation, and across ethnic groups. Poor people face weak incentives to upgrade their skills and knowledge because their leaks and matches come from other poor people.[32]

You Get What You Expect in Traps

Another feature of traps is that expectations matter. Great expectations can get you out of the poverty trap.

Suppose a poor country starts below the poverty trap threshold. The return on investing in knowledge, education, and machines is currently too low to make such investment worthwhile, and so the country would be stuck in the poverty trap. But now suppose that you expect that everyone else will be investing in acquiring skills, knowledge, and machines. Everyone else has the same expectations. It is now worth your while to make the investment, because when the investment matures, it will be matched with the high skills created by everyone else's investment. So high expectations are enough to get the economy out of the poverty trap. Conversely, bad expectations could take a country that was above the poverty trap threshold and send it down into the poverty trap. You won't invest if you think that no one else is going to be investing. Whether an economy gets rich or poor can depend on whether everyone expects it to get rich or poor.

Expectations could be a source of the instability of growth rates that we observe in practice. A single shock to the system could change expectations overnight. You suddenly expect everyone else to stop investing, so you stop investing. The expectations story could explain the Latin American growth crash after the debt crisis in 1982, the Mexican crash in 1995, and the East Asian crash in 1997–1998. Growth changes more violently than is justified by a change in fundamentals because expectations change abruptly.

The increasing returns story of poverty traps says that poverty is a failure of coordination. If only everyone was able to agree in advance that they would make investments until they reached a skill level above the poverty trap threshold, then they would get out of the poverty trap. Unfortunately, the market does not make this coordination on its own, and so poverty persists.

Government Policies and Traps

How would government policy affect incentives in a world of leaks, matches, and traps? First, recognize that government intervention may be necessary to get an economy out of a trap. If there is a minimum required return on investment, low knowledge may make the rate of return too low for the private sector to invest. The public sector could get the economy out of the trap by subsidizing investment in new knowledge.

Second, be careful about how that government intervention affects incentives. It wouldn't help get out of a trap to have massive public investment that is financed by a punitive tax on private investment. If the cause of the trap is a low private rate of return to capital, it does not make much sense to depress that return further. What the state gives with one hand, it takes away with the other.

Bad government policies could even be the cause of the trap. Bad policies imply a lower rate of return to the private sector. If the post-policy rate of return falls below the required minimum rate of return, the private sector won't invest. The private sector facing sufficiently bad policies will not invest in the knowledge and skills that the nation needs to get out of the trap.

The first step in a bad policy situation is to remove the bad government policies. If that is not enough by itself to get the nation out of the trap, then the government should subsidize all forms of knowledge and capital accumulation. This would mean duty and tax exemptions for capital goods, education, technology licensing payments, and even government subsidies for those goods and services.

The subsidies should be financed by taxes that do not themselves discourage knowledge accumulation, like taxes on consumption.

The government can also act to try to solve the coordination problem. If it can convince a number of big players to make big investments even if current incentives are not sufficiently strong, then the nation can escape the trap. This is a plausible story of the government-business collaboration that helped jump-start the East Asian growth miracle.

If the nation as a whole escapes the trap but leaves behind some ethnic or regional group, the government should try to subsidize the acquisition of skills, this time by the poor. Government welfare payments should increase in a matching fashion when individuals increase their incomes. The opposite occurs under most welfare schemes in the industrialized countries, although the U.S. earned-income tax credit is a successful exception that shows how to reward the poor for earning money. The subsidy to skill acquisition by the poor should be financed in a way that does not depress anyone else's return to skill acquisition. Again, putting a tax on consumption is one way to do this.

Having said what policies should be, stories of leaks, matches, and traps still raise the frightening specter of indeterminacy. Policy differences will not be enough to explain all the variation in growth across nations. Some nations will be poor just because they started off poor or because everyone expects them to be poor. The success or failure of government programs does not uniquely determine the fate of the poor. Even knowing fundamentals like how much moral uprightness, thriftiness, and diligence a given group has, and even if a wise government gives them every incentive to succeed, *we do not know what their economic future will look like*. It is sensitive to initial conditions of knowledge and skill and to expectations, all of which are hard to measure.

This chapter has presented a rather gloomy prospect for the poor, those that are stuck in vicious circles. The next chapter considers some other aspects of technology that gives more hope for at least some backward regions and nations.

Intermezzo: War and memory

Jade is a young woman who grew up in Nae-Chon, a village of 240 people fifty miles southeast of Seoul, Korea. Jade was born in 1958, the year after me. Over her lifetime the average income of Koreans increased more than eight times. Over my lifetime, American income has increased less than two times.

The older people in Nae-Chon look back on their youths with a mixture of nostalgia and relief. Jade's mother remembers that there was no store in Nae-Chon when she first moved there in the 1950s; residents to walk three or four hours into Suwon to buy sugar, salt, or lamp oil. Mrs. Kwang adds how everyone would carry a load of firewood on their back on an A-frame to sell in Suwon.

Jade's mother had to carry the laundry all the way down to the river to wash. "You'd have to get up at three o'clock in the morning, there was so much to do," says Mrs. Kwang. "But those old clothes were really lovely," she sighed.

"The poorest people just ate the bark of the trees or what herbs and grasses they could find in the spring," interjects Mrs. Yu. "There was always a time of hunger before the rice harvest."

The conversation turned somber as they remembered the war. Mrs. Kwang's husband worked as a slave laborer in a coal mine in the north and returned with his health broken. In the war against the North Koreans, Mrs. Kwang remembered, everyone fled south, hurrying past the bodies lying along the roads.

Jade's father had a law degree, but twenty years of war had kept him from establishing himself in his profession. He stuck to farming and put his hope in the next generation, sending Jade to Seoul University. She finished her studies, got married, and moved to Japan. Her sister now lives in Inchon, in an apartment filled with appliances like "washer, juicer, dryer, blender." Her mother still lives in Nae-Chon.

But now Nae-Chon itself has all the appurtenances of a consumer society. The roads are paved, houses have TV antennas or satellite dishes, electric and telephone wires. Less appealing is the litter of plastic cartons and soda bottles tossed in the ditches. A polyurethane foam factory gives work to villagers. The young no longer talk of war and politics, but of sports, foreign travel, and clothes. Nutrition has improved so much over recent decades that this generation is four and a half inches taller than their grandparents.[1]

Creative Destruction:
The Power of Technology

I think there is a world market for maybe five computers.
Thomas Watson, chairman of IBM, 1943

The previous chapter painted technological knowledge as a force creating poverty traps. But there are other ways in which the power of technology offers hope for tropical countries, who don't have as much vested interests in old technologies as industrial countries do. At least some tropical countries have the potential to skip some technological steps that are now obsolete and jump right to the technological frontier. However, seizing technological opportunities requires a minimum level of skill, basic infrastructure, some previous technological experience, and favorable government policies

The Shock of the New

I look at the mess on my desk at home and just about everything I see are products that didn't exist a few years ago. Most important, the laptop on which I'm typing these words did not exist as recently as 1985, when I got my Ph.D. I laboriously typed out my dissertation on what now would be a dinosaur mainframe computer. Just a few years earlier, I had been typing high school and college papers on a manual typewriter. Even when I got my first laptop at the World Bank in 1986, it had a habit of kidnapping innocent young computer files that were never seen again. I had to reenter one computer file four different times.

My laptop today corrects my spelling and grammar. It hooks up to a telephone line so I can download my e-mail from work; e-mail, fast modems, and the touch-tone technology that makes it all possible did not exist a few years ago. I can also access the Internet, another new technology, and read thousands of economics papers and check other information web sites. I did a lot of research for this book over the web. I can get the e-mail addresses and telephone numbers of other economists from the web. I store those addresses and phone numbers on a Sharp electronic organizer that is today nearly obsolete compared to the Palm Pilot but did not exist at all a few years ago.

The coffee I guzzle as I work is Starbucks' high-quality coffee, another product unavailable a few years ago. I used to be limited in my supply of good coffee to what I could get on occasional trips to Bogotá, Colombia; otherwise I was stuck with the horrors of the grocery store brand. Now there's a Starbucks on every street corner. My coffee at home goes through a cheap espresso machine to really give me a jolt.

We are living through an amazing technological revolution. We have seen that growth is not explained very well by accumulation of inputs like machines. The major part of growth is the residual, which includes technology.

My computer modem is twenty-two times faster than those of two decades ago.[1] From just 1991 to 1998, the price of a megabyte of hard disk storage fell from five dollars to three cents.[2] Computing power per dollar invested has risen by a factor of 10,000 over the past two decades. The cost of sending information over optical fiber has fallen by a factor of 1,000 over the past two decades. Semiconductor usage per unit of GDP in the United States has grown by a factor of 3,500 since 1980. In 1981 there were all of 213 computers on the Internet. Now there are 60 million.[3]

And it's not just high tech that has made such spectacular leaps. Wheat yields doubled between 1970 and 1994; corn and rice yields also soared, by 70 and 50 percent, respectively. Asian cereal yields have done even better, tripling over the past four decades.[4]

Industry has become more efficient. New technologies like just-in-time inventory management and numerically controlled machines have emerged.

Health advances have been spectacular. To take one example, the treatment of mental illnesses like schizophrenia and depression has leaped with the discovery of new drugs like Risperdal and Prozac, bringing relief to millions of sufferers.

The list could go on and on. Technological change is indeed a powerful force behind economic growth, which is all about creating new goods and new technologies. A side effect of this growth, however, is that it destroys old goods and old technologies. The previous chapter looked at how new technology complements existing technology, which implied depressing prospects for backward nations. Now let me illustrate how new technology can sometimes substitute for existing technology, which will add some potential for backward nations or regions to catch up. First, let's just celebrate the amazing power of technology to get more output out of the same amount of input. Let's illustrate with the history of lighting, a field where we can precisely measure the input (Btu of energy) and the output (lumen hours).

The Story of Light

The first known type of lighting was a campfire, which dates from about 1.4 million years ago.[5] Our slow-witted ancestor *Homo australopithecus* was the inventor of the campfire. As everyone knows who has tried to set up a tent by firelight, a fire consumes a lot of energy without giving much light. The more with-it Paleolithic peoples, of about 42,000 to 17,000 years ago, replaced campfires as a source of light by burning animal fat in stone lamps. This was a major breakthrough by Paleolithic standards: the fat lamp was about twenty-two times more energy efficient as a source of light than campfires.

Moving up the evolutionary scale, the Babylonians of about 1750 B.C. used sesame oil to light up their temples. This was double the energy efficiency of lamps using animal fat. Finally, by the times of the Greeks and the Romans, we have candles, which have about twice the luminosity of sesame oil. Plato wrote by candlelight. No further advances were made for the next 1,800 years.

We at last moved beyond candles at the expense of the whales. Whale oil lamps were about twice as bright as candles for a given amount of energy. The early nineteenth-century whalers hunted the noble mammals relentlessly to get their oil. Just as whales faced extinction, they (and we) were saved by the discovery of petroleum. Edwin L. Drake sank the world's first oil well near Titusville, Pennsylvania, on August 27, 1859. Kerosene lamps were about 20 percent brighter than whale oil lamps for a given amount of energy, and petroleum was cheap compared to whale oil.

Then Thomas Edison came along and gave us the electric carbon lamp, which was a dramatic improvement: sixteen times more energy efficient than kerosene. The electric lamp continued to be improved,

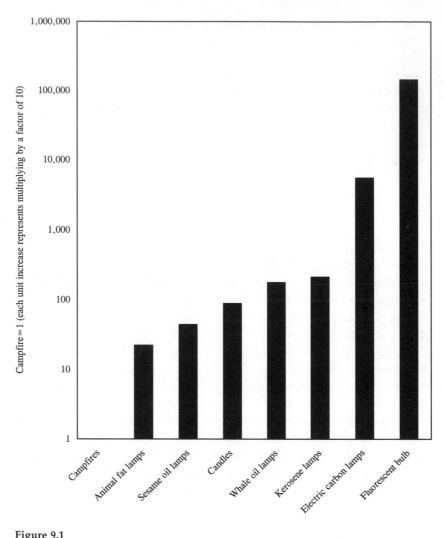

Figure 9.1
Lighting power per unit of energy

all the way to today's compact fluorescent bulb, which as of 1992 was twenty-six times brighter than Edison's lamp for a given amount of energy. So today's lights are 143,000 times brighter than the campfires of the cavemen, for a given amount of energy (figure 9.1).

The dramatic advances in technology and the rise in wages mean that we can buy a lot more lighting for a given amount of labor. We can get 840,000 times more lumen hours today for one hour of labor than could *H. australopithecus*. Even if we shrink our gaze away from the evolutionary time line, we see dramatic changes. We can purchase 45,000 times more lighting for an hour of work today than could the workers of two centuries ago.

Nice But No Panacea

Technology is a wonderful thing, but let's not anoint it as yet another elixir for growth. Technology responds to incentives, just like everything else. When technology exists but the incentives for using it are missing, not much will happen. The Romans had the steam engine, but used it only for opening and closing the doors of a temple.[6] They even had a coin-operated vending machine, used to dispense holy water in the temple. They had reaping machines, ball bearings, water-powered mills, and water pumps but did not attain sustained growth. They also had levers, screws, pulleys, and gears, which they used mostly for war machines.[7]

The Mayans and the Aztecs had the wheel, but used it only for children's toys.[8] Hyderabad, India, was the world's first producer of high-quality steel and exported it to the medieval Islamic empire, which used it to make swords for the holy war against the infidels.

China is the most dramatic example of having technological knowledge but failing to sustain growth of income per head. The Chinese learned to cast iron a millennium and a half before the Europeans. They had iron suspension bridges, which the Europeans would later imitate. Chinese agriculture was a marvel of high-yield rice fields, with hydraulic engineering performing the irrigation and draining of fields. Chinese agriculture used an iron plow, the seed drill, weeding rakes, the deep-tooth harrow, many different types of fertilizer, and chemical and biological pest control. By the time of the Ming dynasty (1368–1644), China had gunpowder, the paddle wheel, the wheelbarrow, the spinning wheel, the waterwheel, printing, paper (even the critical breakthrough of toilet paper), the compass, and triple-masted ocean-going ships.[9] But the Chinese chose not to compete in the world economy with their advanced technology, and they closed their borders. So China remained stagnant through the nineteenth century, when Westerners using these some of these same technologies were able to impose their will on China. (Just think how history would be different if the Chinese had discovered America.)

In the world today, we can get some idea of technological progress by measuring productivity growth: the part of economic growth not accounted for by growth in machinery and labor force. The industrial countries have productivity growth of about 1–2 percent per year. This explains virtually all growth of output per worker in industrial countries. However, even if the technological frontier is moving outward at 1 to 2 percent per year, we do not observe a very strong tendency for many poor nations to benefit from this growth. As we have seen, the growth rate of GDP per capita of the typical poor country was zero between 1980 and 1998. Differences in productivity growth explain over 90 percent of the differences across countries in per capita growth between 1960 and 1992.

Some countries even have negative productivity growth. For example, Costa Rica, Ecuador, Peru, and Syria all saw real per capita GDP fall during the 1980 to 1992 period at more than 1 percent per year. This was at the same time that their real per capita capital stocks were growing at over 1 percent per year and educational attainment was also increasing. I wouldn't argue that Costa Rica, Ecuador, Peru, and Syria had technological regress, but clearly other factors got in the way of technological progress. Technologically driven growth is anything but automatic.

Just as productivity growth explains most of the difference in per capita growth across countries, so differences in technological levels explain most of the differences in income per capita. U.S. workers produce twenty times the output per worker that Chinese workers do. If Chinese workers had the same technology as U.S. workers, then U.S. workers would produce only twice as much as Chinese workers (which would be explained by more education and machinery for U.S. workers). Most of the higher output of American workers compared to Chinese workers is explained by higher technological productivity.[10] Poor countries like China continue to lag behind technologically, despite the widespread availability of advanced technology. Technology by itself does not improve life everywhere.

Technological Progress

Economic growth occurs when people have the incentive to adopt new technologies, being willing to sacrifice current consumption while they are installing the new technology for future payoff. This leads to a steady rise over time in the economy's productive potential and people's average income.

The incentives that are important are the same as I've already discussed. Good government that doesn't steal the fruit of workers' labors is the essence of it. The Romans and the Chinese had centralized authoritarian governments that devoted most of their resources to war and bureaucracy. The Roman empire thought of production as something to be left to the slaves, not a good attitude for technological progress. Nineteenth- and twentieth-century America had (and has) a vibrant private market that rewarded the inventors of new and improved lighting. Ecuador, Costa Rica, Peru, and Syria all had unpredictable government policies that tended to discourage investment in the future through innovation. So we reach the same old conclusion: incentives matter for growth.

But there are a few complications about incentives for technological progress. Technological progress creates winners and losers. Beyond the happy facade of technological creation are some technologies and goods that are being destroyed. Economic growth is not simply more of the same, producing larger and larger quantities of the same old goods. It is more often a process of replacing old goods with new goods. People who were producing the old goods may well lose their jobs, even as new jobs—probably for other people than the people who lost their jobs—are created producing the new goods. In the United States, for example, around 5 percent of jobs are destroyed every three months, with a similar number of new jobs created.[11] Vested interests wedded to the old technology may want to block new technologies.

In our lighting example, high-cost light producers kept getting pushed aside by lower-cost light producers. Candles lost out to whale oil lamps, which in turn lost out to kerosene lamps, which in turn lost out to electric lighting. Candlemakers, whalers, and kerosene refiners have successively been driven out of business by new technologies. This is not a new insight. The economist Joseph Schumpeter noted as long ago as 1942 that the process of economic growth "incessantly revolutionizes the economic structure *from within*, incessantly destroying the old one, incessantly creating a new one. This process of Creative Destruction is the essential fact about capitalism."[12]

The economists Philippe Aghion and Peter Howitt have stressed this kind of approach to growth in recent research.[13] They note that the process of creative destruction complicates incentives for innovation. They give more reasons why a free market economy could have a rate of technological innovation that is too slow. Innovators cannot capture all of the returns to their innovation because others can imitate them (Apple never got the full returns to its innovative graphical user interface because Microsoft imitated it with Windows). Since the social return to innovation is higher than the private return, private individuals do not innovate as fast as would be socially beneficial. Patent protection is one attempt to solve this problem, but it is a very imperfect mechanism that doesn't cover all of the diversion of returns away from the original innovators (as Apple found out). We can call this problem the nonappropriability of innovations. (This is like the "knowledge leaks" principle of the previous chapter.)

Aghion and Howitt also point out another less-well-known way that the cards are stacked against innovation in a free market economy. Today's innovators are acutely aware that future innovations will eventually render obsolete today's inventions. That lowers the return to today's invention and so tends to discourage innovation, an unfortunate circumstance because tomorrow's inventions are going to build on today's invention. As Isaac Newton said, "If I have been able to see further, it was only because I stood on the shoulders of giants."[14]

Today's innovators don't take into account that their innovation will permanently increase the productivity of the economy; they get the returns to their innovation only until the next "new, new thing" comes along. This means once again that the private return to innovation is less than the social return. The extreme case is that no innovation happens because people are afraid subsequent innovation will happen. As Yogi Berra once said about a restaurant, "Nobody goes there; it's too crowded."

For the reason of nonappropriability and obsolescence, the rate of technological innovation will tend to be too slow in a market economy. These disincentives to innovation can be so strong that there is no innovation and thus no growth in a free market economy. The way out would be to create strong incentives for innovation by subsidizing private research and development, subsidizing adoption of best-practices foreign technology, encouraging foreign direct investment from high-tech places, having the government itself do some research and development, and having strong intellectual property rights that allow inventors to keep the profits from their invention.

The Deadweight of the Old

The other new perspective given by the "creative destruction" model is that the deadweight of old technologies could limit the benefits of the new technologies. One reason for the slowdown in growth in the United States and other industrial countries may be due to an exhaustion of the existing technologies without moving fast enough to the new technologies. The incomplete switchover to e-technology may have been what slowed the industrial countries, although it bodes well for their growth in the future.[15] (I just wasted two hours trying to arrange an international flight on-line, before I finally turned to an old-fashioned travel agent to do it for me. The e-revolution is great but has its growing pains.)

A classic paper by the economic historian Paul David (which I just found on the Internet, though after a somewhat tedious search) describes the hindering effect of old technology on an earlier technological revolution: electric engines replacing steam engines.[16] Indeed, the period of gradual adoption of the electric engine coincided with a productivity slowdown in both the United States and United Kingdom. As late as 1910, only 25 percent of American industry was electrified, although Edison had invented the central electricity generating station in 1881. The electric engine was slow to catch on because it required a whole reengineering of the factory floor. With steam engines, there was a high fixed cost for the engine, so a steam engine was put in the middle of the factory floor, and then its power was transmitted by shafts and belts to all of the machines in the factory. The electric engine's big advantage was that it could be installed inside each machine individually, with no need for a central engine. This saved on energy transmission losses through the belts and shafts. It also saved on investment in plant, because the belts and shafts and their heavy supporting infrastructure no longer had to be constructed. The whole system of materials movement within the factory was optimized once location relative to the energy source was no longer a factor. One-story factories replaced multistory factories, which had been desirable from the shafting technology with the steam engine. The multiple power source factory was also less prone to shutdowns. A problem with the steam engine or any of the belts and shafts would shut down the whole factory while the system was repaired. If an electric machine broke down, on the other hand, it affected only the equipment containing it.

However, none of these gains was realized right away because of the heavy investment that had already taken place in the belts-and-shafts factories. In the initial phase of adoption of the electric engine, it merely replaced the steam engine as the central energy source for the belts and shafts. It was only as these old factories depreciated and new ones were built designed around decentralized electric power that the full productivity gains were realized. Ironically, past technological prowess (at steam) can block new technology (power). Backward countries could have an advantage in implementing the new technology because they never had the old one!

Moreover, in a theme that is familiar throughout this book, individual factories' decisions on electric power depended on what other factories were doing. It was worthwhile building a generating station only if a large number of commercial users were in the vicinity. If neighboring users were not adopting electric power, an individual factory was out of luck. This network effect may explain why there was very little electrification at first, and then it happened all in a rush. By 1930, 80 percent of American industry was electrified.

Similarly, the productivity gains of the computer are slow to be realized, because they imply a whole reorganization of the old way we do business. I still have much more of my office space devoted to books and papers than I do to computers. This is because the economy is not yet computer intensive enough to do away with the paper versions of documents. It's already easy to foresee the day when all business and professional documents will be shared on-line, obviating the need for shelves of paper-based materials. But it still hasn't happened because there are still too many traditional people out there with ink and paper. When it does come, the new wave will come with a rush. Probably the rush has already begun. In 1997, there was still only one Internet-linked computer for every twenty-three people in the United States, but the number of Internet-linked computers is growing at 50 percent a year.[17] In many poor countries, the Internet is growing even faster, as they can skip some of the intermediate steps and jump to the frontier. Mexico already has 36

Internet service providers, including one in its most backward state of Chiapas.

Vested Interests and Creative Destruction

Another insight of creative destruction is that there will be losers as well as winners from economic growth. As growth proceeds, old industries die and new ones are created. Growth alters the landscape, turning farms into fast-food restaurants and factory sites. And because growth involves losers as well as winners, it's easy to see why there has always been a vocal antigrowth faction, even aside from the concern for the environment.

On the web is a site for the Preservation Institute, a group that calls for "the end of economic growth."[18] 1999 study warns, "Urban sprawl is undermining America's environment, economy, and social fabric."[19] The historian Paul Kennedy notes that economic change "like wars and sporting tournaments" is "usually not beneficial to all." Progress benefits some "just as it damages others."[20] Browsing the library, I find titles like *Sustainable Development Is Possible Only If We Forgo Growth, Economic Growth and Declining Social Welfare, Developed to Death, The Poverty of Affluence, The Costs of Economic Growth*, and the more restrained *Growth Illusion: How Economic Growth Has Enriched the Few, Impoverished the Many, and Endangered the Planet*.[21] Demonstrators at the Prague 2000 annual meeting of the IMF and World Bank threw rocks and Molotov cocktails to express their disenchantment with global economic growth.

The most obvious vested interest that has an incentive to oppose creatively destructive growth is the group working with the old technologies. I resist the new Palm Pilot palmtop computer because I have all my telephone numbers in the now obsolete Sharp Wizard electronic organizer. More generally, there will be a coalition of workers and corporations in the old industries pleading for protection against the new technology. When the new technology is coming from abroad, this often translates into protection against competing imports made with the new, more efficient technology. Government leaders may also be part of the vested interests in the old technology. Bureaucrats may feel that new technology threatens their control. This may be the story of China's turning inward in the Ming dynasty and China today trying to control the use of the Internet. These vested interests could be so strong as to slow growth significantly.

The economic historian Joel Mokyr argues that the same interests that produced the world's first industrial revolution in England later opposed further technological progress, causing England to lose its technological lead to America. English public schools trained the elite for the professions rather than in science and technology. On the Continent, in contrast, the Germans introduced their *Technische Hochschule*.[22] The American spinning industry went ahead with the introduction of the new technique of ring spinning, while Lancashire stuck with the old technology of mule spinning.[23] After three worker strikes in the 1850s, the English prohibited the introduction of the sewing machine into shoemaking in Northampton. Workers in the Birmingham gun-making industry blocked the introduction of the great breakthrough of interchangeable parts. English workers also blocked new machinery in carpetmaking, glassmaking, and metalworking.[24]

Then we see the same thing happening to America, losing its lead to Japan in the 1970s and 1980s. Now Japan is stagnating, and America—after a big shakeup—is in the lead again, although both America and Japan are growing more slowly than they were a few decades ago.

We can think of the conflict between the old and the new technology as an intergenerational conflict. The old are those who were trained in the old technology, and their skills may be highly specific to that technology; they have every incentive to oppose new technologies. The young are trained afresh in whatever is the current technological frontier; they have an incentive to introduce this new, more productive technology. So whether technological progress continues depends on whether the young or the old are in charge. In a democracy, this may come down to demographics: is the population sufficiently skewed toward the older generations that they form a majority? This in turn depends on population growth. In rapidly growing populations, the young have a majority; in slowly growing populations, the population ages, so the old are in the majority.[25] Poor countries have rapidly growing populations, and so have the advantage of a young majority.

This insight could explain some of the dramatic facts of recent economic experience. The economic growth slowdown in the industrial economies coincides with an aging of their populations. This could explain why the electronics revolution of the past two decades has not yet had the expected productivity payoff: the older generations are resisting having the personal computer permeate the whole infrastructure of modern society. (My mother mightily resists the introduction of e-mail and still types her letters to me on what is probably the last electric typewriter in America.) The U.S. economy may be more dynamic than other industrial economies because of its faster population growth and relatively younger population (thanks in part to immigration).

This perspective could explain another big economic happening: the general failure of transformation in the ex-communist economies of Eastern Europe and the former Soviet Union. These are economies with near zero population growth and old populations. A plausible story (among many others) for their failure to take off after dismantling the planned economy is that the vested interests in the old technology are still in charge. The old enterprise managers still resist the introduction of new Western technologies that would give the advantage to the young over the old.

The late economist Mancur Olson pointed out another feature of economic growth explained by the insight of vested old-technology interests. He noted the curious fact that economies seemed to grow very fast after major wars or other societal revolutions. Examples are the rapid growth in Japan, Germany, and France after World War II. Olson's story was that wartime destruction and revolution dissolved the old vested interests and let new leaders come to the fore. Extending Olson's story a bit, we could say that war and revolution kicked out the older generation and brought in the new generation ready to adopt new technology.

The story of Japan's and America's post–World War II steel industry illustrates the difference between a shakeup to create new leaders (in Japan) and resistance to innovation by vested interests (in the United States). The American occupation in Japan purged the heavy industries of their prewar leadership. A young engineer named Nishiyama Yataro emerged as president of Kawasaki Steel and was one of the technological pioneers of the industry.[26]

In 1952, two Austrian companies invented the basic oxygen furnace to replace the then standard open hearth furnace. They tried to sell their invention both to the Americans and Japanese. The Americans, who produced ten times more steel than the Japanese and had a heavy investment in open hearth technology (by which they themselves had leapfrogged over the British, who used the Bessemer process),[27] declined the offer of the new basic oxygen technology.

Nishiyama Yataro, in contrast, adopted the technology in the late 1950s, soon followed by other Japanese firms. After the technology was perfected, the oxygen furnace reduced production costs relative to open hearth furnaces by 10 to 20 percent and cut refining time to one-tenth of what it was under the old technology. Moreover, technology adoption begat technology adoption. Continuous casting, where production from the steel refining process went directly into the production of slabs, replaced the old process—in Japan in the 1950s, but not in the United States—by which refined steel was cooled into ingots and then reheated to make slabs. Continuous casting was more energy efficient because the ingots did not have to be reheated.

Continuous casting followed naturally from the basic oxygen furnace, because otherwise there was a production line imbalance between the speed of slab making and steelmaking. This innovation in turn led to computerized process control of the whole steelmaking process, which Japan introduced as early as 1962 and was the world leader in this technology in the 1980s.[28] Over 1957 to 1993, the efficiency of resource use in Japanese steel more than doubled, while American steel efficiency remained roughly the same.[29] Over the past four decades, Japanese iron and steel production has quadrupled, while American iron and steel production has grown just 13 percent.[30] Japan's share of the world steel market doubled from 1960 to 1996, while the U.S. share fell by half. And then, as the natural progression would have it, Japan has more recently been losing market share to newcomers like Korea and Taiwan.[31]

As the Japanese steel story illustrates, the tension between vested interests in old and new technologies can give an advantage to the backward economies. The advanced economy will have a big stake in the current technology, having trained its workers in the use of the technology so well that they are more productive sticking with the current technology rather than switching to a new one.[34] Compare this to a backward economy that has not trained its workers in the old technology because it hasn't yet started producing in some industries at all or because the old factories were bombed in a war. The backward economy will find it worthwhile to jump right to the new technology when they move into new industries, overtaking the advanced economy. Again, some think that this is a plausible story for Japan's catching up to the United States after World War II. This is an interesting contrast to the message of the previous chapter that the backward economies will always be at a disadvantage.

Before getting too excited about the blessings of backwardness, though, let's note that the forces identified in the previous chapter are still active. Although backwardness may be an advantage in allowing countries to jump to the frontier technology, there are also disadvantages to backwardness. Countries that are too backward may lack the complementary inputs to new technologies. For example, to move to computerized process control of steelmaking requires familiarity with computers. At an even more basic level are reliable energy supplies, which depend on the transportation infrastructure of the economy. An economy could be "too backward," with no hope of leaping to the frontier technology. The disadvantages of backwardness could explain why Chad didn't catch up to the United States in the same way that Japan did. We have seen that there is no general tendency for the poor countries to catch up to the rich; instead, on average, they are falling further behind.

Imitation Among the Poor

Poor countries are unlikely to be inventors of technology, but they do not have to produce their own Thomas Edisons and Bill Gateses. They have the advantage that they can advance their technological level by adopting inventions from rich countries.

As we saw in the Bangladesh garments example in the previous chapter, poor countries can leap right to the technological frontier by imitating technologies from industrialized nations. Bangladeshi garment workers imitated Korean garment workers during their apprenticeship in Korea, and Bangladeshi managers imitated Korean managers. The result was a multibillion dollar garment export industry in Bangladesh.

One likely vehicle of transmission of advanced technology from rich to poor countries, as was evident from the Bangladeshi garment example, is foreign direct investment. The Bangladeshi technological leap would not have happened unless the Korean firm Daewoo had decided to invest in Bangladesh.

There is indirect evidence that direct foreign investment is good for technological progress. Several empirical studies have found that higher inflows of foreign direct investment as a ratio to GDP raise economic growth in poor countries, possibly reflecting growth through technology adoption.[33] A study of Indonesian firms found that foreign-owned firms had higher output per worker than domestic firms. Foreign-owned firms in Indonesia also raised output per worker in domestic firms, presumably through imitation.[34]

Another channel by which foreign technology enters a country is through imports of machines. It's easy for people in poor countries to jump to the technological frontier in computers: just buy a Dell Latitude CPi laptop with Microsoft Windows Word and Excel installed on it, and off you go. A recent study found that imports of machines do indeed raise growth.[35] If the government is foolish enough to prohibit imports of machines, growth will suffer. For example, Brazil moved more slowly into the computer revolution than necessary because of a government ban on PC imports, a misguided attempt to promote the domestic PC industry, a classic attempt by vested interests to hijack technological progress.

In general, imitation responds to the same kind of incentives that innovation does. The government should subsidize technological imitation because it brings benefits to other firms in the economy besides the imitator. And of course, the business climate has to favor foreign direct investment and imports of machines, not to mention entrepreneurs in general.

Bangalore

Bangalore, India, is the capital of Karnataka state in the south India. It's an inland plateau city, long famous for its refreshing climate and many gardens. It was a sleepy place where honeymooners and retirees went to get away.[36]

But gardening is not what Bangalore is famous for today. The universal cliché is that it's India's Silicon Valley, one of the biggest concentrations of software industry in the Third World. In bars named NASA and Pubworld on Church Street in downtown Bangalore, young software engineers hang out and exchange industry gossip ("Church Street buzz"). Software clients include Citibank, American Express, General Electric, and Reebok.[37] Texas Instruments, Sun Microsystems, Novell, Intel, IBM, and Hewlett-Packard all have offices here. Local firms include Wipro, Tata, Satyam, Baysoft, and Infosys. Some domestic firms have paired off with foreign partners (Wipro with Intel, Tata with IBM). Headhunting firms come to

Church Street to recruit software engineers for the original Silicon Valley. Bangalore accounts for a large share of India's $2.2 billion software industry. Bangalore is a good example of how a backward area can leapfrog to the technological frontier.

But why are Silicon Valleys all over the world so concentrated in particular locations? Like elsewhere, Bangalore's story begins (but does not end) with a government interventions and a university. What Stanford was to the Silicon Valley and MIT to Route 128, the Indian Institute of Science is to Bangalore.

Indian industrialist Jamsetji Nasarwanji Tata founded India's premier science and technology university, the Indian Institute of Science, in Bangalore in 1909. Like everybody else, he was attracted by the beautiful climate. After national independence in 1947, government defense, aeronautics, and electronics agencies located in Bangalore: Hindustan Aeronautics, Bharat Electronics, the Indian Space Research Organization, and the National Aeronautical Laboratory. So we can begin to understand why the software industry gravitated to this spot, but something still seems missing. Software engineers came here because other software engineers were already here, who in turn were here because other software engineers were here. Why does the software industry concentrate in these tight geographic circles all over the world?

I have been treating technological innovation as a conscious decision by innovators, who respond to incentives often reinforced by government intervention. But there's an unconscious side to invention, which is called *path dependence*. An innovator cannot anticipate where a particular innovation might lead. Jamsetji Nasarwanji Tata did not anticipate in 1909 that his technical school would lead to a computer industry concentration in Bangalore (especially since computers weren't yet invented).

Path Dependence and Luck

An individual innovator usually cannot foresee whether a particular invention will lead to a chain of further inventions or whether it's the last gasp of a technological dead end. We have here again the specter of indeterminacy. Some societies may have had the bad luck to implement technologies that made sense for the present but didn't offer much innovation potential. Other societies may just get lucky, having embarked on the first steps of what turn out to be technologically fruitful paths. This is path dependence. A country's future success depends on the path it chose in the past. For example, the eighteenth-century English were much concerned with technological progress in mining, given their abundant coal deposits. One problem they faced was getting the water out of the coal mines.

What happened next was that the miners "worked on developing better pumps, leading to more accurate boring machines and other tools, which eventually helped to develop steam- and modern waterpower. Mining required knowledge of metallurgy, chemistry, mechanics, and civil engineering; the convergence of so many different branches of so many different branches of knowledge ... could not but lead to further technological progress." Many of the great eighteenth-century British inventors came out of the mining industry.[38]

Another example is the West's use of the wheel in transport. There was a natural progression from the wheelbarrow to the horse-drawn cart to the stagecoach to the railroad. In the Middle East and North Africa, in contrast, camel transport replaced wheeled transport after the invention of the camel saddle before 100 B.C. Using camels made economic sense since no roads had to be built for camels going through the desert, but they were a technological dead end. As Mokyr puts it, "Camels conserved resources ... but they did not inspire railroads."[39]

A more recent example is Japan's inventing analogue high-definition television in the late 1960s. Japan was the world leader for a while in HDTV, making its first broadcast in 1989, but it lost its lead to the United States and Europe, which saw that the future of the technology was in digital HDTV. The first digital HDTV broadcasts in the United States came in 1998.[40] In technology, it's hard to anticipate what's going to be the breakthrough technological path. Sometimes you just bet on the wrong horse.

Complementarity versus Substitution

A similar idea is that new technologies are complementary to each other, in that one invention raises the rate of return to a different invention. This is in contrast to the effect that I have been stressing for most of this chapter: that new technology destroys old technology. The complementarity effect has some of the same predictions as the skill-matching game of the previous chapter. Whether complementarity or substitution dominates determines the shape of economic history.

The railroad was a complementary invention to the steam engine. (How far would we have gotten with horse-drawn rail carriages?) The Internet is a complementary invention to the personal computer. (Can you imagine the Internet on mainframes?).

If complementarity of inventions dominates substitution of inventions, the consequences will be similar to the increasing returns story of the previous chapter.

First, invention will tend to be highly concentrated in space and time, like the English Midlands between 1750 and 1830, Silicon Valley in the 1980s and 1990s, and Bangalore India's software industry today. Inventors' activity is spurred by having other inventors around them. Where these concentrations happen can depend on accidents such as university location.

Second, innovation will happen where technology is already highly advanced. (This effect offsets the advantages of backwardness for imitation and leaping to the frontier mentioned earlier. On balance, backwardness seems to be a disadvantage because of the complementary invention effect.) New inventions will happen where they can draw on existing inventions. This is path dependence again.

Third, sometimes new inventions give new life to existing inventions, as opposed to the creative destruction emphasized for most of this chapter.[41] This does not invalidate creative destruction; the two processes can live side by side, with some technologies destroyed by new inventions and other technologies perpetuated by everextending invention.

Finally, technological change will accelerate over time. If new inventions are complementary to existing technology, their rate of return will increase as technology advances, meaning faster technological progress. This seems borne out by experience. In the first millennium after Christ, it was big news to come up with the occasional innovation like the horse collar, which allowed horses to pull loads without the yoke's pressing against their windpipe. Even in the nineteenth century, it took a while to get from the 1.2 million horsepower that steam engines delivered to American industry in 1869 to the 45 million horsepower that electric engines delivered in 1939. That's a forty-fold increase in muscle power over a seventy-year period. In contrast, over the past forty years, we have gone from having 2,000 computers in 1960 with an average processing power of

10,000 instructions per second to having 200 million computers with an average processing power of 100,000 instructions per second— a million-fold increase in information processing power in four decades.[42]

The possible complementarity of inventions introduces a role for history and expectations. History is important, because having advanced technology already makes a country a breeding ground for new invention. Expectations are important, because the return to an invention will be higher if the expectation is that everyone else is making complementary inventions. Computer companies come to Bangalore because they expect other computer companies to locate there.

Again, note that this is a contrary prediction to the creative destruction theory, where anticipating future inventions discouraged an invention by making it obsolete sooner. Once again, both theories can be right for different inventions: some inventions make existing technology obsolete, and others raise the return to existing technology.

A given technology can have both effects at once. For example, Microsoft Windows tended to substitute for Apple's graphical user interface, shrinking Apple to a small percentage of the PC market. On the other hand, Windows raised the rate of return to multiple Windows-based software applications. The word processing program I used for writing this book would not exist without Windows. Microsoft's incentive to invent and improve Windows was stronger because of all the complementary software it expected to be written by other inventors. (Sometimes these are inventors within the software giant itself. The giant is sitting pretty if it can capture all of the complementary inventions within one company—as the Justice Department has noticed.)

Technology also may be complementary to skills. One bit of evidence for this is the increased returns to skills in industrial economies as the electronic revolution proceeded over the past few decades; this is a plausible explanation of the increased inequality in many industrial countries. High school graduates get left behind by the e-economy even as college graduates get a high payoff for their skills.

Complementarity between technology and skills would set up a matching game like that discussed in the previous chapter. People would accumulate high skills where there was high technology and invest in new technology where there was high skills. There would be the same kind of virtuous or vicious circles as in the skill-matching game of the previous chapter or the complementary inventions story of this chapter.

The dependence of invention on history and expectations raises a role for sheer luck, as did the theories of the previous chapter. A critical mass of inventors can happen to coalesce in a particular place, like Bangalore, India, and then sustain itself by continually attracting new inventors. The failures of Roman and Chinese technology to take off despite promising beginnings could be because they lacked a few critical complementary inventions (or enough people with complementary skills). In the end, it could be the luck of the draw. I explore luck further in the next chapter.

The Future of the Tropics

How much the current electronic revolution will create and destroy in the poor countries is very much an open question—will complementarity or substitution dominate? Technological backwardness can be an advantage or a disadvantage. It's a disadvantage to the extent that the ability to use new technology depends on the familiarity with existing technology (i.e., if new technology complements existing technology). It's a disadvantage to the extent that low average skills pulls down the returns to new technology in poor countries. Then it's very bad news that the poorest countries have fewer Internet users relative to population than the richest countries, by a factor of 10,000.

However, we have also seen ways in which new technology destroys existing technology (i.e., if new technology substitutes for existing technology). If this is the case, poor countries' lack of much existing technology could be a blessing in disguise. They can jump right to the frontier technology. One notable phenomenon that travelers to developing countries see today is the amazingly high density of cell phones. Since state-owned telephone companies never really delivered the goods, users have leapfrogged right to cell phones, skipping the intermediate stage of high telephone mainline density.

Moreover, the falling price of communications and transport can create new opportunities for poor nations to borrow knowledge and technology from the rich nations. The decentralized nature of the electronics revolution could be very good for the poor. Electric power, a phone line, and a computer translates to access to a vast store of knowledge on the Internet. The World Bank is investing heavily in distance learning, in which speakers in Washington can give lectures by teleconference to audiences in poor countries (and vice versa).

Falling transport and communications costs will lower the importance of being close to major markets, gradually eliminating the distance factor that has worked against poor countries in the global South trying to be competitive in the markets of the global North. The Bangalore software industry wouldn't exist if it weren't for the dramatic fall in the cost of distance. We can expect new Bangalores as the communications revolution continues.

We have seen that so far, the rich have tended to grow faster than the poor over the past two centuries of technological progress. However, this needn't continue to be true; the changing nature of technology and aggressive government incentives for technological adoption in poor countries could change the equation. Which way the computer revolution goes is an open question.

Conclusion

An understanding that technological creation and destruction is the essence of the growth process yields several new insights about growth. The empirical evidence suggests that technological innovation and research and development should be subsidized. The United States for one is going in the wrong direction: federal R&D spending as a ratio to GDP today is only 0.8 percent, compared to 1.5 percent in the 1960s.

The old technology has its adherents who have to be overcome if the process of growth is to go forward. They will try to erect barriers to the entry of new firms to preserve their competitiveness with the old technology. A favorable climate for new generations of businesspeople and entrepreneurs is essential for growth from the creative destruction point of view.

For poor countries, it's time to turn on the light—the electric light that is 100,000 times brighter than wood fires. The new e-dot economy is a two-edged sword: it could leave behind Third World places that are too unskilled, too backward technologically, or too hostile to enterprise, but it could mean the decentralization of production to other Third World centers and leapfrogging to the frontier.

The combination of this chapter and the previous chapter could help us understand the pattern of many poor economies stagnating, with an exceptional few catching up to the rich economies. Which group a given country falls in depends on both luck and government policy. Let's turn first to luck.

Intermezzo: Accident in Jamaica

A woman in Bower Bank, Jamaica, had eight children. The father was in jail in the United States, no longer sending remittances.

Her fourteen-year old daughter "get burn up from her face, breast, chest down to her legs with boiling water February 2 1999. That night just because I never have any money earlier to cook, me go town and get a money, buy something to cook cause them never eat from morning. Me daughter bend down, to pick up something near the stove and bounce off the pot of boiling water pan herself. Me tek her to hospital and me never have the money fe register her. Me beg somebody the money and register her. Me owe the hospital $10,500 for the bill, a caan [can't] pay it. She's to go back for treatment because her hand caan stretch out or go up, but the hospital will not see her if I don't pay the bill."

Although men flatter themselves with their great actions, they are not so often the result of a great design as of chance.

François de la Rochefoucauld

Nha is a twenty-six-year-old father in Lao Cai, Vietnam. His household has twelve members. Nha's family used to be one of the richest families in the village, but now they are one of the poorest. In recent years they have suffered two disasters. First, his father died two years ago. That left only two main workers in the family: Nha and his mother, aged forty. And two years ago, Nha's daughter, Lu Seo Pao, had a serious illness and had to be operated on in the district and province hospital. His family had to sell four buffalo, one horse, and two pigs to cover the cost of the operation. The operation cost several million Vietnamese dong. Sadly she is still not cured. All the people in his community helped, but no one can contribute more than 20,000 dong. Nha's younger brother, Lu Seo Seng, who was studying in grade 6, had to leave school in order to help his family. Nha says that "if Lu Seo Pao had not been ill, his family would still have many buffalo, he could have a house for his younger brother and Seng could study further."

Sandhya Chaalak is a thirty-year-old mother of four daughters in Geruwa, India. Her eldest child is seven, and the youngest is still in her lap. Her husband used to work in a dairy, cleaning buffalo. Then disaster struck. For over a year now, he has been suffering from diabetes and can no longer work. To raise money for her husband's treatment, Sandhya sold her house and her land to another resident of the village for 1,300 rupees, although the actual value was over

20,000 rupees. She knows she was underpaid, but she feels indebted to the buyer because he has allowed her to retain a small room in the house for her ailing husband and children. She has taken over supporting the family by hauling fuelwood on her head a distance of about 10 kilometers every other day. She has little hope for the future. She lives hand to mouth, for her daily earning barely suffices for two kilograms of rice a day. Her daughters do not go to school, and she is hardly keen that they should do so.

Freda Musonda is a mother of five children in Muchinka, Zambia. Her husband died in 1998. After the funeral, his relatives seized the family's possessions, including the furniture, her husband's sewing machines (he was a tailor), and his bank book. Freda was left with nothing but her children. She was told by her father-in-law to leave the house. Luckily, her husband's friend drove her to her village with the children. She worries about how she will feed her children because she has nothing with which to start earning income. Her parents are very old and poor. She has cultivated her parents' field, but the maize fields are not doing well because she had no fertilizer. The cassava and millet fields are more promising. Her two children started at Mabonde basic school, but they were sent back because she could not afford to pay for them. At the time the interviewer visited, there was no sign that the family was going to have anything for lunch. According to Freda, the family had not eaten anything the previous day because she could not sell her dress. Her children were feeding on unripe mangoes.[1]

Nha, Sandhya Chaalak, and Freda Musonda were thrown into the vicious circle of illiteracy, unskilled work, and poverty by household disasters. Living in rich countries, it is easy to forget how much poor people are at the mercy of nature and disease.

The poverty traps that exist at low incomes make poor households and economies highly vulnerable to shocks. Within the household, the return to skills may depend on complementary household assets and skills of other household members. The ability to use new technologies like the green revolution depends on complementary skills to get the right mix of fertilizer and high-quality seeds. Households with enough resources can invest in skills and technology to get the virtuous circle going. Poor households cannot borrow because they have no collateral, and so they cannot invest in skills or technology even where the return to schooling and technology is high. A disaster can wipe out the liquid assets of the household that it could have used to get ahead. A household can be thrown into a vicious circle of poverty by a disaster.

The Economy of Disaster

Whole economies are also vulnerable to disasters. For example, an economy could be at a high enough average skill level that it pays off for everyone to acquire skills, to match with other skilled individuals. Or the introduction of new techologies could be worthwhile if enough skilled people exist. If a disaster kills off skilled people and wipes out the assets of the survivors, however, the poor will no longer be able to afford skill acquisition and acquistion of new technologies. They could be thrust back into the vicious circle where no one acquires skills because they have only unskilled people to match with. They could fall back into the vicious circle where new technology is not adopted because skills are too low, and skills are not improved because technology is too backward.

Poor countries are more vulnerable than rich countries to natural disasters. Between 1990 and 1998, poor countries accounted for 94 percent of the world's 568 major natural disasters and 97 percent of disaster-related deaths.[2]

Twenty-seven percent of the poorest fifth of nations had famines between 1960 and 1990; none in the richest fifth did. Over 1 percent of the poorest fifth of countries' peoples were refugees from one type of disaster or another; none of the richest countries' peoples were refugees. Eleven percent of the low-risk population in the poorest fifth of countries had the human immunodeficiency virus (HIV); three-tenths of a percent of the low-risk population in the richest fifth of countries had HIV.

The twenty-one countries with the highest HIV prevalence in the world are all in sub-Saharan Africa. The AIDS epidemic has already killed 14 million Africans. In Zimbabwe and Botswana, one in four adults is infected with HIV. A child born today in Zambia or Zimbabwe is more likely than not to die of AIDS.[3] If the children don't die of AIDS themselves, their parents might; there are 11 million AIDS orphans in Africa today.[4] Because of AIDS, life expectancy in the hardest-hit African nations is projected to be lower by seventeen years in 2010: forty-seven years instead of sixty-four.[5] Four million more people became infected with HIV in Africa in 1999. AIDS is not just a human tragedy; it also starves the economy of its prime-age workers. In Botswana, companies take out "key man" insurance to cover the cost of recruitment if a skilled worker dies of AIDS.[6]

Besides the AIDS epidemic there are also natural and man-made disasters. The number of people killed in natural disasters (such as earthquakes, droughts, floods, landslides, typhoons, and volcanic eruptions) and man-made disasters (war, famine, and so forth) worldwide since 1969 is 4.2 million. Of this total, six low-income countries account for two-thirds of the deaths: Ethiopia, Bangladesh, China, Sudan, India, and Mozambique.[7]

The poor countries' sensitivity to disasters could explain why they have a much larger range of growth rates than do industrial countries. The poorest fifteen countries in 1960 had subsequent annual per capita growth 1960 to 1994 that ranged from −2 percent (Zaire) to 6 percent (Botswana). The richest fifteen countries had growth that ranged only from 1.6 percent (Switzerland) to 3.2 percent (Italy).[8]

In the past few years, we have had Hurricane Mitch, causing deadly floods in Nicaragua and Honduras; two earthquakes in Turkey; monsoon-induced flooding in Orissa, India; an earthquake in Colombia; mudslides in Venezuela; an earthquake in Armenia; floods in Vietnam; an earthquake in Taiwan; Yangtze River flooding in China; El Niño in Ecuador; tidal waves in Papua New Guinea; Hurricane Keith in Belize and flooding in Bangladesh and Mozambique. As the new millennium opens, famine threatens people in Sudan, Kenya, and Ethiopia.

To take just one disaster, two weeks of torrential rains in Venezuela caused flash floods and mudslides in December 1999. The disaster killed an estimated 30,000 people, left 150,000 homeless, and destroyed much of the state of Vargas. Estimated economic damage is $10 billion to $15 billion, or 10 to 15 percent of GDP.[9] Red Cross volunteers filed some of the first on-scene reports:

Houses that look like shredded paper. Streets that look like they have been bombed continuously for days. The stench of death. Debris everywhere. The rock and mud remains of rivers that carved their way through towns. Bits of cars and telephone booths that peep out above the ground. It is hard to believe that this is the result of water and not of war. But if you enter what is left of a house or a school or a church, and walk through the corridors, enter what was once a class room or a kitchen, the perpetrator of the crime is unmistakably mud. So thick and so high that every structure is now part funeral home, part morgue, part cemetery. In the town of La Guaira, where 35,000 people once lived, only 5,000 remain.

Survivor Blanca Rosa Giralda, age seventy-four, said, "When I saw the wave [of mud] coming at me, I didn't have time to remember I was an old lady." She ran to higher ground.

Many of the victims were living in tin and wood shacks at the foot of Mount Avila next to Caracas. Government officials had ignored for decades the slums creeping up the dangerous slopes of Mount Avila. "Sure I knew it was dangerous," said slum resident Andrés Eloy Guillen, "but it's the land I live on. Only the rich get to choose."[10]

I traveled to Caracas in February 2000, a month and a half after the mudslides. I shuddered on seeing the shantytowns of the poor clinging to hillsides—those shantytowns that survived. Elsewhere there were red gashes in the hillsides where land and houses had been swept away. There were still many pockets of debris that the government had not yet cleaned up.

Why Luck is Important

Economists on the quest for growth liked to think that growth responded to deterministic factors. But the new views of leaks, matches, and traps said that growth was not so deterministic after all. The new view of technological change said that technology in one part of the economy depends on complementary technological changes in other parts of the economy. The complementarity of technology and skills could set up vicious and virtuous circles that depend on the economy's starting point. Although leaping to the technological frontier could enable backward economies to catch up to advanced economies, an economy can be too backward in skills or existing technology to implement the technology needed for the leap.

Growth depends on initial conditions. If the economy starts from a favorable position, it will take off. If a natural disaster or historical initial poverty has it below the threshold, it won't take off. Growth also depends on expectations. If everyone expects the economy to succeed, then they invest in knowledge and technology for that economy; otherwise they don't. Bad luck could create bad incentives; good luck could create good incentives. People respond to incentives.

Sensitivity to expectations also makes economies vulnerable to luck. An accidental change in initial conditions can make everyone believe that investment in an economy will not pay off. If everyone disinvests accordingly, then investment really will not pay off. The belief that everyone else will not be putting in new knowledge, machinery, technology, and skills is enough to make people not invest in knowledge, machinery, technology, and skills. They lack opportunities for matching their own investments in technology, machinery, and skills to others'.

With increasing returns, a war or a flood could shift an economy from a growing to a declining one. The same is true of abrupt changes in an economy's export prices or import prices, or of a sudden interruption in capital flows, as we saw in Latin America in 1982 and 1994–1995, Asia in 1997–1998, Russia in 1998, and Brazil in 1999. With increasing returns, capitalist economies are inherently unstable. Even the United States was no stranger to financial panics and depressions during its long climb out of poverty to prosperity.

How do accidents change a country's prospects? We've seen that because of leaks and matches, there are strong incentives to invest in knowledge, machinery, and skills where a lot of knowledge, machinery, and skills are already in place. The existing knowledge will leak to any new investors. The existing knowledge, machinery, and skills will create opportunities for profitably matching new knowledge, machinery, and skills to the old ones. If new technology is complementary to existing technology, there are vicious and virtuous circles. So if there is an abrupt drop in the amount of technology, machinery, and skills or a change in expectations for how much there will be in the future—say because of a natural disaster, a war that devastates the economy, or sudden capital outflows, as in the Asian and Latin American crises—then the incentives for growth will quickly worsen.

Luck Keeps Us Honest

I like talking about luck because it's a rival hypothesis that keeps us scientifically honest whenever we test our own favorite hypothesis on what determines growth. Thinking about luck is good for the soul. It reminds us self-important analysts that we might just be totally witless about what's going on. Luck makes us ask ourselves whether we would see the same association between our favorite factor X and economic growth if the true cause was sheer luck. I explore in this chapter some of the subtle ways that luck might operate in the data.

Consider an evolutionary example. We often think of the extinction of dinosaurs as a moral fable on what happens if you don't adjust to changing conditions. We often insult apparently doomed, lumbering organizations by calling them "dinosaurs" (this is pretty presumptuous on the part of *homo sapiens*, since our species has so far lived less than 1 percent as long as the dinosaurs). The fittest survive, and the less fit perish.

This sounds a lot like the traditional idea that the most fit economies succeed in the long run. The similarity is not accidental. Darwin borrowed from Adam Smith the idea that an invisible hand could pick winners in a decentralized system like a market or an ecosystem.

But now there are new views of what happened to the dinosaurs. They were doing fine until the earth got hit by an asteroid. In the words of one evolutionist, it was bad luck rather than bad genes that did them in. The asteroid hypothesis is a good example of the eternal tension between inherent merit and good luck.

Finally, growth rates behaving like luck is important. There is only a weak association between growth for each country between 1975 and 1990 and growth between 1960 and 1975. We have countries like Gabon that had about the best per capita growth in the world between 1960 and 1975 and then had negative growth from 1975 to 1990. Similar cases that were above average between 1960 and 1975 and then disasters from 1975 to 1990 include Iran, Ivory Coast, Nicaragua, Guyana, Peru, and Namibia. Conversely, we have countries like Sri Lanka that had zero per capita growth between 1960 and 1975 and then had above-average growth from 1975 to 1990. Growth in the earlier period is a poor predictor of growth during the later period; growth in the former period explains only 7 percent of the variation across countries in the latter period. Figure 10.1 shows the volatile per capita income of four prototypically unstable countries.

This instability of growth could have a lot to do with these kinds of shocks and the way that countries respond to them. Poor countries may be closer to the threshold of knowledge and skills that in the increasing-returns stories makes the difference between virtuous circles of growth and vicious circles of decline. A disaster that wipes out skilled workers or assets of the population may plunge them beneath the threshold of escaping the vicious circle of poverty. Rich countries are likely safely past that threshold.

Only four countries—Korea, Taiwan, Hong Kong, and Singapore —had exceptional growth in both periods. Because of their consistent high growth, they became known as the gang of four. But even a

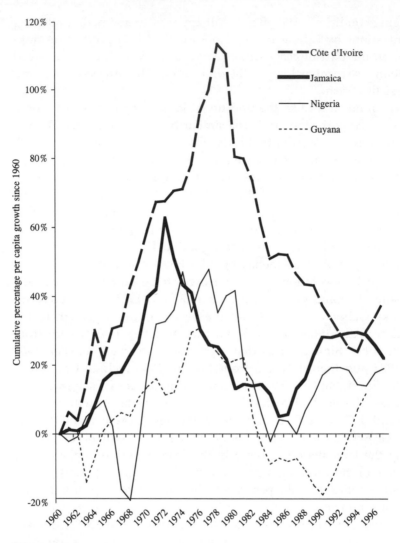

Figure 10.1
Examples of variable per capita income over time

weak correlation of growth rates across periods will produce some countries that stay high performing just by chance. Sooner or later the odds will catch up to them. Remember what happened to East Asia in 1997–1998.

Sometimes the big growth reversals are a consequence of government policy reversals, but generally they are not. Unlike growth, last decade's policies are a good predictor of this decade's policies. Last decade's inflation explains between 25 and 56 percent of this decade's inflation. Last decade's openness (trade share) explains 81 percent of this decade's trade share. Last decade's financial development (money to GDP ratio) explains between 60 and 90 percent of this decade's financial development. Policies are much more persistent than growth and so cannot be the sole determinant of growth.

The instability of growth also drives another nail into the coffin of capital fundamentalism, in either its physical or human capital manifestations. Investment in physical capital—plant and equipment—is highly persistent across decades. Last decade's investment explains 77 percent of the variation in this decade's investment. Something similar is true for educational investments. Last decade's enrollment in primary education explains 78 percent of this decade's. Last decade's enrollment in secondary education explains 85 percent of this decade's. Yet this decade's growth explains very little of the variation in next decade's growth.[11]

This instability of growth extends to long time periods too. Compare the rank a country held in per capita growth over sixty years (1870–1930) against the growth ranking in the next sixty-two years (1930–1992). We see that there is considerable shaking up of the ranks between these two long periods. To give some concrete examples, Argentina had the highest growth (out of twenty-seven countries that had data) for the period 1870 to 1930, but fell to dead last from 1930 to 1992. For an example going the other way, Italy was only fifteenth in growth in the period 1870 to 1930 but jumped all the way to second between 1930 and 1992.

Mean Reversion

If economic growth is pure luck, then obviously it would be impossible to forecast. However, there is one way in which you can pretend to forecast even if luck determines all. It's a parlor trick that you can pull on the unsuspecting. Announce to your friends that you are sure that country X is going to have a fall in growth. Announce also that country Y is going to have an increase in growth. You are almost certain to be right, even if the growth of all countries is completely random.

How can you do this? It's foolproof, as long as you are allowed to pick which X and Y you will make these statements about. Pick X—the country where growth is going to fall—as the country with the highest growth rate in the world this year. Pick Y—the country where growth is going to rise—as the country with the lowest growth rate in the world this year. If growth is random, then the extremely unlucky outcome in Y is unlikely to be repeated. Hence Y's growth will increase. And the extremely lucky outcome in X is unlikely to be repeated, so X's growth will decrease. This is mean reversion.

I used this trick to predict in a 1995 publication that "the strato-spheric trajectory of the [Gang of] Four should be heading back toward earth soon." I didn't know anything about their banking systems, international capital flows, exchange rates, or anything else that brought on the East Asian crisis of 1997–1998. I just knew that the top-ranked growers would revert toward the mean sooner or later.

Roulette

To make mean reversion concrete, think about a roulette wheel. Suppose that a thousand of us are playing roulette. Each of us plays twenty times on the roulette wheel, betting on red or black. It is safe to assume that each time the wheel is spun, each of us has a 50 percent chance of winning.

What would be the range of winning percentages among our group of one thousand after twenty tries? Because we have so many trying our luck, the range is surprisingly wide. On average, out of a thousand, the luckiest among us will have won seventeen times out of twenty (85 percent winning percentage) and the unluckiest one of us will have won only three times out of twenty (15 percent winning percentage). The luckiest will be bragging about his uncanny sixth sense for what color is coming up on the roulette wheel, while the unluckiest will feel like a real klutz.

If the luckiest and unluckiest play more roulette, we know that each still has a 50 percent chance to win every play. Fifty percent is better than the luckiest was doing and worse than the unluckiest was doing. It's a very safe prediction that the unluckiest will start doing better and the luckiest will start doing worse.

This trick still works if there is some ability involved and only a partial role for luck. It's still likely that the best outcome involves a combination of superior ability and good luck, and the worst outcome involves a combination of inferior ability and bad luck. Ability remains, but extremely good or bad luck is unlikely to recur, so the best will have some falling off, and the worst will have some improvement. Making such a prediction will still probably be right.

The principle of mean reversion is universal. All you need to get strong mean reversion is at least some role for luck and selection of the best outcome of the previous period. Mean reversion explains why the Rookie of the Year in the American League has a worse second year (the so-called sophomore jinx—the Rookie of the Year moves back toward the average after an exceptional first year), why the NFL Super Bowl winner seems to fall apart the next year (the team doesn't really fall apart; it just falls back toward the mean), why second novels are disappointing (we pay attention to the second novel only when the first was exceptional), why movie sequels are usually not as good as the original (a sequel is made only after an extremely successful movie, and extreme success is unlikely to recur), and why a stock market prognosticator falls out of favor right after a streak of accurate predictions (she had a lucky streak that got our attention and then reverted to average). In economic growth, mean reversion explains why the success stories of one decade disappoint the pundits the next decade. It also explains why the disasters of one decade do better the next decade.

Mean reversion is often mistaken for the different prediction that success breeds failure. Moralistic sportswriters often write about how the Rookie of the Year let success go to his head, how he spent too much time on the banquet circuit rather than training, and how he got distracted by all his nights on the town with supermodels. The moralistic sportswriters could be right, but the Rookie of the Year will have a worse second year even if he spent the whole off-season in church camp.

One group that does not seem to understand mean reversion is us development experts. In extrapolating continued extreme success for the extremely successful, we are doing the equivalent of forecasting the luckiest person's continued roulette success because he had been successful the first twenty times.

Prediction

Jude Wanniski, in his 1978 best-selling book *The Way the World Works*, celebrated the achievements, as of 1978, of the Ivory Coast. To Wanniski, the Ivory Coast was the star of Africa.[12] A supply-side enthusiast, Wanniski thought the Ivory Coast's economic success was due to low statutory tax rates. (There were already two minor problems with Wanniski's story. The first was that there's no evidence that economic growth has any association with statutory tax rates, as we will see in the next chapter. The second problem was that these taxes applied to the formal private sector, which employed only 1.4 percent of the population.)[13]

Wanniski's star country (now officially known to English speakers as Côte D'Ivoire; the French still call it Ivory Coast) has had among the world's biggest economic collapse since 1978 (look at figure 10.1 again); there were only minor increases in tax rates.[14] Ivorians are now nearly 50 percent poorer than they were in 1978 when Wanniski celebrated the miracle wrought by low Ivorian taxes.[15]

Because of the large random element, forecasting growth is very hard. Korea had poor economic performance in the 1950s. The first World Bank mission to Korea in the early 1960s had this to say about the Korean government's plan for 7.1 percent GDP growth: "There can be no doubt that this development program far exceeds the potential of the Korean economy." As it turned out, Korean growth was 7.3 percent for the forecast period and would get even higher for the next three decades.

Hollis Chenery and Alan Strout wrote in the early 1960s that growth in India would exceed growth in Korea between 1962 and 1976. As it turned out, Korea grew three times faster than India over this period. Another development economist in the early 1960s ranked East Asia below sub-Saharan Africa on "economic culture" and "population pressure." The economist Gunnar Myrdal fretted about future superstar Singapore's "potentially explosive problems," including rapid population growth, which would lead to "a mounting unemployment burden."[16] All that turned out to be explosively mounting in Singapore was GDP.

In Search of Excellence

This failure to appreciate mean reversion in economics is true at scales other than countries. Tom Peters in his mega-best-seller with Robert J. Waterman, *In Search of Excellence*, identified thirty-six highly successful American companies in 1982. They included such stalwarts of American industry as IBM, Digital, General Motors, Wang, and Delta Airlines. One of their criteria for success was above average return on equity, 1961 through 1980.[17]

For Peters and Waterman, the success of this group stemmed from "a unique set of cultural attributes," "values," customer service, and getting the "itty-bitty, teeny-tiny things" right.[18] By sticking to such values, they wrote in 1982, companies like Delta Airlines had remained "remarkably successful." For example, one informant of Peters and Waterman related that his wife had missed out on a super-saver ticket on Delta Airlines because of a technicality. She complained, and Delta's president met her personally at the gate with a new ticket.[19] (Wait while I choke back my disbelief at this last story, as a much-abused airline passenger.) A New York investment firm, Sanford Bernstein & Co., later examined how Delta and the other thirty-five highly successful companies had done since the book. It found that many of the thirty-six *In Search of Excellence* companies, including Delta, had since been in search of the bottom of the stock market. From 1980 through 1994, slightly less than two-thirds of the thirty-six companies yielded below-average returns in the stock market.[20] Mean reversion plagues even mega-best-selling business extrapolators.

In general, it's hard to predict success when there are intangible and unobservable factors behind success.

Which composer in eighteenth-century Vienna was most likely to have his or her work endure for later centuries? At the time, you probably would not have picked the one who was only the eighth most popular composer in Vienna: Mozart.

Who is Sam Bowie? Never heard of him? Neither had I. Yet he was picked ahead of Michael Jordan in the 1984 National Basketball Association draft.[21]

What politician complained about a successful rival, "With me, the race of ambition has been a flat failure; with him it has been one of splendid success. His name fills the nation; and is not unknown, even, in foreign lands"? This is Abraham Lincoln speaking about

Stephen Douglas in 1856.[22] It's very, very hard to predict success in sports, music, and politics—as well as in economics.

Warning: Some Prices Are Beyond Your Control

Another piece of evidence that luck is an important determinant of growth is the high sensitivity of growth to changes in the terms of trade: the ratio of export to import prices. These prices are largely determined in the international marketplace. There is very little that a poor country can do to influence what it gets for its exports or pays for its imports.

In the 1980s, there was a strong association between terms-of-trade shocks and growth. The one-fourth of countries that had the worst shocks—for example, oil exporters that saw the price of oil collapse —also had the worst growth. Their bad shock cost them an average of about 1 percent of GDP per year. Per capita growth for them was actually negative, at −1 percent a year. Countries that had the most favorable shocks to their prices—increases in export prices or decreases in import prices that yielded them about 1 percent of GDP per year—also had the best growth of about 1 percent a year. The effect is about one for one: a terms-of-trade loss of 1 percentage point of GDP will cause a loss of 1 percentage point of growth.[23]

To make things concrete, think about Mauritius and Venezuela. International financial institutions like to point to Mauritius as a great success story, attributing that success to good economic policies. And indeed policy may have had something to do with Mauritian success. But Mauritius also had the most favorable terms-of-trade shock in the entire sample in the 1980s.

Conversely, international financial institutions point to Venezuela as an example of how not to run an economy. Growth has been sharply negative in Venezuela since 1980. This happens to coincide with the collapse of oil prices in the 1980s. Bad policy probably con-tributed to the Venezuelan debacle, but so did bad luck. (And now, higher oil prices are reviving up the Venezuelan economy again, even with a growth-killing populist government in power.)

Terms of Trade Going Up or Down?

There has been a longstanding debate in economics about the trend in the terms of trade of poor countries. In the 1950s, economists postulated that the terms of trade would tend to decline over time. They thought that as income rose, the world economy would have less use for basic commodities like oil and copper. This sounded like a good argument for poor countries to diversify their production away from basic commodities.

In the 1970s, one group of experts postulated just the opposite. The "limits to growth" crowd warned that the world was running out of basic commodities like oil and copper. Although they seldom emphasized the potential benefits of these shortages to the developing countries that produced them—that their terms of trade would improve as prices of goods in short supply shot up—they warned the industrial countries about the doomsday that awaited when these commodities ran out.

So which is it? Are terms of trade of developing countries going up or down? The best answer I've seen is "both." Experts on the left often warn simultaneously about the declining terms of trade of poor countries *and* the coming shortages of raw materials (which would improve terms of trade of poor countries). The prestigious Brundtland Commission, for example, in its report *Our Common Future* in 1987, warned the poor countries that they would face "adverse price trends." But then later they warned that oil production, much of which is concentrated in poor nations, will "gradually fall during a period of reduced supplies and higher prices."[24]

Economists not agile enough to think that something can go up and down at the same time have looked at long-run trends in commodity prices. The current wisdom from such studies is that there is no strong tendency either way. Commodity prices on average do not decline relative to manufactured goods, after adjusting for the rising quality of manufactured goods.[25]

War

Terms-of-trade collapses are but one of the shocks that can throw a developing economy askew. Another shock beyond the control of the economic policymakers is war. It is fairly obvious that war creates bad incentives for growth. No one wants to build a new plant if ravaging armies are going to destroy it.

So nothing much good is going to happen to an economy at war, and the data confirm the obvious. A country at war, with either another country or itself in a civil war, has a per capita average growth rate of −1 percent per year. Peacetime economies have an average growth rate of 1.8 percent per year. For example, the Bangladeshi economy contracted by 22 percent during and after its war of independence in 1971. Ethiopia's per capita income fell by 27 percent during its protracted civil war from 1974 to 1992. Sudanese saw their incomes drop 26 percent during the first civil war between the Islamic north and the Christian south (1963–1973); then income fell 23 percent again when war re-emerged beginning in 1984 and continues to the present. Note that all of these wartime disasters happened to countries that were already among the poorest in the world.

These calculations probably understate the effect of war on the economy, because the worst wars shut down not only the economy but also the statistical office that publishes growth rate numbers. Sudan stopped reporting GDP numbers in 1991; the civil war is still going on today. Afghanistan, Liberia, and Somalia have all stopped reporting GDP during ongoing civil wars; anecdotal evidence suggests that these are not booming economies. So we lack data on the worst wartime disasters.

Chronic civil war explains some countries' underdevelopment. Colombia has a very professional and high-quality civil service and exemplary economic management. Yet Colombia's history since independence has been plagued by civil wars or violent insurgencies: 1839–1842, 1851, 1859–1862, 1876, 1885, 1895, 1899–1902, 1930, 1946–1957, and 1979 to the present. Gabriel García Marquez had his fictional character Colonel Aureliano Buendía continually start new civil wars in his tragicomedy *One Hundred Years of Solitude*.

Comedy is not what one thinks of in Colombia today (Woody Allen says comedy is tragedy plus time). Well-armed guerrillas now control an area the size of Switzerland, and their links to drug lords worsen the violence. Right-wing vigilantes fight against the guerrillas. In 1999 the various armed groups killed 32,000 people.

During my various visits to Colombia, I have had a bomb go off next to my hotel, have witnessed an attempted assassination, and once absent-mindedly walked into the middle of an armed standoff between two rival government military units. During another of my visits, a government minister kindly offered to give my colleagues and me a ride back to our hotel. We were a little skittish because we knew that guerrillas had unsuccessfully tried to denotate a bomb beneath his car the month before. But politeness outweighed fear of death, and we accepted his offer, running red lights all the way back to our hotel. While no estimate of the effect of such recurrent violence on Colombia's economy is possible, it probably has quite a lot to do with Colombia's poverty today.

Industrial Country Growth

Growth in developing countries is also very sensitive to growth in industrial countries in North America, Western Europe, and the Pacific Rim. When the rich countries sneeze, the poor countries get the flu. The statistical evidence is that one percentage point slower growth in the industrial countries is associated with one to two percentage points slower developing-country growth. The growth slowdown in the industrial countries from the 1960–1979 period to the 1980–1998 period could explain some of the slowdown in developing-country per capita growth from 2.5 percentage points over 1960 to 1979 to zero over 1980 to 1998.[26]

Why would developing-country growth be so sensitive to industrial country growth? It may be that industrial countries set the technological frontier and developing countries follow. A slowdown in growth of new technologies slows growth in both leader and follower countries.

In any event, the industrial country slowdown is yet another bit of bad luck that has afflicted developing countries over the past two decades. The irony is that they had finally begun to improve their policies, on average, in the 1990s, only to be rewarded with zero growth. This may reflect the increasing returns that penalizes poor countries, or the bad world economic conditions, or both. If industrial economies accelerate their growth thanks to the e-revolution, as some predict, then developing countries could reverse their luck in the next decade.

Don't Try This at Home

Let's fantasize for a moment about what the world would look like if growth depended only on luck. Let us consider two countries that for the moment I will call Venambia and Singawan. Venambia increased its per capita income by 50 percent between 1960 and 2000, while Singawan's per capita income tripled (figure 10.2). What were the factors behind Singawan's economic miracle and Venambia's economic misery? Rivers of ink from us experts could flow. The

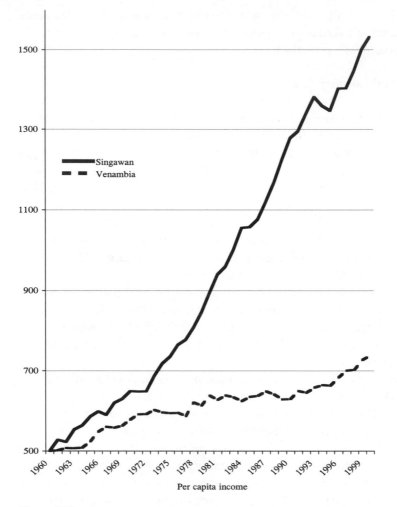

Figure 10.2
A tale of two countries

differing factors could have been different institutions, different cultures, or different government policies. They could have been adept government intervention, adept laissez-faire, or intervention and laissez-faire at the same time.

They could have been, but they weren't. What is the real identity of Singawan and Venambia? I created Singawan and Venambia from a random number generator. I allowed growth of per capita income to fluctuate randomly between −2 and 6 percent each year for 125 simulated countries. Then I took the country with the fastest growth (Singawan) and the country with the slowest growth (Venambia). The country with the fastest growth naturally boomed, while the country with the slowest growth was by construction mediocre. But the difference between the fastest-growing country and the slowest-growing country in this example was completely random.

Mathematicians point out that random numbers often do counterintuitive things. For example, if you flip a coin repeatedly and count the number of heads and tails, it's likely that one of the two will be in front for long periods of time. In addition, if you flip a coin for long enough, it is likely there will be long runs of heads (and of tails). For example, in the Singawan and Venambia example, Singawan had a streak of twenty-two years without a recession. Gamblers are very aware of these "lucky streaks." So are basketball players, who have a "hot hand" when they hit a number of baskets in a row. But we know that it's all just completely random. In reality, studies have shown that basketball players are no more likely to hit a basket after a string of made baskets than after a string of missed baskets.

Think of how all of us economists would feel to discover that differences between the swift and the dead were just random. This little exercise should make all of us pretentious analysts very, very humble about our powers of analysis.

We forget how selective we are being when we talk about growth miracles and growth disasters. There is a natural tendency to focus on the best growth miracles and the worst growth disasters when trying to illustrate what causes growth differences. But we cannot hope to explain the difference between the best and the worst completely if there is any random element at all. The laws of probability ensure that the best will have had at least some good luck and the worst will have had at least some bad luck. A strong dose of randomness could explain why it is so very difficult to predict who is going to succeed and who is going to fail, as we saw earlier.

Conclusions

The Romans had a goddess of luck, Fortuna, who was the first-born daughter of Jupiter. She was usually pictured with a cornucopia, as the bringer of prosperity, and with a rudder, as the controller of destinies. Priestesses in the temple of Fortuna gave worshippers predictions based on rolling of dice and drawing of lots. A wheel sometimes figured in her portrayal, anticipating Vanna White and the Wheel of Fortune by two millennia.

The medieval version of Vanna White was found at the Benedictine abbey in Fécamp, Normandy, around 1100:

I saw a wheel, which by some means unknown to me descended and ascended, rotating continually.... The wheel of Fortune—which is an enemy of all mankind throughout the ages—hurls us many times into the depths; again, false deceiver that she is, she promises to raise us to the extreme heights, but then she turns in a circle, that we should beware the wild whirling of fortune, nor trust the instability of that happy-seeming and evilly seductive wheel.[27]

For the poor, the cycle of good and bad luck takes on a tragic cast, because they have so little to fall back on. In Ghana, the *sondure*, or hungry period, recurs annually in some regions and may last five or sixth months, depending on the erratic rainfall. Health is often bad during the *sondure*. In Zambia, the demand for labor is at the highest just before the harvest, when food shortages and malaria reduce the energy of workers. In Nigeria, the poor farmers borrow at high interest rates during the "hungry season" when food prices are high, then sell the crop at low prices after the harvest to repay the loan.[28]

Whether we look at the comic attempts of economists to explain randomness or the tragic vulnerability of the poor, luck is a constant influence on the quest for growth. I don't really believe growth is completely random. I hope that evidence elsewhere in this book will convince you that government policies and other factors have a strong association with growth and prosperity in the long run. Luck causes fluctuations around a long-run trend determined by more fundamental factors. Keeping in mind the role of luck in economic development will keep us from paying too much attention to short-run fluctuations around this long-run outcome. It also allows us to be more charitable toward countries where growth has taken a dive. Bad government policies are usually partly to blame, but so is bad luck. To see how bad governments affect growth, let's turn to the next chapter.

Intermezzo: Favela Life

Carolina, age twenty-seven, lives in the favela *of Piu Miudo, one of the worst slums outside Salvador, Brazil. Carolina had grown up in the village of Guapira in northeast Brazil. Her family of eight lived in a mud-and-wattle palm-thatched hut. Their daily diet was black beans, rice, and cassava flour. Drinking water was sometimes contaminated with worms that caused schistosomiasis, and cockroaches in the mud wall of the hut carried fatal Chagas' disease. The nearest doctor was ten miles away over a dirt road. Not surprisingly, villagers embraced many superstitions even as they prayed to St. George for protection. They believed that God could turn sinners into werewolves, that the fertility of their fields was governed by the moon, and that a menstruating woman who stepped in a field would curse the crop.*

As soon as she was old enough, Carolina moved to the big city, Salvador, and became a housemaid for a wealthy family. But Carolina's quest for a better life went wrong. Her wealthy family asked her to leave after she became pregnant. Then the father of her child, a dockworker named Afrodizio, abandoned her. She moved into the hut of a friend in Pau Miudo, supporting herself and her child by taking in laundry. She washes the laundry in a canal each day, earning about twenty dollars a month.[1]

11

Governments Can Kill Growth

Politics is the art of looking for trouble, finding it, misdiagnosing it, and then misapplying the wrong remedies.

Groucho Marx

Bad governments as well as bad luck can kill growth. Because becoming rich—that is, growth—is so sensitive to the incentive to lower present consumption in return for higher future income, anything that mucks up that incentive will affect growth. The prime suspect for mucking up incentives is government. Any government action that taxes future income implicitly or explicitly will lower the incentive to invest in the future. Things like high inflation, high black market premiums, negative real interest rates, high budget deficits, restrictions on free trade, and poor public services create poor incentives for growth. We have evidence that these government policies lower growth. In this chapter I will look at this evidence. In the following chapter I will look at one form of bad government— corrupt ones. Then in the next chapter I will look at the deeper reasons governments in some societies go bad.

Creating High Inflation

I first visited Israel in November 1997. When most people think of the land of Israel, they think of its rich history, its giving birth to three great religions, its tragic conflict between Jews and Palestinians. Macroeconomists, who always have a strange perspective on things, think of consumer price inflation.

Israel had one of the worst cases of high inflation in the world from 1973 to 1985. After 1985, it had one of the most successful treatments of high inflation in the world. To macroeconomists, Israel is a great laboratory for studying what happens to a country's growth rate when it gets the high inflation disease.

The story begins in late 1973, when OPEC's oil price increase hit Israel as well as many other countries. Unlike most other countries, Israel was in a war at the same time: the Yom Kippur war of October 1973.

Throughout much of history, inflation has been an expedient that governments use in wartime. When governments have to spend a lot of money in a hurry and with no extra tax revenue lying around, they resort to printing money. Both sides of both world wars printed money. The U.S. government printed money like never before during the Civil War, but not as fast as the even more revenue-starved Confederate States government. The pre-U.S. Continental Congress paid Revolutionary War soldiers with paper money. The 1790s French revolutionary government kept itself afloat with paper *assignats*. Even in ancient times, Cleopatra financed her Egyptian military adventures using the B.C. analogue to printing money: reducing the precious metal content of the coinage below face value.

Israel, following all of these good historical precedents, printed money during 1973–1974 to get through the shocks of oil price hikes and war. The government's reliance on printing money was understandable. But when the war was over, the government kept inflation going. It was going to take twelve years to unwind the inflationary chaos that began in late 1973. What happened?

High inflation is easy to start and not so easy to stop. Workers demand and often get the indexation of their wages to consumer prices. Savers demand the indexation of their deposits. All this indexation creates inertia in the inflation rate. Even if inflation falls this year, wages are going to increase at the rate of past inflation, wages drive up inflation, and so the inflation keeps going. Israel became the land of indexation during its high inflation.

What's more, governments find it difficult to give up printing money to finance budget deficits. The government of Israel ran an annual budget deficit, on average, of 17 percent of GDP between 1973 and 1984.[1] The per capita growth rate, which had been an impressive 5.7 percent per year from 1961 to 1972, fell to 1.2 percent between 1973 and 1984.

For economists, Israel has another distinction besides being a great laboratory for inflation. For many economists, it is home. Israel has a remarkably high percentage of the international economics profession's members for such a tiny country. All of these great economists were not listened to at the beginning of the high inflation, but they would be in on its ending.

One of those distinguished Israeli economists was Michael Bruno, who became the governor of the Central Bank of Israel during the fight to end inflation. He later became the chief economist of the World Bank, which is where I had the pleasure of working with him. Michael died all too young, soon after he left the World Bank, and the occasion of my first visit to Israel was a conference in his memory.

Bruno in 1985 was a member of a five-member team that secretly prepared a comprehensive stabilization package, hiding out in a room of the Israel Academy of Arts and Sciences, which, as he later put it, "no one suspected could have anything to do with practical policy matters."[2] The program was approved at the end of a twenty-hour cabinet meeting in the early morning hours of July 1, 1985, and officially launched on July 15.

Bruno and his colleagues brilliantly engineered the shutdown of the inflationary engine. They got the labor unions to agree to a freeze on wages, they froze prices and the exchange rate, and they got a steep reduction in the budget deficit from the government. (One of Bruno's chief fears during the plan's preparation was that the United States would prematurely give aid to the government, which would lessen the urgency of reducing the deficit.) The budget deficit fell from 17 percent of GDP between 1973 and 1984 to 1 percent of GDP between 1985 and 1990.[3] Bruno participated actively in making the program stick after his appointment as Central Bank governor in June 1986.[4] Inflation fell from 445 percent in 1984, to 185 percent in 1985, to 20 percent in 1986.

Bruno and his colleagues had stopped high inflation. Growth began to recover, with average per capita growth of 3.4 percent in the first three years after inflation started on its way down.

Israel was not unique in allowing such high inflation to develop. In the 1970s, 1980s, and 1990s, the disease of peacetime high inflation spread like never before in economic history. Argentina, Bolivia, Brazil, Chile, Costa Rica, the Dominican Republic, Ecuador, Ghana, Guinea-Bissau, Iceland, Jamaica, Mexico, Nigeria, Peru, Suriname, Turkey, Uruguay, Venezuela, Zaire (Congo), and Zambia all had bouts of inflation above 40 percent per year that lasted two years or more (as did many ex-Communist countries, as we saw earlier.)[5]

High inflation crazily inverted the lecture your grandfather gave you on how compound interest could multiply savings. In your grandfather's lecture, saving your pennies makes you rich if you wait long enough. In the inverse version, high inflation reduces riches to pennies if you wait too long.

Argentina sets the record for highest and longest inflation, with an annual average inflation of 127 percent per year from 1960 to 1994. Thus, Argentines had the most potential in the world for money meltdown. If an Argentine with the equivalent of $1 billion in savings had kept all of his money in Argentine currency since 1960, the real value of his financial holdings in 1994 would amount to a thirteenth of a penny. A candy bar that cost 1 Argentine peso in 1960 cost 1.3 trillion pesos in 1994. To avoid having to use trillions in prices for candy bars, Argentina had done numerous monetary reforms where it asked the public to exchange 1 zillion "old pesos" for 1 "new peso." Then prices were thereafter quoted in "new pesos."

It's not a big mystery why inflation creates bad incentives for growth. Because of the money meltdown, people try to avoid holding money during high inflation. Inflation is effectively a tax on holding money. But this avoidance of money comes at a price, because money is a very efficient mechanism for economic transactions. We can think of money as being one of the inputs into efficient production. Inflation is then like a tax on production.

Moreover, inflation diverts resources away from producing things to producing financial services. A study has found that financial systems, measured by the share of financial services in GDP, get bloated during high inflation, and so productive sectors get short shrift. This makes sense: individuals devote a lot of resources to protecting their wealth during high inflation, resources that get taken away from productive uses. People respond to the incentives to divert resources toward protecting their wealth and away from creating new wealth. Trying to have normal growth during high inflation is like trying to win an Olympic sprint hopping on one leg.

Is this the way things work out in practice? Just to remove any suspense, growth experiences during high inflation are not happy. For a sample of forty-one episodes of high inflation (above 40 percent), here is what per capita growth looks like before, during, and after a high-inflation episode:[6]

Before the episode	1.3 percent
During the episode	−1.1 percent
After the episode	2.2 percent

We see that Israel's experience was typical. Growth falls sharply during a high-inflation episode, then recovers nicely afterward. This pattern is robust to different definitions of the *before*, *during*, and *after* episodes; it is robust to exclusion of extreme observations; and it is robust to different time periods. Inflation creates bad incentives for growth; people respond to incentives, and growth suffers accordingly. One easy way for the government to kill growth is to print money to cause high inflation.

Creating a High Black Market Premium

I was lounging on Negril Beach in Jamaica, recovering from the rigors of a consulting assignment in Kingston, when a local entrepreneur made me an attractive proposition. He offered to trade me Jamaican dollars for American currency at a rate 65 percent more favorable than the official exchange rate I get at the hotel. (Since such a transaction was illegal under Jamaican law, I'm not going to tell you whether I accepted his offer.) But why would he make such an offer?

The Jamaican government did not allow its citizens to buy American dollars except in small amounts for tourist travel. Jamaicans would have liked to hold dollars as a hedge against devaluation of the Jamaican dollar, so there was more demand for U.S. dollars than could be satisfied through official channels at the official exchange rate. The official exchange rate did not price U.S. dollars high enough compared to the value that Jamaicans placed on them—hence, the offer of the local entrepreneur to pay a higher price for my U.S. dollars than the official rate the Jamaican banks were offering.

The same phenomenon is common around the world. How does the existence of a black market premium affect the incentives for growth? First, there is obviously a strong incentive to get access to U.S. dollars at the official rate and resell them at the black market rate. This creates fierce competition for licenses to buy U.S. dollars. Anytime the main profit opportunity in the economy is to get around government rules, not much good is going to happen in the real economy.

It gets worse. The black market premium acts as a tax on exporters. Exporters are forced to deliver the U.S. dollars they earn to the central bank at the official exchange rate. Their imports are effectively purchased at the black market exchange rate. There are two possibilities: either they are not given enough currency to buy imports at the official exchange rate, or they are. If they are not given enough foreign exchange at the official exchange rate, then of course they will have to buy U.S. dollars on the black market. Even if they are given enough U.S. dollars at the official rate, they know that they have the possibility of selling these dollars on the black market, so they will place a value on U.S. dollars that reflects the black market rate and use some of these precious dollars to buy their imports. They effectively buy their imports at the high black market rate and sell their exports at the low official exchange rate. With a high black market premium, that is a punitive tax on exporters—not a good incentive for growth.

The black market premium had a lot to do with the collapse of cocoa in Ghana, which I will discuss more in a later chapter. Cocoa accounted for 19 percent of Ghana's GDP in the 1950s but only 3 percent of GDP in the 1980s. Ghana had a world-record 4,264 percent black market premium in 1982 and had consistently had the premium above 40 percent for eighteen of the previous twenty years. The black market premium was a tax on cocoa because the farmers had to sell their cocoa to the government marketing board at a price reflecting the official exchange rate. They had to buy their inputs at black market prices many times higher. By 1982, cocoa farmers were receiving only 6 percent of the world price for their cocoa. The incentives to smuggle it to neighboring countries and sell it at the world price were overwhelming. People respond to incentives. Trying to fight the incentives, the Ghanaian military leader at the time, Jerry Rawlings, decreed the death penalty for "economic crimes" like smuggling.

As we saw in a previous chapter, it was not only cocoa that was suffering in Ghana in those years. In those twenty years of the high black market premium, the income of the average Ghanaian dropped by nearly 30 percent.

The Ghanaian premium reached such alpine heights through a combination of bad policies. The nominal exchange rate was kept fixed. The government financed its deficit by printing money, which led to inflation. Exporters evaded delivering their foreign exchange

Table 11.1
The years of living dangerously: Episodes of black market premium above 1,000 percent

Country	Years black market premium over 1,000	Median black market premium	Median per capita growth (%)
Ghana	1981–1982	2,991	−7.7
Indonesia	1962–1965	3,122	−0.7
Nicaragua	1984–1987	4,409	−5.6
Poland	1981	1,404	−11.4
Sierra Leone	1988	1,406	−0.4
Syria	1987	1,047	−2.9
Uganda	1978	1,046	−6.9

so official exports fell. By 1982, the official exchange rate had become so fictitious that Ghanaian prices hardly rose at all when the long-awaited devaluation came.

When we look at the data for other countries, we see similar ruinous effects of the black market premium. Countries that had the black market premium above 40 percent in some years had average per capita growth of 0.1 percent per year during those years. (Countries with a zero black market premium had average growth of 1.7 percent over the same time period.) Especially bad governments that let the black market premium go above 1,000 percent had average growth of −3.1 percent per year. Table 11.1 shows all the episodes above 1,000 percent.[7]

The association between a high black market premium and negative growth is strong. Let us assume that the black market premium causes the low growth. Then another easy way a bad government can kill incentives for growth is to keep the nominal exchange rate fixed in the face of high inflation until it reaches a really outlandish black market premium.

Creating High Budget Deficits: A Tale of Three Crises

Mexico enjoyed macroeconomic stability from 1950 to 1972, an era that earned the moniker "stabilizing development." The exchange rate of pesos for dollars stayed fixed for all of those years. Inflation was low. The country had robust per capita growth of 3.2 percent per year. But when Luis Echevarría took over the presidency in 1970, there was a feeling that all was not well. Many Mexicans questioned whether the growth had helped the lot of the poor. Echevarría responded by instituting a new program of "redistribution with growth."

We economists heartily endorsed Echevarría's response, and "redistribution with growth" became a popular slogan throughout the community of us economists working on poor countries. Unfortunately, we were venturing from an area where we still understood little—the determinants of growth—into one where we knew almost nothing—how to redistribute income toward the poor without harming growth. (Since then, the cycle swung back to growth, but now we once again are shifting toward redistribution, still lacking much knowledge about how to achieve it.)

Even more unfortunate, Echevarría's program caused him to lose control of the government's budget deficit, which was going to cost the poor far more in the long run than any short-run benefits they derived from "redistribution with growth." Echevarría's choices from 1970 to 1976 caused damage that still affects Mexico today, three decades later. The sins of one president are visited upon later presidents, unto the fourth generation. The budget deficit went from 2.2 percent of GDP in the first year of his administration to over 5 percent in 1973–1974, and then to 8 percent in 1975. Inflation at the same time accelerated to over 20 percent.

Budget deficits and high inflation rates didn't make it easy to keep a fixed exchange rate. Mexican exports suffered a profit squeeze as their peso costs kept increasing but the dollar prices they received stayed unchanged. Exports fell. Imports seemed relatively cheap compared to the rising prices of Mexican products, and so imports boomed. There was a high external deficit (more imports than exports), which meant external debt accumulation to finance the excess imports. Speculators started to keep their assets in dollars, becoming wary of an imminent major devaluation.

Finally, in 1976, the expected crisis arrived. With capital fleeing the country and foreign exchange reserves falling, Echevarría announced that he was devaluing the currency, whose exchange rate had remained unchanged for over two decades, by 82 percent.[8] Per capita growth fell to under 1 percent in 1976–1977.

The crisis would have been prolonged except for the serendipitous discovery of new oil reserves around the Bay of Campeche. Between 1978 and 1981, the economy boomed as oil riches gushed out, with per capita growth at 6 percent.

Unfortunately, the government of López Portillo, Echevarría's successor, used the oil riches to go on a spending spree. The official motivation once again was "redistribution with growth," but the oil riches seemed so boundless that all kinds of spending increased.

López Portillo somehow managed to outrace oil revenues with even faster spending. Using the oil revenues as collateral, the government's foreign debt increased sharply from $30 billion in 1979 to $48.7 billion by the end of 1981 (compared to only $3.2 billion in 1970; López Portillo and Echevarría were nothing if not big spenders).[9] There was no mystery where the new debt was coming from. López Portillo brazenly ran budget deficits of 8 percent of GDP in 1980, 11 percent in 1981, and 15 percent in 1982. By 1981–1982, speculators once again honed in on the Mexican peso as a currency soon likely to lose its shirt. Billions of dollars flowed out as Mexicans put their money into dollar assets abroad, even as their enterprises were borrowing in dollars. As Lopez Portillo said plaintively after the inevitable devaluation caused huge enterprise losses but capital gains for individuals, "poor enterprises, rich individuals."

After vowing to defend the currency "like a dog," López Portillo let the currency float on August 9, 1982. The currency immediately lost 30 percent of its value. (Disillusioned but witty Mexicans dubbed the opulent hilltop home of the president *colina del perro*—hill of the dog.) A few days after the devaluation, finance minister Jesus Silva Herzog announced that Mexico could not service its debts. It was a turning point not only for Mexico, but for many other poor countries. Mexican per capita growth during the subsequent "lost decade," 1982 to 1994, was −1 percent per year.

The government finally brought inflation under control after 1988 and refixed the exchange rate. It also instituted economic reforms that caused a sort of boomtown atmosphere in Mexico in the 1990s. Nobody seemed to notice that while the official budget deficit was well under control, lax banking regulations were leading to bank losses that the government would have to cover (much like what would happen in East Asia's growth crash three years later). For the third time in two decades, credulous international investors got burned in Mexico in December 1994 as the peso went down in flames. For the third time in two decades, the Mexican people suffered through a crisis caused by fiscal mismanagement. Growth in 1995 fell to −8 percent per capita.

Mexico was not alone in having fiscal mismanagement kill growth. Many other high-debt countries had also gotten into trouble because of public sector red ink and overborrowing. There is a strong relationship between budget deficits and growth in the data. The worst fifth of countries with extremely high deficits have per capita growth of −2 percent per year, while budget surpluses are associated with 3 percent per capita growth (figure 11.1).

High budget deficits create bad incentives for growth because they create the anticipation of future tax hikes to reduce the deficit and service the public debt. They raise the possibility of inflation that will tax money holdings. They lead to general macroeconomic instability, which makes it hard to tell which projects are good and which firms should get loans. People respond to incentives. For all of these reasons, high budget deficits are another easy way for a bad government to kill growth.

Killing Banks

Yet another way to kill off growth is to kill off banks that allocate credit for investment. How do you kill banks? Banks need to have people deposit money in them in order to make loans for investment—but people will deposit money in the banks only if they get a good return on their savings.

We saw earlier that high inflation causes bloated financial systems, but this was assuming that market forces determined interest rates. However, many poor countries put controls on their nominal interest rates even while inflation was soaring out of control. The result was that depositors were not protected against the erosion of the real value of their deposits.

Say that the nominal interest rate was subject to a ceiling of 10 percent. Suppose inflation was 30 percent. Then a depositor who reinvested interest earnings in a savings account would still have real savings declining at 20 percent a year. The nominal interest rate minus the inflation rate is the real return that depositors get on their savings. If this real interest rate is sharply negative, that will certainly lower the incentives to put money in the bank. People are much more likely to put their money abroad or into real estate or not save at all. A negative real interest rate policy is usually called "financial repression," because it represses financial savings in banks.

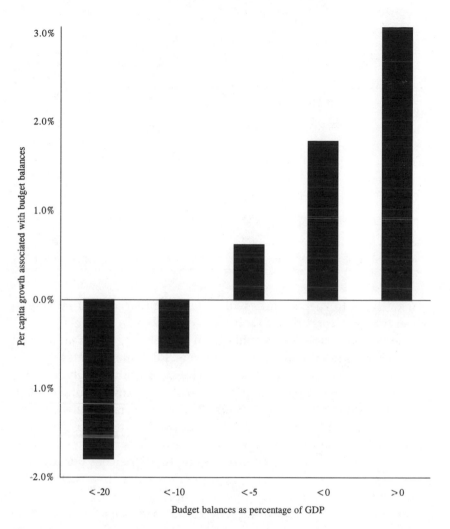

Figure 11.1
Budget deficits and per capita growth, 1960–1994

Table 11.2
Examples of severely negative real interest rates

Country	Years	Real interest rate (%)	Per capita growth (%)
Argentina	1975–1976	−69	−2.2
Bolivia	1982–1984	−75	−5.2
Chile	1972–1974	−61	−3.6
Ghana	1976–1983	−35	−2.9
Peru	1976–1984	−19	−1.4
Poland	1981–1982	−33	−8.6
Sierra Leone	1984–1987	−44	−1.9
Turkey	1979–1980	−35	−3.1
Venezuela	1987–1989	−24	−2.7
Zaire	1976–1979	−34	−6.0
Zambia	1985–1988	−24	−1.8

Banks trying to keep savings with a negative real interest rate are in effect trying to carry water with a sieve.

The evidence supports the view that sharply negative real interest rates are associated with growth disasters. Real interest rates that are −20 percent or even more negative go together with sharply negative growth: −3 percent per capita per year. Interestingly, milder financial repression is not so disastrous. Real interest rates between −20 and 0 go together with modest but positive per capita growth— a little below 2 percent per capita. Positive real interest rates are most favorable for growth, with a growth rate of 2.7 percent per capita.[10] Table 11.2 shows some examples of severely negative real interest rates and the accompanying growth performance.

Strongly negative real interest rates are bad for growth because they tax those who put their financial savings in banks. Most people do not. People respond to incentives, so the amount put in banks will decline. The ratio of the amount of savings put in banks to GDP in countries with strongly negative real interest rates (less than −20 percent) is little more than half the ratio in countries with mildly negative or positive interest rates.

How does that affect growth? If banks provide valuable services to the economy when they provide credit, then the economy is going to suffer when banks have little credit to give. In the words of economists Robert King and Ross Levine, banks:

evaluate prospective entrepreneurs, mobilize savings to finance the most promising productivity-enhancing activities, diversify the risks associated with these innovative activities, and reveal the expected profits from engaging in innovation rather than the production of existing goods using existing methods. Better financial systems improve the probability of successful innovation and thereby accelerate economic growth. Similarly, financial sector distortions reduce the rate of economic growth by reducing the rate of innovation.

King and Levine find a strong relationship between a country's level of financial development (as measured by the ratio of the financial savings in banks to GDP in 1960) and growth over the next three decades. Per capita growth shifts down by 2.3 percentage points from the most developed quarter of financial systems to the least developed quarter. Killing off banks is another easy way that a misguided government can kill growth.

Closing the Economy

Another unfortunate legacy of the first generation of research on poor countries was to close many poor economies to international trade. Countries went to great lengths to produce goods at home rather than import them. A case in prereform Ghana gives the most nonsensical lengths to which this could go. The Ghanaians were so eager to have domestic automobile production that they imported kits with a complete set of auto parts from Yugoslavia. They then assembled the cars and sold them. But the international price at which they bought the kits was greater than the international price of the fully assembled vehicle!

The argument for protectionism was twofold.[11] First, many first-generation development economists believed that the price of export commodities like oil, copper, and tin had a long-run downward trend. Hence, a country should avoid getting stuck in the position of importing manufactured goods and exporting commodities. Rather, they should throw barriers in the way of manufactured imports so as to develop their own industries. Many countries in Latin America, Africa, and Asia followed this advice and tried to do "import substitution," where domestic production would replace the proscribed imports.

The idea that commodity prices were doomed to trend down has not held up very well. The typical change in terms of trade of poor countries has been negative but nothing major—only about −0.6 percent per annum.[12] Even this is spurious, because the consensus is that the rise in manufacturing prices is overstated by underestimating quality improvements in manufactured goods.[13] Commodities, by contrast, are measured in standard units that don't change in quality over time. Anyway, countries that had a comparative advantage in commodities could always diversify their commodity price risk using financial instruments like hedging contracts.

Second, the first generation of development economists believed that allowing manufactured imports in would kill off any poor countries' industries before they had a chance to begin. The idea was that there was a learning curve to developing industry. Allowing imports in from countries that were already ahead of the curve would prevent poor countries from doing their own learning to establish industry. This was an old argument in economics, known as the "infant industry" argument.

The case for free trade is also an ancient one in economics. Free trade allows economies to specialize in what they are best at doing, exporting those things and importing the things they are not so good at producing. Interference with trade distorts prices so that inefficient producers will get subsidized. This distortion could affect growth because inefficient resource use lowers the rate of return to investing in the future.[14]

The free trade arguments are now supported by the experience of the past few decades, which has found that more open economies are richer and grow faster. Openness to trade has many dimensions, and all of these dimensions are positively associated with growth.

Jeffrey Sachs and Andrew Warner defined countries as closed if they had any of the following: nontariff barriers covering 40 percent or more of trade, average tariff rates of 40 percent or more, a black market premium of 20 percent or more, a socialist economic system, or a state monopoly on major exports. They found that closed poor economies grew at 0.7 percent per capita per year while open poor economies grew at 4.5 percent per capita per year. When a previously closed economy became open, they found that its growth increased by more than one percentage point a year.[15]

My colleague David Dollar examined economies where prices of traded goods in dollars at the prevailing exchange rate were higher than U.S. prices for the same goods. He interpreted the higher prices in these economies as reflecting restrictive trade policies, like a tariff that would drive up domestic prices relative to foreign ones. He found that economies with distorted prices in this sense grew more slowly than economies that were not so distorted.[16]

The Korean economist Jong-wha Lee finds that high tariff rates have a negative effect on growth when the tariff rate is weighted by the importance of total imports in GDP.[17] He found in separate work that imports of machines are particularly helpful to economic growth.[18] Columbia University economist Ann Harrison finds that a variety of measures of restrictions on free trade tend to lower growth.[19] UCLA economist Sebastian Edwards finds that a variety of measures of interfering with free trade (tariffs, nontariff barriers, collected trade taxes, and others) tend to lower productivity growth.[20]

Harvard economist Jeffrey Frankel and Berkeley economist David Romer find a positive effect of the share of trade (exports plus imports) in GDP on income levels. They argue that this is a causal relationship, by identifying the geographic component of trade (the tendency for neighbors to trade more with each other and the tendency for larger economies to have more internal trade).[21] The effect is large: a 1 point rise in the share of trade in GDP raises income per capita by 2 percent.

Maryland economist Francisco Rodriguez and Harvard economist Dani Rodrik express a contrarian view. They argue that many of these measures do not really capture trade interventions and that they are not robust to changes in the sample period or other control variables (they did not study all of the results mentioned here, however).[22] Still, few variables in the research on growth capture exactly a specific policy or are robust to all possible control variables. It is too easy to drive out individual associations with other control variables. What does hold up well is that the whole set of policy distortions of free trade is negatively related to growth.[23] This evidence tells us that governments that mess around too drastically with free markets and macroeconomic stability, whether in trade, foreign exchange, banking, budget deficits, or inflation, will have lower growth.

Government Disservice

I am arriving in Islamabad, the capital of Pakistan, on a World Bank mission to look at public services. Public services leave something to be desired in Pakistan. Social indicators like infant mortality and female secondary enrollment are among the worst in the world in Pakistan. There is also substantial variation within Pakistan. Female literacy ranges from 41 percent in urban Sindh to 3 percent in rural North-West Frontier province and Baluchistan. Pakistani economist Ishrat Husain notes that fewer than a third of Pakistan's villages have access to wholesale trading centers, and where there are roads, poor road quality raises transport costs by 30 to 40 percent.[24] Just over the short period 1990 to 1998, vehicles per kilometer of road doubled. Public irrigation services are also in crisis. Nearly 38 percent of publicly irrigated land suffers from salinity and flooding; the crop loss due to salinity alone may approach 25 percent.[25]

A study of public services in Uganda found that firms had power outages amounting to eighty-nine days a year. Firms invested in backup power generators, which raised their investment cost by 16 percent. It costs about three times more to buy and run a generator than to get publicly supplied electricity. Phone services were no better: it took 4.6 attempts on average to complete a long-distance within Uganda and 2.8 attempts to complete an international call. Similar problems occurred with water supply (thirty-three days of outages a year), waste disposal (77 percent of firms disposed of their own wastes), and postal services (only 31 percent of business correspondence was delivered by the post office).[26]

In Nigeria, the government has failed almost completely to provide basic services, despite $280 billion in government oil revenues since the discovery of reserves in the late 1950s. The government has preferred to spend its money instead on things like the $8 billion steel complex that has yet to produce a bar of steel and a new national capital built from scratch, not to mention the breathtaking amount of money stolen by the rulers. The southern delta region where the oil is produced suffers from oil spills and lacks roads, schools, and health care. The government high school in the delta fell into ruins a few years back due to a tropical squall; the government has never bothered to replace it. (The plight of the delta got some international attention thanks to the campaign of the Ogoni people for better treatment led by Ken Saro-Wiwa, who was executed for his pains by the late dictator Sani Abacha.) The slums of Lagos are no better off: shacks on stilts set on black lagoons that also serve as odiferous sewers, admid scraps of land piled high with mounds of garbage. Doctors and nurses have long since abandoned the health clinics in the slums due to lack of funds and medicines. The men of the Lagos lagoons eke out a living from snagging rafts of logs floated down the Niger River into the lagoons. Despite Nigeria's abundant energy reserves, the National Electric Power Authority (NEPA, said by Nigerians to stand for Never Ever Power Always) frequently cuts power to the sawmills that process the logs, so that they stand idle much of the time.[27]

So far I have covered very specific quantifiable actions that governments take that kill growth. However, there are some less quantifiable ways that they also hinder growth. As the Pakistan, Uganda, and Nigeria examples showed, they may fail to provide quality public services like electric power, telephone lines, roads, health, water, sewerage, irrigation, postal services, waste disposal, and education (and interfere with the private sector's providing such services). They may be corrupt, which I save for a separate chapter all its own. They may create a maze of regulations that kill off private enterprise.

A survey of private businesses in sixty-seven countries gives some insight into the regulatory burden. In countries as diverse as Bulgaria, Belarus, Fiji, Mexico, Mozambique, and Tanzania, firms cited "the regulations for starting new businesses/new operations" as a strong obstacle to doing business.[28] To take a well-known example, the Peruvian economist Hernando de Soto registered a small clothing factory in Lima as an experiment and decided in advance not to pay bribes. During the time it took to get registered, government officials asked for bribes ten times. In two cases, he had to break his own rule and pay the bribes, or the experiment would have come to a halt. In the end, it took ten months to register the clothing factory. A similar procedure takes four hours in New York.[29]

In judging government services like electric power supply, firms surveyed in Azerbaijan, Cameroon, Chad, Congo, Ecuador, Georgia, Guinea, Guinea-Bissau, India, Kazakhstan, Kenya, Moldova, Mali, Malawi, Nigeria, Senegal, Tanzania, and Uganda report that they experience power outages at least once every two weeks. In Guinea, the average firm reported a power outage at least once a day. Firms turn to high-cost generators to cope with the unreliable power supply. According to a survey, 92 percent of Nigerian firms had generators.[30]

More than a third of developing countries have a waiting time for a telephone line of six years or more.[31] Guinea again stands out because people literally die waiting: the waiting time for a phone line is ninety-five years.

Roads are a problem in many countries. Firms surveyed in Albania, Azerbaijan, Bulgaria, Cameroon, Chad, Congo, Costa Rica,

Guinea-Bissau, India, Jamaica, Kazakhstan, Kenya, Kyrgyz Republic, Moldova, Malawi, Nigeria, Togo, Ukraine, and the West Bank rated road quality as 5 or worse on a scale of 1 (very good) to 6 (very poor). In Costa Rica, cuts in road operations and maintenance during the fiscal austerity program of the 1980s left 70 percent of the roads in poor condition.

Another area where governments often fail is elementary public health services. The same firm survey found that firms rated quality of public health services as 5 or worse on a scale of 1 to 6 in eighteen of sixty-seven developing countries. Poor Guinea again makes the news by spending only 3 percent of its health budget on drugs for its health clinics, as compared to 34 percent for health workers wages. This comes out to spending on drugs per capita of eleven cents. As a result virtually all clinics lack drugs.[32] Medical workers without medicines are not helpful to promoting the basic health services crucial to development.

In contrast, good governments that spend their money on essential public services realize very high rates of return. One study estimated that each additional 1 percentage point of GDP in transport and communications investment increased growth by 0.6 percentage point.[33] Other studies found that the number of telephones per worker had a strong, positive impact on growth.[34] The rate of return to infrastructure projects such as irrigation and drainage, telecommunications, airports, highways, seaports, railways, electric power, water supply, sanitation, and sewerage averages 16 to 18 percent per year.[35] The returns to maintenance spending on existing infrastructure (such as road maintenance) are even higher, perhaps as much as 70 percent.[36] Governments can kill growth by doing too much regulation and too little public service provision.

The Missing Policy

There is one government policy that has been conspicuously missing from my short list of ways to kill growth: tax rates on income. I said at the beginning that a high tax rate was the most obvious disincentive to invest in the future, since it directly lowers after-tax return. Many of the policies we have just reviewed imply a tax that lowers the return to investing in the future.

Surprisingly, there is no evidence that higher *explicit* tax rates lower growth. High-tax-rate countries like Sweden seem to do fine, while low-tax-rate countries like Peru run aground. The United States kept growing at about the same rate after the income tax was introduced in 1913 and after the tax rate was increased sharply in the 1940s. U.S. income tax revenues increased from under 2 percent of GDP in 1930 to nearly 20 percent of GDP by 1989, yet growth remained unchanged.[37] There is no statistical association between the statutory tax rate and economic growth, either across time in the United States or across countries in the world.

This example shows the value of subjecting every theoretical prediction to empirical testing. We can only guess why the theoretically compelling "taxes lower growth" story does not work out. It may be that the statutory tax rate does not really capture the true tax rate on income. The latter is affected by the opportunities for legal evasion (such as deductions, tax credits, or different tax rates on different kinds of income) or illegal evasion.

In the developing countries, actual tax collected is a small fraction of that which should be collected at the official tax rate. To take the Peru and Sweden comparison again, Peru collects only 35 percent of what it should take in given the tax rate and the size of the tax base; Sweden collects nearly all. The collection rate varies considerably from one country to another, and so the value-added tax rate or revenue collected is a poor measure of the disincentives that producers face.

Chicken and Egg to Go

So far I have identified several government actions that are associated with low economic growth: high inflation, high black market premiums, high budget deficits, and strongly negative real interest rates. However, I have been careless with my language so far. By saying "governments kill growth," I am saying that bad government actions *cause* bad growth. But I have only established that government actions are associated with growth, not that government actions cause growth.

There are many stories about going astray mistaking correlation for causality. The most common story involves nineteenth-century Russian peasants. Supposedly the peasants noticed that villages with a lot of smallpox also had more doctors' visits than villages without smallpox. They drew the natural conclusion and started shooting the doctors.

Another story along the same lines comes from the great American historian Francis Parkman. This one is a little more subtle. French Catholic missionaries in Canada mounted a major effort to convert the Huron Indians in the seventeenth century. They were not terribly successful, perhaps because the Hurons correctly suspected that the Great Spirit of the priests wanted their land as well as their souls. The indefatigable priests nevertheless persisted. They figured they could get at least deathbed conversions, so as soon as they heard a Huron was mortally ill, they rushed to his bedside and administered the conversion rite of baptism shortly before the sick Huron died. This association between baptism and the subsequent demise of the baptized did not escape notice. The Hurons had every reason to suspect that the holy water the priest sprinkled on the baptized contained some deadly poison. (Whether this is related to the martyrdom of some Jesuits at the hand of the Hurons, Parkman doesn't say.)

How do we avoid making similar mistakes of confusing causation with correlation? Could it be that negative growth causes governments to take desperate measures? Say the government resorts to high inflation as a means of financing high budget deficits during bad economic times. We would have an association among low economic growth, high deficits, and high inflation. Then the government is not killing growth; it is low growth that is killing the government. Causality could go both ways, so what do we say comes first, the chicken or the egg?

Economists have resorted to several strategies to tease out causality of the growth-policy relationship. One is to see if the initial value of the policy variable is correlated with subsequent growth. For example, King and Levine established that a well-developed financial system in 1960 is associated with good economic growth over the subsequent thirty years. The thinking goes that the past can cause the future, but the future cannot cause the past.

This is not foolproof, because sometimes you can anticipate the future (as the priest-Huron example showed). However, we saw in the previous chapter that it is very difficult to anticipate growth. Therefore, using initial values of policy variables does help the presumption that government actions cause changes in growth.

Another strategy to establish causality is to identify the part of the policy variable that is correlated with some outside events and then see if that part is correlated with growth. For example, Ross Levine has found that adopting a French rather than English legal system adversely affects banking system development. Having a French legal system presumably has nothing to do with economic growth except insofar as it affects the financial system. So we can decompose the measure of banking system development into a first part that was caused by the French legal tradition and into a second part that could be caused by other factors, including low growth. If the first part is still correlated with growth, then we can have increased confidence that banking system development causes growth. Economists have followed similar strategies to establish at least tentative causality from the black market premium and inflation to growth.[38]

Growth Across Continents

Policy effects on growth are not just theoretical possibilities. Ross Levine and I examined the income difference between East Asia and Africa as explained by policies and other factors. For each policy, we calculated the difference in that policy between Africa and East Asia and then multiply it by that policy's effect on growth. I apply the growth difference to initial income to get the income differences. Africa's higher government budget deficits, higher financial repression, and higher black market premium explain about half of the growth difference between East Asia and Africa over three decades. If policies truly do cause growth, then Africa would have been $2,000 richer per person if African economic policies had been at East Asian levels (figure 11.2).[39]

On the brighter side, Latin American governments changed incentives for growth in the early 1990s by correcting all of the above, and they gained an additional 2.2 percentage points of growth in response.[40] They lowered inflation, lowered the black market premium, moved toward free trade, and lifted repression of banks. They closed the growth gap with East Asia in the early 1990s by reforming more than the East Asians (who at that time did not need to reform as much as the Latin Americans did).

Conclusion

So here we finally have something constructive coming out of our motto: people respond to incentives. Knowing this, governments can avoid killing growth by avoiding any of the following actions that

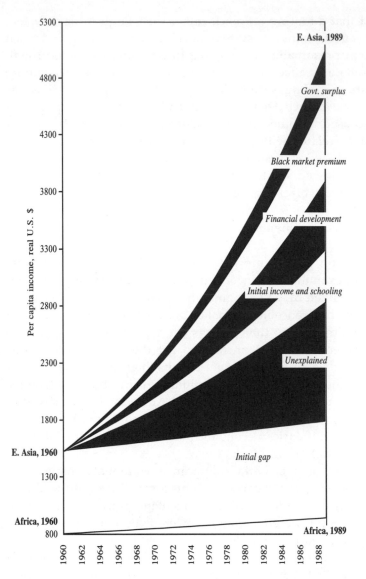

Figure 11.2
Decomposing the growth gap between East Asia and Africa. *Source:* Easterly and
Levine 1997

create poor incentives for growth: high inflation, high black market premiums, high budget deficits, strongly negative real interest rates, restrictions on free trade, excessive red tape, and inadequate public services. The tragedy is that governments so often cause lost growth. We will look at how governments come to follow such irrational policies in the succeeding chapters.

Before anointing macroeconomic policy reforms as the elixir of growth, however, note that we still have the possibility of poverty traps—as discussed in earlier chapters. Indeed, all poor countries' growth in the '90s was below what their macroeconomic policy reforms would have predicted. And institutional reform is also very important. We look at one type of institutional failure—corruption—in the next chapter.

Intermezzo: Florence and Veronica

Florence and Veronica Phiri once lived with their parents in a small but comfortable house in Lusaka, Zambia. Their father was an electrician. But both their parents died when the girls were eight and six. Their father's family took all of the Phiris's possessions, including the house, and sent the girls to live in a rural village with an aunt. The children worked hard there fetching water and collecting wood. Often they were beaten for not working hard enough.

After two years, their mother's relatives brought Florence and Veronica back to Lusaka to live with their maternal grandmother in a dilapidated house. Their grandmother earns a precarious living by selling vegetables at a market stand. When she has a bad day, the family goes without food. Four other orphans also live with the grandmother, in a country full of orphans because of deaths from AIDS. Florence and Veronica play in streets full of dust with their four cousins.

A community group donated money for Florence to pay school fees, buy a school uniform, and buy shoes. There wasn't enough money to do the same for Veronica.[1]

There is no distinctly American criminal class, except Congress.

Mark Twain

The urge to steal everything not bolted to the floor is the most obvious growth-killing incentive that government officials face. Requiring private businesspeople to pay bribes is a direct tax on production, and so we would expect it to lower growth. Corruption is one of the problems most likely to be mentioned by casual visitors to poor countries or by investors in those countries. In a poll commissioned by the agency Roper Starch International in nineteen developing countries, corruption was the fourth out of fifteen top national concerns of citizens, after crime, inflation, and recession.[1]

Despite the obvious importance of corruption in economic development, it has not attracted much attention from economists until recently. The prestigious four-volume *Handbook of Development Economics*, published from 1988 to 1995, does not mention corruption anywhere in 3,047 pages of text. A recent leading textbook on development economics does not mention corruption (or politics for that matter) anywhere.[2]

Moreover, the international financial institutions like the World Bank and International Monetary Fund paid virtually no attention to corruption for decades. Only recently has corruption become a hot issue for these institutions. Even then we are often reluctant to utter the word *corruption; problems with governance* is the bureaucratic jargon we use instead.

Once we acknowledge the importance of corruption to growth, there are unresolved questions. Why do some governments face stronger incentives to steal than other governments? Why is corruption more damaging in some countries than in others? In this chapter, I discuss the scale of corruption, its effect on growth, its determinants, and some possible solutions.

Life on the Run

When I lived in Mexico City for a year, I played a constant cat and mouse game with the Mexican police. I was the mouse, and the very corrupt Mexican police were the cats. Driving my car with its American license plate in Mexico City was like having a sign, "I'm an American tourist. Please extort bribes from me."

Before I caught on to how corrupt the police were, *I actually stopped and asked a policeman for directions*. When I told my Mexican friends that I had done this, they exploded in laughter. As they surmised, the policeman whom I asked for directions immediately shouted, *"Alto"* (halt) and ran to get several fellow officers to share in the booty. I used the time-honored technique of pretending not to understand the language. I pretended that I thought *alto* meant "proceed in your car at a high rate of speed away from the corrupt policemen, who are fortunately on foot."

I wasn't so lucky in my next encounter with the police. This time a motorized policeman pulled me over. Asking him what my infraction had been, he told me I had committed the serious offense of *transporting books without a license*. The offending cargo was a box of books in my trunk. I had the nerve to carry these in my Volkswagen Rabbit. What did I think I was? A professional moving company? This serious offense required a trip to the station house (my Mexican friends told me, "Never let them get you to the station house"). I offered to pay the fine for my outrageous offense on the spot, and that resolved matters. (I'm embarrassed to tell you how much I paid for the bribe. I got caught with only large denomination notes on me.)

After that I developed several techniques for evading police sting operations. I continued to act like an idiot as far as comprehension of Spanish went whenever the policeman was on foot. The next time I encountered a motorized policeman, I simply refused to pull over and kept driving until I got to the private university I was going to. Private property was apparently safe refuge, and the policemen gave up the chase at the gates.

Things were not so amusing for poorer inhabitants of Mexico City, whom the police regularly shook down for bribes. Supposedly each precinct had a quota of bribes to collect every month, from which the higher-ups would get a cut. Everyone knew about this corruption, but attempts to deal with it proved futile. This phenomenon of venal police is not limited to Mexico; in countries ranging from Jamaica, Uganda, India, to Moldova, the poor report police brutality and corruption as one of their main worries.[3]

The All-World Corruption Tour

Corruption occurs in rich countries and poor countries, tiny countries and gigantic countries, Christian countries and Islamic countries, African countries and Asian countries, Old World countries and New World countries. Although it appears everywhere, there are some careful measures of the severity of corruption across countries that we can use. I will first give some anecdotes to illustrate the ubiquity of corruption and then present some measures to distinguish corruption across countries.

Denver brewery owner Joseph Coors was a big financial backer of Ronald Reagan. When his beer can manufacturing plant had to dispose of some hazardous waste, Reagan appointed several members of the Coors clan to the Environmental Protection Agency, which then lifted restrictions on dumping of toxic waste in Colorado. There was a public outcry against Coors for his buying the right to dump toxic waste, if not for his watery beer.[4]

The psychologist Dr. Don Soeken alleged in 1988 that he had been asked to declare as mentally unbalanced American civil servants who had uncovered corruption in the State and Defense Departments. Their superiors were trying to discredit them by claiming they were insane (the civil servants, not the superiors).[5]

In Japan, a government prosecutor uncovered a scheme where businessmen who needed a government favor would provide expensive free entertainment for the officials concerned. Showing their determination to stamp out corruption, the Japanese government reassigned the prosecutor in August 1998 to a remote coastal city.[6]

In Ecuador in February 1997, agents for President Abdala Bucaram allegedly walked off with $3 million in Ecuadorian currency from the Central Bank. They delivered the loot to his office shortly before his term of public service was to expire.[7]

The brother of Mexican president Carlos Salinas was implicated in payoffs for drug running, which may explain the $132 million in his Swiss bank account. Meanwhile, the personal secretary of President Salinas, Justo Ceja Martinez, was unable to explain how he accumulated $3 million from 1988 to 1994 on an annual salary of $32,400.[8]

In a South Indian state in the late 1970s, corruption permeated the system of official irrigation. Among the many types of corrupt payoffs, there was one euphemistically called "savings on the ground." A government contractor would do less work than called for in his contract—like removing only 1 inch of silt from the irrigation canal instead of 3 inches of silt. The contractor would split the "savings on the ground" with the government's executive engineer, who had already gotten a kickback of 2.5 percent of the contract for awarding the contract to that particular contractor. The savings on the ground and kickbacks ranged from 25 to 50 percent of the value of what was supposed to be put on the ground. The executive engineer's earnings from corruption were as much as nine times his official salary. Little wonder that these lucrative posts were bought and sold within the irrigation bureaucracy. The executive engineer in this example might pay a lump sum of five times his annual salary for a two-year posting, still leaving him an attractive net income. The rampant corruption had more than a little to do with the poor performance of the irrigation system.[9]

In Korea, four unqualified bone setters paid the equivalent of $11,000 to the Bureau of Health and Social Affairs in one province for fake licenses. There has been no word on how their patients survived amateur bone setting.[10]

On a more spectacular scale, the former mayor of Beijing and member of the Politburo, Chen Xitong, was sentenced to sixteen years in prison for corruption. He allegedly diverted as much as $2.2 billion in Beijing city funds during his time of public service, using kickbacks on construction contracts and many other devices. Chinese television showed some of the trappings of the high-living Chen: "a gold ring, a gold tortoise, a silver carriage and horses, a house in the countryside equipped with massage chairs and an extensive bedroom complex."[11]

One government agency in the Philippines was said to be so corrupt that even the janitors were receiving payoffs.[12] Marcos initially promised to clean up corruption. His lack of success can be measured in the zillions of dollars that he himself stole. To give one example, Westinghouse allegedly paid Marcos $80 million to get the contract to build a new nuclear plant. A presidential commission approved General Electric's much lower bid, but President Marcos overruled them. His secretary of industry complained that the country was getting "one reactor for the price of two."[13] (Nor has democracy been a panacea for corruption: the current democratically elected president is facing impeachment on corruption charges.)

Nigerian dictator Sani Abacha allegedly accumulated billions of dollars from kickbacks on construction contracts and from diverting oil revenues to his personal account. He also diverted $2 billion from state oil refineries, leaving them unable to produce gasoline, and then, with real chutzpah, pocketed commissions on imported gasoline. Only his sudden death in June 1998 put an end to his imaginative plunder.[14]

In Zimbabwe, the cabinet awarded the contract for the airport at Harare to Air Harbout Technologies from Cyprus. In a startling coincidence, the local agent of Air Harbout Technologies was President Mugabe's nephew. The cabinet overruled the tender board that placed this company fourth. Two other facilitators allegedly received $1 million.[15]

President Mobutu Sese Seko of Zaire, not satisfied with his personal fortune of billions of dollars, stole the entire gold-mining region of Kilo-moto. Kilo-moto covers 32,000 square miles and has reserves of 100 tons of gold. In another transaction Mobutu, who never seemed to think small, gave the West German rocket company OTRAG the rights to an area of southeast Zaire as large as West Germany itself.[16]

Rating Corruption and Its Consequences

This selection of anecdotes may suggest that government officials everywhere are no better than highwaymen on the road to growth. All countries can furnish anecdotes, but some countries are more corrupt than others.

The *International Credit Risk Guide* surveys businesspeople for their perception of corruption in countries around the world on a rating between 0 (most corrupt) and 6 (least corrupt). In 1990, the countries that distinguished themselves with a 0 for exceptional graft in the line of duty were: the Bahamas, Bangladesh, Indonesia, Liberia, Paraguay, and Zaire. (The Philippines under Marcos had earned a 0, but by 1990 the country under a reformist government had climbed all the way to 2.) The countries with a 6 are all industrial countries, although not all industrial countries have a 6 (the United States and Japan, for example, are both 5s).

The data show that corruption and growth are inversely related. (This sample includes growth in the 1980s against corruption in 1982 and growth in the 1990s against corruption in 1990.) Similarly corruption and the investment ratio to GDP are inversely related. (This sample is investment to GDP in 1982 on corruption in 1982 and investment to GDP in 1990 on corruption in 1990.) Nobody wants to invest in a corrupt economy, and nobody wants to do all the other things that make for a growing economy.[17]

Corruption not only has a direct effect on growth; it also has an indirect effect because it makes other policies that affect growth worse. For example, many of the corruption anecdotes describe diversions of funds from public revenues or blowing up public expenditures through kickbacks. It's not a surprise, then, that more corruption is associated with larger budget deficits. The average budget deficit in the quarter of the sample that is least corrupt is 3.1 percent of GDP; the average deficit in the most corrupt quarter of the sample is 6.7 percent of GDP.

Still, the relationship of corruption with growth is not a simple one. Notice that the list of most corrupt in 1990 includes both growth disasters (Zaire) and growth miracles (at least a miracle until recently, Indonesia). Could the effect of corruption be different in different countries?

The effect of corruption could even be different over time in the same country. The 1990 survey by the *Internation Credit Risk Guide* did not include much data on the postcommunist countries, since communism was not yet post- everywhere in 1990. A World Bank survey of sixty-nine countries in 1996 did include many postcommunist countries. Firms in the sixty-nine countries were asked whether "irregular payments" were a common practice in their industry. The possible answers ranged from 1 (always) to 6 (never). While the communist countries had always had some corruption (the Soviet Union got a 4 on the 0–6 scale of the *Credit Risk Guide* in 1990), it was clear from this new survey that corruption had become more pervasive in the postcommunist countries. The two most corrupt countries were Azerbaijan and Bulgaria. Postcommunist countries accounted for 10 of the top 20 most corrupt in the 1996 survey, although they accounted for less than 30 percent of the sample. The disastrous output decline occurring in the postcommunist countries, while having many other causes, is another hint that corruption is not good for growth.

Varieties of Corruption

Two different kinds of corruption could affect growth: decentralized corruption and centralized corruption. Under decentralized corruption, there are many bribe takers, and their imposition of bribes is not coordinated among them. Under centralized corruption, a government leader organizes all corruption activity in the economy and determines the shares of each official in the ill-gotten proceeds.

Decentralized corruption is like the multiple roadblocks by soldiers that one would encounter in traveling in, say, Zaire. Each soldier at a roadblock is an individual predator, without taking into account the effect of his actions on other predators. The wealth of the travelers is a common resource that all of the independent thieves try to appropriate.

We have the classic common pool problem. The bribes demanded will be higher as each soldier thief tries to get as much revenue from the hapless traveler as possible before other thieves get it. The total "theft rate" implied by decentralized bribes will be higher than under centralized corruption. Indeed, the theft rate under decentralized corruption may be so high that total corruption revenues are lower than they would be with a lower theft rate. As the tax rate climbs, individuals put more effort into avoiding bribe opportunities for the military thieves. They travel by roads with fewer roadblocks, carry less money with them, and conceal the wealth of goods they are shipping. Decentralized corruption ironically results in lower total bribe revenues than centralized corruption even though it has a higher bribe "tax rate" on private activity. Decentralized corruption creates the worst incentives for growth.

There is yet one more reason that decentralized corruption is damaging. The likelihood that someone will be punished for corrupt behavior is positively related to the strength of state enforcement and negatively related to the number of corrupt officials. With decentralized corruption, the state is weak and many officials are corrupt. Even if the state prosecutes some corrupt officials, the likelihood of being caught is low because there are so many corrupt officials from whom to choose when the state prosecutes. There are thus virtuous and vicious circles in corruption. The virtuous circle occurs when, for whatever reason, decentralized corruption is low and so anyone who does steal will likely get caught. Thus, corruption stays low. The vicious circle occurs when decentralized corruption is high, and so the likelihood of being caught is low. Thus, corruption stays high.

Under centralized corruption, one leader seeks to maximize the take from the corruption network as a whole. This leader is more solicitous of his victims' prosperity, because he knows that stealing too much will cause the victims to take evasive action that will lower bribe collections. So the centralized corruption mafioso, like Suharto in Indonesia, will set the bribe "tax rate" at all of the roadblocks at lower levels that maximize the total take of the system. Under centralized corruption, there is monitoring of the size of the rake-off at each level; anyone trying to rake off more than the center prescribes will be punished. Because of this supervision, there are no vicious circles. Centralized corruption is less damaging than decentralized corruption.[18]

More generally, a strong dictator will choose a level of corruption that does not harm growth too badly, because he knows his rake-off depends on the size of the economy. A weak state with decentralized corruption doesn't have this incentive to preserve growth. Each individual bribe taker is too small to affect the overall size of the economy, so he feels little restraint on getting the most out of his victim.

This tale gives us insight into why corruption was more damaging to growth in Zaire than in Indonesia. Zaire is a weak state with many independent official entrepreneurs. Indonesia under Suharto was a strong state that imposed bribes from the top down. Zaire had negative per capita growth, while Indonesia had exceptional per capita growth (until recently).

There was also a shift in the type of corruption in the post-communist countries. The communist countries had always had some corruption, but under the centralized party dictatorship, it was mostly top down. The postcommunist countries, by contrast, have many independent power centers and so have shifted to decentralized corruption. This helps us to understand why corruption has been much more damaging after communism than during communism.

Determinants of Corruption

It is clear that the incentives for corruption are stronger in a decentralized government than in a centralized one. In a decentralized government, such as a coalition government among interest groups, the theft rate will be higher. Moreover, any piles of money that become available through commodity windfalls or foreign aid are more likely to be stolen in a decentralized weak government than in a strong centralized government.

I will discuss in the next chapter one circumstance that leads to multiple interest groups: a high degree of ethnic diversity. Stockholm University's Jakob Svensson has indeed found that corruption is higher with more ethnic diversity, as Paolo Mauro of the IMF also did in earlier work.

Svensson also found that corruption increases with more foreign aid in an ethnically divided society though not in an ethnically homogeneous one. Foreign aid is a common resource that each ethnic interest group will try to divert to its own pockets. Svensson too found that countries that were both commodity (like cocoa or oil) producers and ethnically divided were more likely to be corrupt. Multiple ethnic interest groups will each try to steal as much as they can from the common pool of commodity revenues.[19]

I already hinted in the previous chapter that one motivation for many bad policies is to create opportunities for graft. This is most obvious for a policy like the black market premium, where any government official with a license to get dollars at the official rate can make a corrupt profit by reselling the dollars at the black market rate. It's not a big surprise, then, that corruption and the black market rate are associated.[20] Causality in this association likely goes both ways: there is incentive among the already corrupt to create a high black market premium and an incentive to be corrupt if there already is a high black market premium.

In the same vein, restrictions on trade create opportunities for corruption. If there is a high tariff on an imported good, there is an incentive to bribe customs officials to import the good at a lower tariff. And, if a license is needed to import the good and the good is in great demand, the license seeker will have to pay a bribe. One study has found that countries that restrict the freedom of international trade are indeed more corrupt.[21]

The quality of institutions in a country also affects corruption. A high-quality civil service organized on meritocratic lines will provide some checks on corruption. A government that itself obeys the laws rather than putting itself above the law will create a poor ecosystem for corruption. The *International Credit Risk Guide* measures four aspects of the quality of the institutional environment for business: rule of law, quality of bureaucracy, freedom from government repudiation of contracts, and freedom from expropriation. Each of these captures a different aspect of the institutional environment that will affect corruption. To stamp out corruption and create good incentives for government officials to promote growth, each of these institutional aspects must be strong.

The rule of law measure captures the ability of government official to enforce or ignore the law selectively so as to get payoffs. Government officials take corrupt payoffs to have the law interpreted creatively in the bribe payer's favor. The *Guide* measures both it and freedom corruption on a 0 to 6 scale. For example, Haiti in 1982 was a place where the law meant about as much as the king's dictates in *Alice in Wonderland*. Haiti had a 0 for rule of law and a 0 for freedom from corruption. Those with a 6 for rule of law are all industrial countries (except Taiwan). All of them except Portugal get either a 5 or a 6 for freedom from corruption.

A low-quality bureaucracy is one where reams of red tape slow business to a crawl. The opportunities for decentralized corruption in such circumstances are obvious. The *Credit Risk Guide* measures this on a 0 to 6 scale, but no country in 1990 got a zero. Bangladesh got a 1 on the quality of bureacracy in 1990 and a 0 on corruption. In Dhaka, you can wait for a cold front in hell to get your business permit, or you can pay a bribe. The countries with a 6 for high-quality bureaucracy are all industrial economies, except for Hong Kong, Singapore, and South Africa. The United States, for example, gets a 6 on high-quality bureaucracy, which may come as a surprise to those who have stood in interminable lines at federal agencies. Still, everything is relative. Standing in line is not as bad as having to go to fourteen different departments to complete paperwork. All countries with a 6 for bureaucratic quality had either a 5 or a 6 for freedom from corruption (except Portugal again).

Freedom from repudiation of contracts measures a different aspect of business and government relationships. A high expected rate of repudiation makes corruption more possible, as private individuals feel the need to bribe officials in order to have their contract honored. (And they will include the cost of this bribe in their contract, so the government winds up overpaying because it threatens not to pay.)

Freedom from repudiation of contracts is measured on a 1 to 10 scale. The worst countries on this measure in 1990, with a 1 or a 2, are Myanmar, Liberia, Lebanon, Iraq, Haiti, Sudan, Zambia, and

Somalia—not exactly honest economies, as it turns out, with an average freedom from corruption score of 1.67 on the 0 to 6 scale. The countries with a 10 are all industrial countries, again with the exception of newly industrializing Taiwan. All of the 10s have a 5 or 6 on freedom from corruption, with the exception of Taiwan and Italy.

Finally, freedom from expropriation strikes right at the heart of business-government relations. With a high risk of expropriation, corruption will flourish as businesspeople make protection payments to those who might expropriate them. The worst countries on this measure in 1990, with a 1 or a 2 on a 1 to 10 scale, were New Caledonia, Iraq, and Namibia. Those with a 1 or a 2 in 1982 were Iran, Libya, Syria, Iraq (again), and Lebanon. The average freedom from corruption score of these economies was 1.9.

All countries with a 10 on the freedom from expropriation measure are industrial countries, and all industrial countries have a 10 except for Australia, which has only a 9. All of these industrial countries have a freedom from corruption rating of 5 or 6, except for Spain and Italy.

In general, the data show a strong association between institutional quality and corruption. (This sample includes corruption in 1982 against institutional quality in 1982, and corruption in 1990 against institutional quality in 1990.) Countries with the worst institutions have corruption that is between 2 and 4 ratings below countries with the best institutions. Corruption is high in countries with any of the four kinds of poor institutional quality. It is low in countries with any of the four kinds of the best institutional quality.

These strong relationships need to be interpreted cautiously. They are subjective ratings, and so the businesspeople surveyed may simply perceive a worse bureaucracy in a corrupt economy than in an honest economy. There may be some third factor, like bad government policies or low per capita income, that causes countries to have both corruption and poor institutions. Still, the strong association between institutions and corruption is at least consistent with the view that institutions can influence corruption.[22]

Policies to Control Corruption

Institutional reform is difficult but not impossible. Ghana, for example, increased its quality of bureaucracy from 1982 to 1990 from 1 to 4 (on a 0 to 6 scale). It increased its rule of law from 1 to 3 (also on a

0–6 scale). The government reduced the black market premium all the way from 4,264 percent in 1982 to 10 percent in 1990. So it was probably no accident that Ghanaian freedom from corruption increased from 1 in 1982 to 4 in 1990 on a 0–6 scale.

The findings in this chapter point to a way out of corruption and its growth-killing effects. First, set up quality institutions. Eliminate red tape, establish rules that government honors contracts and does not expropriate the private sector, and create a meritocratic civil service. These institutions create checks and balances on officials instead of opportunities for payoffs.

Second, establish policies that eliminate incentives for corruption. A high black market premium or a highly negative real interest rate practically guarantees massive graft. Eliminating both is not only good for growth, as we saw in the previous chapter; it is also good for controlling corruption.

Too often we have treated government as if it were some beneficent agent that we could advise on how to benefit the public weal. The knowledge that governments are often corrupt gives pause to such an attitude. Knowing that governments are corrupt, we should be cautious about relying on them to do interventions on behalf of growth. For example, we wouldn't want to recommend industrial policies that subsidize certain sunrise industries, because governments are likely to take payments when they decide whose sunrise to subsidize. The best course would be to eliminate government's discretionary power over households and businesses as much as possible and set up hard and fast rules of the game for government operation. Too long we have ignored corruption on the quest for growth.

Intermezzo: Discrimination in Palanpur

Palanpur is a small village in Uttar Pradesh state in northern India. It is unusual in that it has been studied by development economists at several distinct periods over the past five decades: in 1957–1958, 1962–1963, 1974–1975, 1983–1984, and 1993. Peter Lanjouw and Nicholas Stern published a book about these five decades of studies of Palanpur in 1998. The following description of life there is based on the first chapter, by Jean Drèze and Naresh Sharma, which describes features that have remained relatively unchanged over the period.[1]

Palanpur had a population of 1,133 in mid-1993. Palanpur is a poor village, with 160 babies out of 1,000 births dying before their first birthday in 1993. The literacy rate is only 37 percent for men and just 9 percent for women.

There are 117 men for every 100 women, reflecting systematic discrimination in health care against girls and women. The scholars witnessed "several cases of infant girls who were allowed to wither away and die in circumstances that would undoubtedly have prompted more energetic action in the case of a male child." The high-caste Thakurs in Palanpur practice child marriage, seclusion of married women from public view (purdah), a ban on women's work outside the home, and in some extreme cases even female infanticide and sati (burning of widows on their husband's funeral pyre).

The other group in Palanpur that suffers discrimination is the low-caste Jatabs. All of them live in a group of "shabby mud houses" on the edge of the village. Jatabs own little land and most frequently work as day laborers or on their own subsistence plots. Only 12 percent of the Jatab men and none of the Jatab women are literate. The school teacher in Palanpur was a Thakur, who considered any contact with a Jatab pupil to be repulsive. The urban managers of the local credit cooperative frequently try to extort money from Jatabs. The Jatabs have great difficulty borrowing money in any case. They try to avoid the higher castes and behave with deference when they do encounter them.

13   Polarized Peoples

So strong is this propensity of mankind to fall into mutual animosities, that where no substantial occasion presents itself, the most frivolous and fanciful distinctions have been sufficient to kindle their unfriendly passions and excite their most violent conflicts.

James Madison, Federalist Paper No. 10

I was once on an airline flight that was canceled owing to mechanical failure. There was another flight immediately following to the same destination. Both the original flight and the next flight were close to being full. These circumstances instantly created two polarized factions: the canceled flighters and the later flighters, both competing for a fixed number of seats on the later flight. The canceled flighters argued that they should have priority on these seats, since they had been on an earlier flight whose cancellation was the airline's fault. The later flighters argued that they should have the seats, since their right to a seat should not be affected by what happened to some other flight. It was amazing how quickly animosity developed between these two factions, just as solidarity developed within each faction—even though these were complete strangers. The canceled flighters exchanged remarks with each other about how unfair, aggressive, and arrogant were the later flighters. The later flighters grumbled to each other equally uncomplimentary remarks about the canceled flighters. The situation almost got violent. In the end, the airline favored the later flighters. Meanwhile both groups lost because the later flight was also delayed while this heated argument was going on. Factions seem to spring out of nowhere in human society.

Factions help explain the part of poor growth that is attributable to government policies. Why would governments ever have the incentive to choose policies that kill off growth? Why would they kill off growth through corruption, when their take from a growing economy would be greater? And if the poor need to have their investments in future income subsidized to participate in growth, then why don't governments always provide those subsidies? We will see that divided societies' governments face incentives to redistribute existing income. In more cohesive societies, governments face incentives to promote development. The fundamental difference between redistributionist and developmentalist governments is social polarization. Societies divided into factions fight over division of the spoils; societies unified by a common culture and a strong middle class create a consensus for growth—growth that includes the poor.

Going After Cocoa

Let's go back to the story of Ghana's main export crop, cocoa. Production of cocoa is concentrated in the region of the Ashanti group, who make up 13 percent of the population. The Ashanti Empire was dominant in precolonial times, to the resentment of other groups such as the coastal Akan groups (30 percent of population). Beginning with the run-up to independence in the 1950s, cocoa replaced historical resentments as a bone of contention between ethnic groups.[1]

In the early 1950s Kwame Nkrumah, from one of the coastal Akan groups, split off from the traditional Ashanti-based independence party. He pushed a bill through the colonial legislature in 1954 to freeze the producer price of cocoa. An Ashanti-based opposition party to Nkrumah ran against him in the 1956 elections with the less-than-subtle slogan, "Vote Cocoa." The Ashanti region even tried to secede prior to independence. With most of the other ethnic groups favoring Nkrumah, these efforts failed.

Nkrumah continued to tax cocoa heavily into the 1960s. The state-run Cocoa Marketing Board bought low from the cocoa farmers and sold high at the world price. The high black market premium on foreign exchange meant the price paid to farmers was worth little in dollars. Farmers were forced to sell their dollars at the official exchange rate, but could buy dollars only at the black market rate.

Between 1969 and 1971, Kofi Busia led the only Ashanti-based government in modern Ghanaian history, having co-opted some of the coastal Akan groups as allies. One of Busia's first acts was to raise the producer price of cocoa. In 1971, he instituted a large devaluation that raised the domestic currency price of cocoa at a time when the world cocoa price was falling. The military overthrew him three days later and partially reversed the devaluation. That was the last chance the Ashantis had at getting market prices for their cocoa.

Although ethnic coalitions rotated with dizzying speed through the 1970s and early 1980s in Ghana, they all seemed to concur on punitive taxation of Ashanti cocoa exports through the ludicrously overvalued official exchange rate, reflected in a high black market premium on dollars. The government handed out its cocoa profits to political and ethnic supporters by giving out licenses to import goods at the official exchange rate. These goods could then be resold at an enormous profit on the black market. The black market premium reached its historical peak in 1982, with the black market exchange rate at twenty-two times the official exchange rate.[2]

The cocoa producers had received 89 percent of the world price of cocoa in 1949.[3] By 1983, they received 6 percent of the world price. Cocoa exports were 19 percent of GDP in 1955; by 1983 they were only 3 percent of GDP.[4] Ghanaian cocoa is one of the classic examples of killing the goose that laid the golden egg. The story of Ghana suggests that the interest groups' struggle to get profits from a commodity like cocoa has something to do with the choice of growth-killing policies—like an overvalued exchange rate resulting in a high black market premium.[5]

Politicians Are People Too

Hard as it may be to believe, there was a time when economists' analysis of tropical countries left out politics. They ignored the politics of the growth disaster in, say, Ghana.

Looking back through the time capsule left by the National Bureau of Economic Research case studies of the 1970s, we find works like a 1974 analysis of trade restrictions in Ghana.[6] The work is amazingly silent about politics, recommending policies to the Ghanaian leaders as if they were the beneficent philosopher-kings of Plato. Nowhere in this work do we find a clue that Ghana was run by corrupt military bosses and its politics were torn apart by ethnic divisions. Nowhere do we find a clue that trade restrictions in Ghana were pretexts for thievery through the buying and selling of import licenses, licenses that were sometimes awarded to the girlfriends of the military strongmen.

It was only later that we economists realized that government officials are people too. Like other people, they respond to incentives. If government leaders feel the incentive to follow growth-creating policies, then they will follow them. If they don't, they won't.

Only after admitting that government leaders must respond to incentives like anyone else could we face the hard question. If government policies like high inflation, high deficits, high black market premiums, and negative real interest rates are so destructive to growth, why would any government have the incentive to pursue them? In this chapter we will look at why politicians sometimes face perverse incentives to destroy growth.

The Wrong Answer

The casual answer to why politicians destroy growth is that they are stealing the public blind during their time of community service. High inflation and high deficits could result from government officials' high spending, spending that winds up in the officials' own bank account. High black market premiums and negative real interest rates certainly make corruption possible. The leader gets foreign exchange at the official rate and sells it at the black market rate. He finances his purchase of foreign exchange using loans at the negative real interest rate and invests the money in foreign assets with a positive real interest rate.

It is plausible that these policies breed corruption, but this is not an adequate explanation of why politicians choose growth-killing policies. The politicians' opportunity for graft is greater the higher is the average income of the economy. You can steal much more from a rich economy than from a poor economy. So politicians' use of growth-killing policies to steal is self-defeating. Even politicians who are stealing want their economy to grow faster, so they can steal more. So if politicians are also people who respond to incentives, why do they choose growth-killing policies?

Many Out of One

The key insight we are missing is that government is not a single, all-knowing actor. Government instead is a coalition of politicians representing different factions. It is this multiplicity that leads to the choice of growth-killing policies.

Think of the following analogy. Suppose there is an underground pool of oil that crosses the boundaries of my property and your property. The law says that whoever owns the land above the pool of oil has the right to withdraw oil from the pool. So both of us have the right to withdraw oil from the single pool. It is also a characteristic of oil field technology that the faster the oil is withdrawn from a field, the lower is the total yield of the field. So do you and I refrain from rapidly extracting oil to preserve the potential of the field? Of course not. You and I engage in a scramble to get as much oil as possible before the other one gets it. The field yields less than its potential because we extract the oil so fast. Pundits will pontificate about our self-defeating greed as we are consuming too fast a nonrenewable resource, but we are acting perfectly rationally. This situation has been called "the tragedy of the commons."

Contrast this with the case where the oil field lies below my property alone. I will carefully withdraw the oil at a rate that preserves the total potential of the field. It was the existence of multiple claimants to the field in the previous example that caused self-defeating behavior that left both of us worse off.

This is the key insight of the field of political economy. The existence of polarized interest groups that each act in their own interest is responsible for bad government policies. Societies that are more polarized have worse government policies than societies that are more unified. Any factor that breeds polarization will worsen policy, and thus cause lower growth. For example, interest groups in multi-ethnic coalitions in Ghana may have reached the following compromise: each interest group representative will be in charge of one policy. One will determine the black market exchange rate, another will determine the rate of money creation and inflation, a third will determine the budget deficit, and a fourth will determine the negative real interest rate.

Under this compromise, each interest group representative will choose its policy so as to maximize its own take, without considering how its choice will affect the take of the others. For example, the highly negative real interest rate chosen by official 4 creates incentives to keep money outside the country. Ghanaian exporters, for example, will understate their true sales and deposit the difference in a bank account outside the country. This lowers the take of official 1, in charge of the black market premium, because his revenue base comes from exporters forced to deliver their sales at the official exchange rate. Official 1 resells the proceeds at the black market exchange rate to get his profits. If less money is being brought into the country from exporters, he will get less of a profit.

Official 2 also has a lower take, because there is more revenue from money creation the higher the amount of money kept in the country. With money kept outside the country, official 2 gets less revenue from the "inflation tax." And official 3 is not able to set as high a budget deficit, because domestic financing of the budget deficit also comes from financial assets kept inside the country. Official 4 set the real interest rate at a level to yield the maximum profits to him from cheap loans, not taking into account the effect of his actions on officials 1, 2, and 3. So official 4 makes the real interest rate more negative than he would have if he had considered how his actions affect the other officials.

We could turn the story around and say that official 1 also does not take into account the effect of his black market premium on official 4. At a high black market premium, the incentive is strong again for exporters to sell part of their products under the table and deposit the proceeds in a foreign bank account. This means less money in domestic banking accounts, which means less is available for official 4 to get in cheap loans to reinvest in higher-yield assets. Official 1 makes the black market premium higher than he would have if he had considered how his actions affect official 4. All officials are drawing from a common pool, without taking into account the effect of their withdrawals on the others' withdrawals.

Compare this result to what would have happened if the Ghanaian leader had been powerful and interest groups weak. He would have controlled the black market premium, the rate of money creation and inflation, the budget deficit, and the real interest rate in Ghana. He would take into account the effects of one on the take from the others, because he gets revenue from all. He will choose a lower real interest rate, a lower inflation rate, a lower budget deficit, and a lower black market premium than those in the four-official case. Polarization between distinct interest groups creates multiple actors. These multiple actors choose more growth-destroying policies than a single actor would.

Don't jump to the conclusion that autocracy is the best system for economic development. Autocrats may be placating multiple interest groups just as much as democracies do. The crucial distinction is not between autocracy and democracy (anyway there's no evidence that one is better for growth than the other). It is between a weak central government made up of a coalition of polarized factions and a strong central government made up of supporters in consensus.

Polarization in weak governments explains why governments so often appear to defeat themselves by killing the goose that lays the golden egg. Such polarization could explain how cocoa exports in Ghana were killed off, going from 19 percent of GDP in the 1950s to 3 percent of GDP in the 1980s. Each government interest group got its take from taxing cocoa exporters without taking into account its effect on other groups. Perhaps one group set up the marketing board on cocoa and determined the price that the cocoa producers would get. Suppose that another faction controlled the black market premium and so determined how much the producer price meant in hard currency. If these two factions operated independently, they would tax cocoa producers more heavily than if a single official had determined the tax on cocoa. Each faction tried to get the most out of cocoa. Killing off cocoa is the Ghanaian analogy to extracting oil as fast as possible from a common pool.

Time for Lunch

A similar story can explain how budget deficits get out of hand in polarized economies. I will throw out another analogy. Suppose six of us go out to lunch and decide beforehand that we will split the check equally. When we order lunch, I know that I am going to bear only one-sixth of the cost of any dish that I order. If I get the $24 lobster instead of the $12 ravioli, I'm only out two dollars. Each of us does a similar calculation, with the result that our total spending is higher than it would have been if we had each paid for our own order. This is a variation on the common oil pool problem. I take into account the effects of my actions on my own budget, not on the group budget.

A similar situation exists with multiple interest group representatives determining a national budget. If there are six interest groups of equal size, then I will bear only one-sixth of the cost of any pet project that I propose for my interest group. Each of the other five representatives thinks the same way. So we have a larger budget and budget deficit than we would have had with a single actor determining the budget. Each of us representatives is just responding to incentives, but the result for the nation is none too good.

Wars of Attrition

Alberto Alesina of Harvard and Allan Drazen of the University of Maryland pointed out another way that multiple actors can lead to the persistence of bad policies. Their insight was that there were wars of attrition between multiple interest groups.

Suppose the economy has high inflation, which is destroying growth. Suppose that there are two distinct interest groups. You and I each head interest groups. Either of us could bring down the inflation by giving up some of our own pet projects financed by money creation. Will one of us do so? Not necessarily. Each of us hopes that the other will give up pet projects and bring inflation to an end. That way, the one of us that didn't give in will gain the benefits of lower inflation while holding onto his pet projects. The two of us are in a war of attrition, hoping that the other will run out of soldiers first.

To see how this works, think about a real war of attrition: the Vietnam War. At first, the war was popular with the U.S. voters, while the North Vietnamese and Vietcong were equally determined to persevere. As time wore on and the measure of success in the war became the ratio of enemy KIAs (killed in action) to our KIAs (the notorious body counts), more about the political weaknesses and strengths of the two opponents was revealed. Even with a lot of KIAs, the North Vietnamese and Vietcong drew on a large and nationalistic population to keep sending in fresh soldiers. The U.S. KIAs generated discontent at home, with the public very unwilling to send soldiers to the killing fields endlessly. Ho Chi Minh caught on to this sooner than did Lyndon Johnson. Eventually after these gentlemen left public service, it became clear to both parties that the North Vietnamese could outlast the United States in a war of attrition. Both parties came to the peace table and concluded an agreement for U.S. withdrawal.

In policy wars of attrition, we also gain knowledge about each other as the war of attrition goes on. If the war of attrition has already lasted two years, then we know that both of us are sufficiently unwilling to give in that we will wait two years. Finally either you or I reach a point where we realize that the other is going to wait longer than we are willing to wait. You or I, whoever suffers more from inflation or places the lower value on its pet projects, will give in first, and the war of attrition will come to an end.

Note, however, that the economy went through a long period of growth-destroying inflation before the war of attrition ended. The war of attrition came about because of polarized interest groups. A single government actor on inflation will bring it down as soon as its cost to society exceeds its benefits. The war of attrition story with multiple interest groups gives an explanation for why bad policies last so long even when their costs in forgone economic growth are obvious to everyone.

In Defense of the Status Quo

Raquel Fernandez of New York University and Dani Rodrik of Harvard tell another clever story of how, with multiple interest groups, a bad policy might persist even though a majority would benefit from reform. Suppose again there are two interest groups. My interest group, accounting for 40 percent of the population, benefits for sure from the change in the bad policy. In your interest group, accounting for 60 percent of the population, one-third of the group will benefit. If the reform is decided by majority voting, there is a winning coalition of all of my group and one-third of your group. We will have 60 percent of the vote in favor of reform.

But suppose that each member of your group is unsure whether he or she will be in the one-third that benefits. Suppose each member of your group is equally unsure about his or her chance of being in the lucky one-third. So each member of your group will face odds of two to one against benefiting from reform. All of the members of your group will vote against reform. Reform will go down to defeat 60 percent to 40 percent, even though a 60 percent majority of the population would have benefited from the reform. A bad status quo persists because of uncertainty about who will benefit from reform. This uncertainty was fatal because of multiple interest groups with different benefits from reforms.

Inequality and Growth

Incentives go awry for government policymakers when there are multiple interest groups. What circumstances tend to create multiple interest groups? Looking around the world, we see societies torn apart by two kinds of polarization: class warfare and ethnic conflict.

The first culprit is high inequality. Suppose that the population consists of a poor majority who own only their own labor and a rich minority who own the other inputs to production: capital and land. Suppose there is democratic voting on policy, or at least effective interest group representation in a nondemocracy. In a near-democratic setting, the poor workers are going to determine policy since they are in the majority. A tax on the rich may be an attractive proposition to this poor majority.

What determines how attractive the proposition is? There are two offsetting effects. First, the tax on the rich lowers the growth rate of the economy, which hurts both workers and capitalists. (We have seen that statutory tax rates do not determine growth, but I am using *tax* here as shorthand for any redistributive device, like a high black market premium.) Second, the tax on the rich redistributes income from the rich to the poor. The potential for redistribution is greater, the higher the cliff between the income of the land-owning capitalists and the income of the workers. A big difference in income—high inequality—means more potential for redistribution from a tax on capital, which offsets the loss of growth potential. So poor majorities in highly unequal societies will vote for a high tax, sacrificing some growth in favor of redistribution. Even in undemocratic societies, the government and its supporters will try to get their hands on loot from the upper class instead of favoring future growth. We have some direct evidence for this: countries that have higher inequality also have a higher black market premium, higher repression of the financial system, higher inflation, and a less favorable exchange rate for exporters than countries with less inequality.

A contemporary example is Venezuela. As of late 2000 a democratically elected populist named Hugo Chavez has explicitly promised his poor majority followers to redistribute the wealth from the oligarchy. Caracas, Venezuela, is the poster child for inequality, with skyscrapers built by the elite with the huge oil riches, yet surrounded by shantytowns precariously poised on steep hills, some of them washed away by the recent floods. Despite $266 billion in oil profits over the last three decades and the continual discovery of new oil reserves, the average Venezuelan has 22 percent lower income today than in 1970.

Inequality may also have been the story in Ghana, where ethnic coalitions taxed the relatively rich Ashanti cocoa farmers. In more equal societies, the poor majority will vote for a low tax on capital because the potential for gains from redistribution is not as great as the potential for gains from growth. This story predicts that high inequality goes with low growth.

This is indeed what researchers have found: higher inequality in income or land is associated with lower growth. Let's look at the relationship between land inequality and economic growth. I am measuring inequality with the Gini coefficient, which goes from 0 (everyone has equal land) to 1 (1 person has all the land). The fourth of the sample with the lowest inequality (average Gini coefficient of .45) had the highest average growth. This fourth includes such growth superstars as South Korea, Japan, and Taiwan. (Korea had the highest growth rate and the most equal land distribution in the sample.) The fourth of the sample with the highest land inequality (average Gini coefficient of .85) had the lowest growth. This highly unequal fourth includes such growth disasters as Argentina, Peru, and Venezuela.[7] In Argentina, for example, it was the policies of Juan and Eva Perón to redistribute income toward the *descamisados* (shirtless ones) that sent the Argentine economy spiraling downward until recently. Hugo Chavez may be the Juan Perón of Venezuela today.

Note that this redistribution is different from the subsidies to the poor that I've argued are necessary to wipe out poverty traps. The subsidy to the poor should be on their future income creation. The redistribution that happens under high inequality would be of current consumption. This is because under high inequality, there is little incentive to invest in the future, including the future of the poor.

One of the explanations of the growth difference between East Asia and Latin America is that East Asian land was distributed much more equally than Latin American land. How did the unequal distribution in Latin America come about?

The Choices of the Oligarchy

There are more subtle dynamics among growth, democracy, education, and inequality. Suppose a rich elite holds exclusive power and restricts voting to those big landowners. Such an arrangement was common in the United States in the early nineteenth century, in many European countries through the late nineteenth century, and in Latin American countries into the twentieth century. Now the question becomes, Does the oligarchy vote for free mass education? How does the degree of inequality affect the answer?

The voting elite faces some trade-offs. On the one hand, implementing mass education will raise growth, because education will raise the productive potential of the poor majority. On the other hand, mass education breeds mass political participation. The newly educated poor will agitate for the right to vote. And then the poor majority may vote for redistribution of land away from the elite toward the majority, which would lower growth. The outcome depends on the degree of initial inequality.

In a highly unequal society, the oligarchy will vote against mass education. Outside the rich elite, the average level of income remains low. So a highly unequal society remains highly unequal and undemocratic. The data confirm this prediction: more unequal societies are indeed likely to be less democratic and to have less civil liberty.[8]

In a relatively equal society, on the other hand, the elite would vote for mass education. They are confident that the newly educated masses, even if they agitate for the right to vote, will not vote for redistribution because the gains from redistribution are low in a relatively equal society compared to the gains from growth. Everyone will benefit from the greater productivity of the masses with more education. Indeed, we find that countries that have a large middle class also have more schooling compared to countries with a small middle class.

Economic historians Ken Sokoloff and Stanley Engerman have argued that a story like this explains the very different development of North America compared to South America. In the United States and Canada, the endless supply of land supported a large population of family farmers. The large middle class of family farmers guaranteed relatively low inequality in North America. (Growing up among farmers in Ohio, little did I suspect that those guys in feedcaps were part of our secret to prosperity.) In South America, on the other hand, the money was in mining and sugar plantations. The oligarchy staffed their mines and sugar plantations with slaves and illiterate peasants. The ownership of mines and plantations was concentrated in the hands of the elite few from the beginning—as was inevitable with such large-scale operations combined with favors from the crown. (It remains true today that economies made up of mines and plantations are more unequal than other societies.)

So North America developed into a rich land with mass education and a voting franchise for all. South America remained poor outside the confines of the elite few, inequality remained higher, there was no mass education until recently, and political power was long restricted to the elite.

The story of South America is not unique in the Third World. In rural Pakistan, the literacy rates—in particular, female literacy rates—are among the lowest in the world. As one author put it, "The ruling elites found it convenient to perpetuate low literacy rates. The lower the proportion of literate people, the lower the probability that the ruling elite could be displaced."[9]

To sum up, polarization because of inequality is a recipe for continuing underdevelopment. Either populist governments will seek to redistribute income to their supporters, or the elites will suppress democracy and mass education. In the worst of all worlds, government will alternate between populist democracies and oligarchic dictatorships, destroying the predictability of policy altogether (which itself hurts growth). The data confirm that countries that are more unequal are also more politically unstable; they have more revolutions and coups.[10] Societies with a large middle class, on the other hand, have incentives favorably aligned for growth, political stability, and democracy.

Ethnic Hatreds and Growth

Polarization by income is not the only kind of social division that can split society up into warring interest groups. Another common phenomenon is ethnic polarization. The Ghana story already highlighted the role of ethnically based interest groups in creating bad policies. Although ethnic conflict is an obvious theme in history, economists have paid remarkably little attention to it. This omission became even stranger when the theory of political economy began to coalesce around the idea of conflict between polarized interest groups. Who better suits the definition of polarized interests than ethnic groups that hate each other?

The most obvious sign of ethnic polarization is bloodshed. Ethnic groups killing other ethnic groups is a staple of today's headlines, from Rwanda to Bosnia to Kosovo. Ethnic cleansing is at least as old as the Romans, who were both cleansers and cleansed. In 146 B.C., the Romans captured Corinth in Greece. They razed it to the ground, killing many of the inhabitants, raped many women, and then sold all surviving Corinthians into slavery. What goes around comes around. In 88 B.C., King Mithradates VI of Pontus invaded Roman territory in Asia Minor. He encouraged Asian debtors to kill their Roman creditors. The Asians massacred 80,000 Romans.[11]

The list of ethnic massacres is a long one. A nonexclusive list of victims of ethnic massacres since the Romans includes: the Danes in Anglo-Saxon England in 1002; the Jews in Europe during the First Crusade, 1096–1099; the French in Sicily in 1282; the French in Bruges in 1302; the Flemings in England in 1381; the Jews in Iberia in 1391; converted Jews in Portugal in 1507; the Huguenots in France in 1572; Protestants in Magdeburg in 1631; Jews and Poles in the Ukraine, 1648–1954; indigenous populations in the United States, Australia, and Tasmania in the eighteenth and nineteenth centuries; Jews in Russia in the nineteenth century; the French in Haiti in 1804; Arab Christians in Lebanon in 1841; Turkish Armenians in 1895–1896 and 1915–1916; Nestorian, Jacobite, and Maronite Christians in the Turkish empire in 1915–1916; Greeks in Smyrna in 1922; Haitians in the Dominican Republic in 1936; the Jewish Holocaust in German-occupied territory, 1933–1945; Serbians in Croatia in 1941; Muslims and Hindus in British India in 1946–1947; the Chinese in 1965 and the Timorese in 1974 and 1998 in Indonesia; Igbos in Nigeria in 1967–1970; the Vietnamese in Cambodia in 1970–1978; the Bengalis in Pakistan in 1971; the Tutsis in Rwanda in 1956–1965; 1972, and 1993–1994; Tamils in Sri Lanka in 1958, 1971, 1977, 1981, and 1983; Armenians in Azerbaijan in 1990; Muslims in Bosnia in 1992; Kosovars and Serbians in Kosovo in 1998–2000.[12] To show how far from exhaustive this list is, the political scientist Ted Gurr counted fifty ethnically based conflicts in 1993–1994 alone.[13]

The new millennium has already brought its first ethnic wars. The February 16, 2000, *Washington Post* reports on the Congo:

In this country where much of Africa has come to fight and no one seems to govern, the consequences of chaos are emerging in the starkest possible terms. As many as 7,000 people have been killed and 150,000 forced from their homes in the remote forest villages above Lake Albert in northeastern Congo since June, when residents and aid workers say brutal ethnic warfare erupted over who owns a particular hill. Lendu tribesmen armed with machetes and arrows have moved from village to village, killing and maiming. Miles of burned out huts line the roads. The conflict between the agrarian Lendu and the herding Hema reflects the combative atmosphere that plagues Congo, which is sinking further into a civil war that began in 1996.

Meanwhile, the February 22,2000, *New York Times* reported dozens killed in riots between Muslims and Christians in northern Nigeria.[14]

The Muslims from the north are demanding Islamic law for northern states; the Christians from the south living in the north protest. The north-south division has bedeviled Nigeria since independence, with the Muslim north in power most of the time. Southern Christians tried unsuccessfully to secede as Biafra in 1967. Now a southern Christian is president after a democratic election in February 1999, and the ethnic violence continues: thousands have been killed since the election.

Muslims and Christians are killing each other as of April 2000 in the Moluccas in Indonesia. Muslim youth in Jakarta are organizing a jihad to go fight on behalf of Muslims.

Historians and journalists pay attention to ethnic conflict only when it erupts into bloodshed. But there is pervasive ethnic antagonism and discrimination virtually everywhere that different ethnic groups share a common nation.

Take the economic discrimination against gypsies (Roma) in Bulgaria. The city of Dimitrovgrad has a more or less excellent infrastructure—which, however, does not apply to the poor quarters and, in particular, the gypsy ghetto. The latter has nothing to do with "official" Dimitrovgrad. There are neither roads nor telephones, the plumbing is disastrous, many houses have no electricity, and there's a bus only every three hours. The situation is the same in Sofia. The Roma quarters there are entirely different from other Sofia quarters. There is no sewage, the shafts are clogged, drinking water is dirty and stinks, and there is no garbage collection or other communal services. The thus segregated Roma feel truly stigmatized, victims of discrimination, "treated like dogs."

The predominantly Orthodox Christian community of Dibdibe Watju, Ethiopia, does not mix with the Protestants in the village. They do not allow the Protestants to bury their dead in the Orthodox Christian church yards. The dead have to be carried to town, where they have a separate burial site. Even the Orthodox Christian members of the same *idir* (funeral association) do not attend a Protestant member's funeral.

In Ecuador, an indigenous man complained that teachers discriminated against his children. They would tell children who struggled with schoolwork, "You are an ass, this is why you can't. You are an animal." The indigenous children struggled with a nonnative language, hindering their scholastic success and future prospects.[15]

Other ethnic groups that complain of discrimination range from Hindus in Bangladesh to lower castes in India to Pomaks in Bulgaria to Tajiks in Uzbekistan to Khmer speakers in Vietnam. This list is far from exhaustive. As *Scientific American* said in September 1998, "Many of the world's problems stem from the fact that it has 5,000 ethnic groups but only 190 countries."

Social scientists have documented extensive problems in economic policymaking when there is ethnic diversity. First, we need to measure the tricky concept of ethnic diversity. Different languages is one possible measure of ethnic differences. A language-based measure of ethnic diversity that social scientists use is the probability that two individuals from the same country will speak different languages. This probability is higher the more distinct linguistic groups there are and the more equal the size of the groups. To calculate this measure of diversity, we need data on the number of language speakers within each nation of the hundreds of languages spoken worldwide.

One determined group of scholars collected such data from census reports in the early 1960s. This group of scholars belonged to a research institute in the former Soviet Union. For whatever obscure purpose, cold war or otherwise, they roamed the globe collecting data on language speakers by nation. We can use their data to calculate the probability that two individuals in a nation will speak different languages.

This measure of ethnic diversity is highest in sub-Saharan Africa, with its many small tribes in each nation. It is lowest in East Asian nations like Korea and Japan, where everyone speaks the national language except visiting American college students.

Ethnic (linguistic) diversity does not automatically imply ethnic conflict, violent or otherwise. It merely reflects the potential for such conflict, if opportunistic politicians try to exploit ethnic divisions to gain an ethnic power base. Apparently such opportunism is common. As shown in table 13.1, high ethnic diversity is a good predictor of civil war and genocide. The risk of civil war is two and a half times higher in the most ethnically diverse quarter of the sample compared to the least ethnically diverse quarter. The risk of genocide is three times higher in the same comparison.

Ethnically diverse societies also have fewer public services. Table 13.1 shows that the most ethnically diverse societies have half the schooling, one-thirteenth of the telephones per worker, nearly twice the electric power losses, and less than half of the share of roads that are paved compared to the most ethnically homogeneous societies. All of these outcomes depend in good part on provision of public

Table 13.1
Ethnic diversity, violence, and public services, 1960–1989

	Average, quarter of sample least ethnically diverse	Average, quarter of sample most ethnically diverse
Ethnic diversity (probability of two people speaking different languages)	5%	80%
Violence		
Probability of civil war	7%	18%
Probability of genocide	5%	16%
Public services		
Average years of schooling of labor force	5.3	2.6
Percentage of roads paved	53.9	24.2
Percentage of power system losses	12.4	22.8
Telephones per 1,000 workers	92.8	7.4

services. Why would public services provision be low in ethnically polarized societies?

For the government to supply a public service, interest groups have to agree on what kind of public service they want. Even for such an innocuous public service like roads, ethnic groups that are in different regions will want roads in their region and will place little benefit on roads in the other groups' regions. And if ethnic groups do not associate much with each other, this means that there would be little interregional travel. Since all groups place a low value on a national road network, politicians will not invest as much in roads as they would in a more ethnically homogeneous society.

For a public service like mass schooling, different linguistic groups would each prefer that schooling be conducted in their language. A compromise may be reached where schooling is given in a lingua franca like the language of the former colonial master. But each group is less satisfied with the compromise than it would have been with schooling in its own language. They are less ready to support mass schooling than they would be in a more homogeneous society.

The new views of economic growth might reinforce this lack of support for mass schooling. Suppose that people in linguistic groups associate primarily with people from their group and not with people from other groups. Then the knowledge creation coming from highly educated people is valuable to you only if those people consist of your own group. Knowledge leaks within ethnic groups and not across ethnic groups. So you support schooling for your own ethnic group because of the beneficial knowledge leaks you will get, but you do not support education for the other groups. Each group feels the same way. Everyone places less value on universal education in a heterogeneous society than in a homogeneous one. A study of rural western Kenya confirms this result. Districts with more ethnic diversity, measured by language, had sharply lower primary school funding and worse school facilities than more homogeneous areas.[16]

Similar arguments can be made with the other public services, and so public services are restricted in ethnically polarized economies. As perhaps an indirect reflection of this, infant mortality, life expectancy, birthweight of infants, access to sanitation, and access to clean water are all worse in more ethnically heterogeneous societies.[17]

That's not the end to the damage. We saw that distinct interest groups may get into a war of attrition over a beneficial reform. Ethnically based interest groups make such destructive wars of attrition more likely. Ironically, with all the attention paid to ethnically based violence, it is the ethnically based policy wars that may be more relevant for most countries.

If one group is richer than the others, then redistributive policies will also be tempting. We saw in a previous chapter that ethnically based business elites are common throughout the world. There would be the same trade-off in policymaking that we saw with general inequality. On the one hand, policies like negative real interest rates and high black market premiums redistribute income from the business elite to the party or parties in power. On the other hand, these policies lower growth because they lower the incentive to invest in the future. Which way the party in power goes depends on the extent of the income gap between the ethnic coalition in power and the ethnic business elite. A combination of ethnic diversity and large income gaps between ethnic groups could lead to growth-killing economic policies. For example, governments in East Africa, dominated by Africans, chose bad policies to tax the Indian business elite.

Table 13.2 shows the association between ethnic diversity and two measures of policy: the black market premium and the ratio of broad money to GDP (reflecting whether there are negative real interest rates that will depress the holding of money). This, together with higher violence and fewer public services, may help explain why growth is two percentage points lower in the more ethnically diverse countries than in the least ethnically diverse countries.

Table 13.2
Ethnic diversity and its consequences for policies, 1960–1989

	Average, quarter of sample least ethnically diverse (%)	Average, quarter of sample most ethnically diverse (%)
Ethnic diversity (probability of two people speaking different languages)	5	80
Per capita growth rate per annum	3.0	0.9
Policies		
Black market premium	10	30
Financial depth (broad money[a]/GDP)	47	22

a. Total assets of the banking system

The association of lower public services with ethnic polarization is a problem even in rich economies like the United States. In the United States, let's define distinct ethnic groups the way that the census does: white, black, Asian, Native American, and Hispanic. Ethnic diversity is measured by the probability that two randomly selected individuals in a county will belong to different ethnic groups.

We find that U.S. counties that are more ethnically diverse spend a lower share of their budgets on core public services like roads and education. The differences are statistically significant.[18] Since whites constitute a voting majority in virtually all counties, the logical interpretation is that racist whites were unwilling to spend as much on public goods like schools when they were shared with other races.

What about those subsidies to the income of the poor that are so necessary for eliminating poverty traps? Unfortunately, higher ethnic diversity is also associated with a lower share of spending on welfare in U.S. counties and metropolitan areas.[19] Another study has found lower support for public schooling among the elderly when the elderly and school-age population are from different ethnic groups.[20] A like-minded study found that the expansion in high school education that happened early this century in the United States happened more in areas with "more ethnic and religious homogeneity."[21] An earlier study compared U.S. social services unfavorably to Western Europe's and attributed the difference to "historic racial antagonisms."[22] The big failure to lift African Americans out of poverty has everything to do with ethnic conflict.

As the noted sociologist William Julius Wilson puts it, "Many white Americans have turned against a strategy that emphasizes programs they perceive as benefiting only racial minorities.... Public services became identified mainly with blacks, private services mainly with whites.... White tax payers saw themselves as being forced, through taxes, to pay for medical and legal services that many of them could not afford."[23]

Foreign Assistance and Ethnic Conflict

Aid donors have been remarkably oblivious to ethnic polarization. They don't sufficiently monitor how aid resources might disproportionately benefit a particular ethnic group, worsening ethnic tension.

A case study of a project in Sri Lanka makes this point. There is a long history of tensions between minority Tamils and majority Sinhalese in Sri Lanka. In 1977, a new Sinhalese-dominated government initiated a massive irrigation and power project called the Mahaweli Project. The World Bank and bilateral donors gave huge amounts of foreign aid to help finance the project; aid per year increased sixfold over the 1978 to 1980 period compared to the period 1970 to 1977.[24] Unheeded by the donors, Mahaweli took place mainly in the Sinhala area and had mainly Sinhalese beneficiaries. Foreign aid utilization in the Tamil city of Jaffna was zero between 1977 and 1982. The feeder canal that was going to serve the Tamil North was canceled early in the project's history. Even worse, the project was going to resettle Sinhalese farmers into Tamil majority areas, diluting the Tamil majority and weakening their ability to articulate their interests at the local government level.

The Mahaweli project was ethnically symbolic; it promised the resurrection of the hydraulic civilization of the Sinhalese Buddhist kings, which had been destroyed by medieval Tamil invaders.

There were many other triggers to the ethnic tensions that escalated into a civil war after 1983. However, the ethnic polarization caused by the project didn't help the delicate process of reaching an interethnic compromise. Civil war and terrorism has continued intermittently ever since. The March 11, 2000, *Washington Post* reports that a suicide bomber in Colombo, Sri Lanka, killed twenty people and injured sixty-four. The *Post* says, "Military officials blamed Tamil separatists for the blast, which came as Parliament discussed extending emergency rule in northern Sri Lanka, a measure that gives broad powers to the army and police fighting Tamil rebels there."

Polarized by Both Class and Race

The worst case for good policymaking and political freedom is to have both high inequality and high ethnic diversity. In the Mexican state of Chiapas, the Zapatista rebellion broke out on January 1, 1994. The rebels, most of them indigenous inhabitants of the area, took seven municipalities, including the famous indigenous city of San Cristóbal de las Casas. The Mexican (nonindigenous) army responded in force, with 25,000 troops, and the Zapatistas retreated on January 2. The army executed some of the rebels it captured and bombed the mountains south of San Cristóbal.

In February 1995, the Mexican government ordered a new military offensive against the Zapatistas. There were widespread reports of rape and murder committed by Mexican troops. The government finally halted the offensive in response to the outcry within Mexico.

In the years since the rebellion, there has been a low-level "dirty war" between the Zapatistas, on one side, and the Mexican military and paramilitary bands, on the other. On December 22, 1997, in Acteal, Chiapas, paramilitary bands allied with the white landowners attacked and massacred a band of forty-five unarmed indigenous people, including many women and children. The national police were nearby but did not intervene.

There have been numerous unsuccessful peace attempts in Chiapas. In January 2000, in response to peace efforts, the Mexican government initiated deportation proceedings against forty-three international human rights observers in Chiapas.[25]

The Zapatista rebellion was only the latest installment in a long-running conflict between (generally white) landowners and (generally Indian) peasants in Chiapas. Chiapas governor Absalón Castellanos Domínguez noted in 1982 that "we have no middle class; there are the rich, who are very rich, and the poor, who are very poor." This statement was all the more poignant since Castellanos himself belonged to an old and wealthy landowning family and, as a military man, was involved in an army massacre of Indians in 1980.[26] Many observers have noted the "sordid association" among landowners and their *pistoleros*, party bosses, the army, and the police, all of whom agree on the use of force to repress Indian peasant rights (for example, depriving Indians of land to which they are legally entitled). Amnesty International noted "a pattern of apparently deliberate political killings" of supporters and leaders of independent peasant organizations. At one point, four successive leaders of the peasant organization Casa del Pueblo were assassinated.[27]

Chiapas is not an isolated case of oppression of the poor by the rich. In Bihar state, India, upper-caste landowners "are terrorizing— through selective murder and rape—the families of laborers 'tied' to their lands." In Samalankulam Village, Sri Lanka, the poor get into the same kind of debt peonage: "The poor borrow money from wealthy people and as a means of repayment work gratis for them." The countryside of Pakistan "is marked by uneven feudal power relationships."[28]

Development failures like Chiapas, Guatemala, Sierra Leone, and Zambia are examples of the fatal mixture of ethnic and class hatreds. In contrast, development successes like Denmark, Japan, and South Korea (recent crises notwithstanding) have benefited from high social consensus associated with low inequality and ethnic homogeneity.

The American Race Tragedy

The United States is no stranger to ethnic and class hatreds. It is telling that the region most polarized by black-white income and ethnic differences—the South—has historically been the most backward economically.

The horrible tradition of lynching in the South for decades violated the most basic human rights. One description of a lynching goes, "In April 1899, black laborer Sam Hose killed his white boss in self-defense. Wrongly accused of raping the man's wife, Hose was mutilated, stabbed, and burned alive in front of 2,000 cheering whites. His body was sold piecemeal to souvenir seekers; an Atlanta grocery displayed his knuckles in its front window for a week."[29]

During the Jim Crow era in the South, blacks endured not only the risk of lynchings but countless daily humiliations. They had separate and inferior schools, drinking fountains, swimming pools, train carriages, lunch counters, and hotels. A black had to make way for a white on the sidewalk. In shops that served both races, blacks had to wait until all the whites were served. White bullies would humiliate blacks by forcing them to drink whiskey and dance minstrel style.[30] As the Jim Crow laws were overturned by the civil rights movement in the 1960s, it is probably not coincidental that the "new South" has begun to catch up to the North.

The United States as a whole is a paradox in that it has managed to prosper despite the sad history of ethnic hatreds. This may be due to its success at creating a middle-class society within the majority of the population, even though it marginalized minorities. In the famous opening words of de Tocqueville's *Democracy in America*, who was obviously thinking only about the white population: "Amongst the novel objects that attracted my attention during my stay in the United States, nothing struck me more forcibly than the general equality of conditions."

The evidence within the United States shows that where groups are more polarized by race and class, prosperity is slower to arrive. The overall success of the United States despite its racial polarization may be because of institutional stability.

Countering Polarization

There is no magic balm that can heal polarized societies. It takes time—maybe decades—for interest groups to overcome their differences and form a consensus for growth. For example, in Argentina the war of attrition over high inflation lasted for two decades, until the government finally brought down inflation in the 1990s. In Africa, the interest group deadlock has still not been broken in many countries, as countries enter into their fourth decade after independence.

Still, never at a loss for words, economists have proposed some institutional arrangements that will create incentives for the government to pursue better policies.

One, which is most relevant for countries struggling with high inflation, is central bank independence. Recall that a war of attrition between interest groups prolongs high inflation. A central bank that does not belong to either group is more likely to stand up to interest group pressure for the credit creation that fuels inflation. An independent central bank is more likely to share the burden of stabilization among interest groups.

Laws that limit credit to the government and create an independent board of governors are one way to define independence of the central bank. Another definition, more pragmatic, is how often the governor of the central bank is changed. Rapid turnover of the governor implies little scope for him or her to defy the government. Researchers have indeed found that independent central banks are associated with lower inflation and higher growth. The results are based on the legal definition of independence for industrial and ex-communist economies and on the pragmatic definition for developing countries.[31]

An independent budget-setting authority can resolve the common pool problem that leads to high government deficits and debt. Having a strong executive finance minister dictate the size of the budget short-circuits the process of each group's ordering a lavish lunch at the other groups' expense. The process of budget setting is also important here. The best arrangement is to have the executive first set the total budget and then have the legislature (the representatives of the interest groups) fight it out over budget composition.[32]

Good Institutions

More generally, institutional restraints make it less likely that class or ethnically based interest groups will unrestrainedly milk the public cow.

Good institutions like those described in the previous chapter (measured by the International Credit Risk Guide) directly mitigate polarization between factions. Ethnically diverse countries with good institutions tend to escape the violence, poverty, and redistribution usually associated with ethnic diversity. Democracy also helps neutralize ethnic differences; ethnically diverse democracies don't seem to be at an economic disadvantage relative to ethnically homogeneous democracies.[33]

Specifically, societies with the highest-quality institutions do not have high black market premiums, low financial development, or low schooling regardless of their level of ethnic heterogeneity. Societies with the highest-quality institutions do not have wars, regardless of their level of ethnic heterogeneity. Good institutions also eliminate the most extreme form of ethnic violence: genocide. There have been no genocides among countries ranked in the top third of institutional quality. In contrast, a number of countries ranked in the bottom third of institutional quality and in the top third of ethnic heterogeneity have had state-sponsored genocidal killings over the past few decades. Examples include Angola, Guatemala, Indonesia, Nigeria, Pakistan, Sudan, Uganda, and Zaire.[34]

The institutional solutions leave us a good way short of definitively resolving the polarized politics that kills off growth. After all, a society polarized by class or race will be less likely to create an independent central bank, an independent finance minister, and high-quality institutions in the first place. But at least we have identified the incentives that government officials face in polarized societies as the root of bad policies. This is a big improvement over endless preaching at poor countries to change their policies. We know some institutional remedies that help matters, even if they are no panaceas. If only rule of law, democracy, independent central banks, independent finance ministers, and other good-quality institutions can be put in place, the endless cycle of bad policies and poor growth can come to an end.

The Middle-Class Consensus

Aristotle said it best in 306 B.C.: "Thus it is manifest that the best political community is formed by citizens of the middle class, and that those states are likely to be well-administered, in which the middle class is large.... Where the middle class is large, there are least likely to be factions and dissension."

One way to summarize the conditions favorable for growth is that progrowth policies are more likely when the two most common forms of social polarization, class conflict and ethnic tensions, are absent. Let's call a situation of a high share of income for the middle class and a high degree of ethnic harmony a middle-class consensus. Societies with a middle-class consensus are more likely to have good economic policies, good institutions, and high economic growth. Examples of countries with a middle-class consensus and high growth are Korea, Japan, and Portugal. Countries polarized by both race and class include Bolivia, Guatemala, and Zambia—all with low economic growth.

Figure 13.1 shows the general pattern: countries with a high middle class share and low ethnic heterogeneity (as measured by language) are rich; those with a low middle class share and high ethnic heterogeneity are poor.

When we examine the data across countries, societies with a middle-class consensus are more likely to have high schooling, high immunization rates, low infant mortality, denser telephone networks, more access to sanitation, better macroeconomic policies, more democracy, and more stable governments. All of these conditions lend themselves to higher economic growth and development. Just

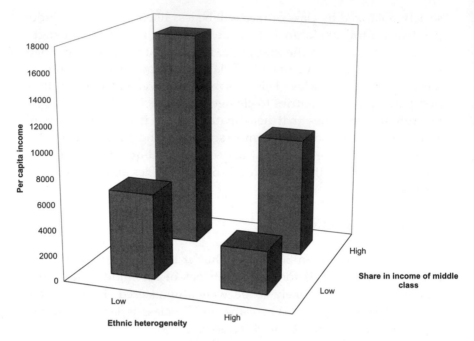

Figure 13.1
Economic development and social polarization

as a middle-class consensus explained the difference in North and South America's development, it helps explain development successes and failures around the world.

The output collapse in Eastern Europe and the former Soviet Union has been linked to destruction of the old middle class before a new middle class could be established. Milanovic describes the "hollowing out" of the old state-sector middle class. Moreover, the presence of sizable ethnic minorities in these new states complicates the achievement of consensus for growth.

We could speculatively blame the lack of middle-class consensus for the failure of societies like ancient Rome, Ming dynasty China (1368–1644), and the Mughal empire in India (1526–1707) to industrialize despite promising beginnings. The Romans were capable of formidable engineering projects like roads, but it was all for the sake of the elite and the military; remember that one-third of the Roman population were slaves.[35] The Ming dynasty spent 200 years renovating the Great Wall. The Mughals gave us the Taj Majal, built for the elite.[36] This is just like the diversion of state revenues to monuments for the elite in many modern economies that lack a middle-class consensus—for example, the late president of Côte d'Ivoire building the largest cathedral in the world in his home town of Yamassoukro.

Preindustrial empires were authoritarian and had little human capital accumulation outside the elite, who were often ethnically distinct from the majority. There is a common misconception that preindustrial societies were more egalitarian than industrializing ones (this became the basis of the famous Kuznets curve hypothesis that inequality first worsens and then improves with industrialization). Casual observation of preindustrial empires suggests otherwise, and in fact more recent evidence suggests that inequality steadily declines with industrialization.[37] More generally, as Marx famously noted, the industrial revolution began as social revolutions abolished slavery, feudalism, and rigid class systems, creating a middle-class bourgeoisie for the first time in world history. Regions in which slavery or feudalism lingered longer were slower to industrialize. In some backward regions of the developing world, like Chiapas, Mexico, parts of rural Pakistan, and Bihar state, India, a form of feudalism is still alive today.

Conclusion

I'm walking with my friend Manny through the Egyptian Museum in Cairo. We are stunned by the masterful three-millennia-year-old gold work of King Tut's tomb, just as a visit to the pyramids erected nearly 5 millennia ago had overwhelmed me earlier. We are here at a conference to bring together researchers from developing countries to study the wealth and poverty of nations. Cairo itself is throwing a big question at us: Why is Egypt still so poor four millennia after building the pyramids? Why didn't an industrial revolution happen under the pharaohs? Some quick back-of-the-envelope analysis provides an answer: income distribution. The pharaohs had everything, and the oppressed masses had nothing. Rich elites can do a fine job erecting monuments to themselves, with the help of labor from the masses. As in other oligarchical societies, the rich elite in Egypt chose to keep the masses poor and uneducated. So prosperity for the few has lasted for millennia, but prosperity for the many remains elusive in Cairo today.

Intermezzo: Violent for Centuries

Tonio, age thirty-eight, lives in the village of Tulungatung, Mindanao, in the Philippines. The village is on the coast, with stilt houses garnished with bougainvillea. The village has no electricity or paved roads, and during the rainy season everything becomes mud. The hills used to be forested with mahogany, but slash-and-burn agriculture has left many gashes in the forest. Tonio grows rice on two and a half acres rented from a teacher in the big city. His wife, Maria Elena, teaches at the village school. Paying rent to the absentee landowner and feeding their three children uses most of Tonio's rice crop.

Tonio's rice crop is not only barely adequate, it fluctuates a lot from year to year. His first crop used the new "miracle rice," and he harvested six tons on his rented plot. But the new rice was also more susceptible to insects, and Tonio could not afford the necessary pesticides. In following years, the army worms, stem borers, and green leaf hoppers reduced the crop to three and a half tons. Then a new government program offered loans to buy seeds, insecticide, and fertilizer. Tonio took a loan of $172 and bought the new miracle seeds, insecticide, and fertilizer. Once again he harvested a crop of six tons and also benefited from a 50 percent increase in the price of rice. He could pay off his loan, buy a mechanical thresher and three pigs, and marry Maria Elena. But his temporary prosperity was again short-lived. The price of fertilizer and insecticide soon rose faster than the price of rice, and Tonio felt compelled to cut back on their use. Once again his harvest fell back to three and a half tons.

Rice is not the only uncertainty facing Tonio. Mindanao has a divided population of Muslims and Christians. Bands of Muslim and Christian terrorists fight each other in a vicious guerrilla war in the countryside around Tulungatung. Muslims and Christians have been killing each other around Tulungatung for hundreds of years. Although Tulungatung has so far escaped the violence, Tonio fears that peace could be broken any time.

Tonio's religion, a mixture of Catholicism and pagan beliefs, comforts him during bad times and sometimes explains why bad times come. When Tonio developed a fever, he felt haunted by a dwarf in the shape of a beautiful woman. While he was bewitched, he went amok. Finally, Tonio went to an old woman in the village for help. She tied him down and cured him with the help of herbs and a magic fire.[1]

Tonio's life in Tulungatung is a mixture of the modern and the traditional in many ways. The stilt houses give the village a look that hasn't changed in centuries. Yet transistor radios blast forth American-style pop music without end. Tonio enthusiastically pursues a traditional Filipino hobby: cockfighting. He once owned a rooster imported from Texas. It won eight times as Tonio placed bets using money borrowed from his father and uncles. The ninth time, the valuable rooster got its throat cut. Tonio nevertheless was grateful that the rooster had gained him honor among the macho cockfighting crowd.

The vicissitudes of life in the village eventually got to Tonio. "Everything is getting worse again in the barrio. I don't know what you have to do to have a good life here. What is God doing up there ?"

14   Conclusion: The View from Lahore

I'm homesick for a country
To which I've never been before.

American folk song

Here I am again in Lahore, capital of Punjab province, Pakistan. I am here in April 2000 on an analysis of public spending in Punjab province for the World Bank. The provincial government depends for more than three-quarters of its revenues on a national government that has a debt of 94 percent of GDP and large expenditures on things like nuclear weapons and national expressways that nobody uses. The national government hence is squeezing all noninterest, nondefense spending, non–show project spending like transfers to the provinces. With no previous experience of Pakistan besides the scary statistics I have read in World Bank reports, I feel like the clueless advising the helpless.

Lahore has so much vitality, it's overwhelming. Traffic on the roads is a stream of donkey carts, bicycles with two or three people on each one, pedestrians walking in the road, motor-scooters with two to five people on each one (often with a toddler clinging to the handlebars), cars, hand-pushed carts, trucks, motor rickshaws, taxis, tractors pulling overloaded wagons, garishly painted buses packed with people clinging to their sides, all weaving in and out at their respective maximum speeds. People throng the markets in the old city, where the lanes are so narrow that the crowds swallow the car. People buying, people selling, people eating, people cooking. Every street, every lane crammed with shops, each shop crammed with people. This is a private economy with a lot of dynamism.

The Old Fort in Lahore is a reflection of its rich history. Lahore's successive conquerors include the Hindus, the Mughals, the Sikhs, the British, and the Pakistanis. I admire the beautiful mosque and the touching devotion of the believers.

I am invited to attend a wedding in Lahore. The ceremony prior to the wedding, called a *mehndi*, is like a window into another world. In the backyard of a house, there are carpets laid everywhere, with a long red carpet where the groom and then the bride are to enter. The red carpet is flanked by candles and flowers, illuminated by bright lights strung overhead. The groom greets his guests wearing a long white robe with a yellow sash around it. The bride then enters, her face covered with a cloth, another cloth held above her head by four attendants. Her attendants lead her to a hanging swing completely covered with orange flowers, where the groom sits with her. The parents of the bride and the groom take turns feeding sweets to their new in-law.

Throbbing drums start up, and the guests of the groom and those of the bride take turns in wild dancing, each trying to outdo the other. I do my best to participate with my own jerky dancing, like a John Cleese routine.

There is a power outage, and things go dark, but a generator they keep for such emergencies quickly restores the action. There is a lavish meal of Pakistani specialties. I talk to the guests, many of them with Ph.D.s and M.B.A.s from the United States, making money in Lahore. They are elegant, witty, courteous. They only reinforce my image from previous contacts with the Pakistani diaspora of a well-spoken, well-educated, courtly people. This is a beautiful, wonderful culture, with so much potential for creativity and prosperity.

Lahore Amiss

And yet so much has gone wrong in Lahore, Punjab, and Pakistan. Wonderful people, terrible government. The majority of the population is illiterate, ill housed, and ill fed. The government alternates between military dictators and corrupt democrats, each more interested in keeping power at all costs than in bringing prosperity to the masses. The government cannot bring off a simple and cheap measles vaccination program, and yet it can build nuclear weapons. The powerful military endlessly obsesses about disputed territory in Kashmir held since 1947 by their bitter enemy India. Every day the headline in the local paper has something about Kashmir. Yet they make no assault on their own unoccupied territory of prosperity for the masses.

I'm here to lead a fifteen-member team reviewing public services provided by the government of Punjab. I'm fortunate to have a team of field-hardened, well-informed, hard-thinking World Bank staff. It quickly becomes apparent that a corrupt, hierarchical, autocratic bureaucracy has done a miserable job providing public services. The bureaucracy has little incentive to provide services as opposed to filling its own wallets. For example, there were only 102 convictions for irregularities of all kinds in anticorruption courts during the entire period 1985 to 1999, a rather unusual number for a 1-million-strong provincial civil service universally agreed to be corrupt.

Despite decades of foreign aid to improve the lot of the masses, Punjab has some of the poorest social indicators in the world. Although most health problems in the Punjab are easily preventable and despite a major effort to increase services under a donor-supported eight-year-long campaign called the Social Action Program, the province is spending only $1.50 per capita on health. Only half of children are immunized. Only 27 percent of pregnant women receive prenatal care. Tuberculosis is not under control. Half of primary health care facilities reported stock-outs of more than two essential drugs during the last quarter of 1999.

The achievements of the elementary education system of the Punjab are disappointing, even after eight years of intensive efforts to improve the coverage and quality of services under the Social Action Program. The total amounts being spent on education have not risen significantly in inflation-adjusted terms since the program began in 1992: a classic example of reducing domestic spending as aid-supported spending increases. The adult literacy rate remains at about 40 percent in the Punjab, and the rate for women remains at only about 27 percent. The definition of literacy employed almost certainly falls far short of the level of literacy skills required in modern life. Only 41 percent of the highly selective group that made it to the tenth grade passed the matriculation exam in 1999.

The annual per student direct spending on elementary education was the equivalent of $27 per student in 1997–1998, which is on the low side even for poor countries. There is an allocation for teaching materials of about $0.36 per student and $0.36 for operations and maintenance per student. Only 3 percent of the budget goes for nonsalary costs in both elementary and secondary schools. High dropout rates imply that approximately a third of resources devoted to basic education are not contributing to the development of sustained literacy and numeracy skills and thus are being squandered.

Much of the population depends on agriculture, which is also suffering from decrepit public services. The Punjab is blessed with abundant water supplies from the Indus River basin, which it has tapped for over a century with the world's largest irrigation system. Yet highly centralized public sector management of the irrigation system had led to inadequate funds for routine and preventive maintenance and major repairs. As a result, only 35 percent of the water gets from the canal head to the root zone. Inadequate investment in drainage has led to waterlogging and salinity in the soils, lowering crop yields. The price of water is kept artificially low for rich and poor alike, leaving few funds for maintenance. The gap between operations and maintenance requirements and actual expenditure is between 30 and 40 percent. Powerful landlords are assured of getting water, while poor farmers often can irrigate only part of their lands.

The government officials we meet seem genuinely well meaning. The panacea offered by the government is decentralization: let local beneficiaries of public services determine how money should be spent on improving those services. Let mayors be elected by the local people, and so be democratically accountable for their performance. It certainly sounds like an improvement on the overcentralized, top-down bureaucracy that micromanages over 4,000 projects like "canal bridge near village Abbianwala Nankana Sahib." Maybe incentives could improve with decentralization. And yet decentralization is no panacea without more fundamental reforms to the civil service and the system of semifeudal land ownership. The wily civil servants could provide the show of local participation while retaining their all-powerful fiefdoms. Powerful feudal landlords could capture the local governments through their well-honed skills of dominating the peasants. Once again, it is devilishly difficult to get incentives right for creating growth.

I went on an officially sponsored visit of a primary school for girls in Sheikhupura district near Lahore. The school was in a village at the end of a one-lane dirt road. As we arrived, a preschool girl and boy gave each one of us a bouquet of flowers. The older girls were lined up in two columns, each holding a paper plate full of colorful flowers. As we walked between the two columns, they pelted us joyfully with the flowers. Flower covered, we walked into the school.

Other children were sitting politely quiet in their classrooms as we entered the school. Each room was used for two different grades. They were short a room even then, so the first grade held their class outside. Each class stood up as we came into the room. They had no textbooks and no paper or pencil. The headmistress told us that their parents couldn't buy the textbooks and paper until the end of the month, when they get paid. And this was the school the district shows off for visitors!

Incentives for the Players

The rich are different from the poor: they have more money. Trekking through the tropics trying to make poor nations rich has raised more questions than it has answered.

Why if I jet to Geneva do I encounter a shiny prosperity, while a few hours more by plane brings me to Lahore and its poor masses? How did some people (about 900 million of them) in Western Europe, North America, and parts of the Pacific Rim find prosperity, while 5 billion people live in poor nations? Why do 1.2 billion people live in extreme poverty on less than one dollar per day?

We have learned once and for all that there are no magical elixirs to bring a happy ending to our quest for growth. Prosperity happens when all the players in the development game have the right incentives. It happens when government incentives induce technological adaptation, high-quality investment in machines, and high-quality schooling. It happens when donors face incentives that induce them to give aid to countries with good policies where aid will have high payoffs, not to countries with poor policies where aid is wasted. It happens when the poor get good opportunities and incentives, which requires government welfare programs that reward rather than penalize earning income. It happens when politics is not polarized between antagonistic interest groups, but there is a common consensus to invest in the future. Broad and deep development happens when a government that is held accountable for its actions energetically takes up the task of investing in collective goods like health, education, and the rule of law.

To explain development failures, I have told a sequential story of failed incentives. Private firms and families did not invest in the future because government policies such as high black market premiums or high inflation penalized such investments. The poor within each society did not invest in the future because they were matched with other low-productivity people; they require subsidies to their income in order to grow. Governments failed to provide subsidies to the poor and chose policies that penalized growth because polarized factions fought over redistribution of existing income rather than investing in future incomes. Donors weakened government incentives to reform by propping up nonreformist governments with politically motivated aid. Faction-ridden governments faced inadequate incentives to provide subsidies to the poor and to provide public health, education, communications, and transportation services, all of which are crucial for quality of life.

The solutions are a lot more difficult to describe than the problems. The way forward must be to create incentives for growth for the trinity of governments, donors, and individuals.

First, the government. Does the government of each nation face incentives to create private sector growth, or does it face incentives to steal from—and thus repress—private business? In a polarized and undemocratic society, where class-based or ethnically based interest groups are in a vicious competition for loot, the answer is probably the latter. It may not show up as outright corruption; it may mean an interest rate below the inflation rate that implicitly steals the savings of the populace, or it may mean a black market exchange rate many times the officially controlled rate that steals the profits of exporters. In a democratic society with institutions that protect the right of minority interest groups, institutions that protect the rights of private property and individual economic freedoms, governments face the right incentives to create private sector growth. We can envision a world in which governments do not devote themselves to theft, but one in which governments do provide national infrastructure—health clinics, primary schools, well-maintained roads, widespread phone and electricity services—and they do provide assistance to the poor within each society.

Second, the donors. Does each donor give a vested amount of aid to each country, so as to justify next year's aid budget? Do the International Monetary Fund and the World Bank give loans to the Mobutus of this world, or support aid to governments that can present credible intentions to build national infrastructure and help the poor? If both institutions and the other donor organizations are left to themselves, they will likely revert to internal bureaucratic politics determining loans. The act of making loans will be rewarded rather than the act of helping the poor in each country. The solution is to have publicly visible "aid contests" in which each government vies for loans from a common pool on the basis of its track record and its credibly and publicly stated intentions. We can envision a world in which international donors do not give aid just to justify next year's aid budget, but give aid where it will help the poor the most.

Third, private individuals. Private households and businesses sometimes face poor incentives because they have bad governments that expropriate their investments in the future. Even when society-wide incentives for growth are good, the poor face low incentives to grow because one's productivity depends on one's fellows, and the fellows of the poor are usually other poor people. Aid that offers matching grants to the poor with increases in their own income (as opposed to the penalties on increased income in most welfare systems) can help correct these poor incentives. We can envision a world in which the poor are given the benefit of the doubt that they will respond to incentives just as much as the rich do.

I have criticized some actions by the World Bank and International Monetary Fund in this book. You will not be surprised if I nevertheless say there is a need for these institutions. Both institutions include many dedicated, smart, and hard-working people, who spend many arduous days away from home in some tough places around the globe. The World Bank can be a powerful institution to subsidize the world's poor, and the IMF can play a useful role in bailing countries out of the short-run crises that even healthy capitalist economies can encounter.

At a minimum, if we learn nothing else from the quest for growth, we economists who work on poor countries should leave aside some of our past arrogance. The problem of making poor countries rich was much more difficult than we thought. It is much easier to describe the problems facing poor countries than it is to come up with workable solutions to their poverty. The recommendations I have just given are themselves no panacea—they will take patient incremental work and further money to implement. Nothing would be sadder than to give up the quest altogether.

As I think back to my visit to the Pakistani girls' school, in the middle of the beautiful countryside of ripening wheat fields and rushing canals, I think of the flower-pelting schoolgirls without textbooks—hoping the future would bring them better. May the quest for growth over the next fifty years succeed more than it has for the last fifty years, and may more poor countries finally become rich.

Notes

Chapter 1

1. Filmer and Pritchett 1997.

2. This list is from table B.2 of the World Bank; *World Development Report*, 1993, listing those communicable diseases that have higher disability-adjusted life years (DALYs) lost for developing countries.

3. UNICEF 1994, p. 6.

4. World Bank, *World Development Report*, 1993, p. 224.

5. Demographic Data for Development Project 1987, p. 23.

6. UNICEF 1993, p. 4.

7. World Bank, *World Development Report*, 1993, p. 74.

8. UNICEF 1994, p. 26.

9. World Bank, *World Development Report*, 1993, p. 77.

10. UNICEF 1994, p. 6.

11. World Bank, *World Development Report*, 1993, p. 73.

12. UNICEF 1993, p. 12; 1995, p. 13

13. UNICEF, 1994, p. 26.

14. World Bank, *World Development Report*, 1993, p. 74.

15. Muhuri and Rutstein 1994, table A.6.4, p. 67.

16. Narayan et al. 2000a.

17. Demographic and Health Services, 1994, p. 55.

18. Narayan et al. 2000a.

19. Narayan et al. 2000a.

20. Narayan et al. 1999, chap. 2, p. 9; chap. 6, p. 10.

21. Narayan et al. 1999, chapter 6, p. 12.

22. Kidron and Segal 1995.

23. Narayan et al. 1999, chap. 6, p. 24.

24. UNICEF, *State of the World's Children*, 1996, p. 14.

25. Humana 1992; Dollar and Gatti 1999. Easterly 1999a found educational equality for women improved strongly with higher income in the long run, but did not necessarily improve with growth in the short run.

26. All of these quotes are from Narayan et al. 2000a, chap. 5.

27. Ravallion and Chen 1997.

28. Dollar and Kraay 2000.

Intermezzo: In Search of a River

1. Jacob 1881.

2. Cresap and Cresap 1987, p. 31.

3. Cresap and Cresap 1987, p. 32.

4. Bailey, 1944, p. 34.

5. Bailey, 1994, p. 40.

6. Bailey, 1994, p. 179.

7. Bailey, 1994, p. 51.

8. Cresap and Cresap 1987, p. 79.

9. Cresap and Cresap 1987, p. 76.

10. Rorabaugh 1981, p. 141.

11. Cresap and Cresap 1987, p. 91.

12. Cresap and Cresap 1987, p. 87.

13. Fischer 1991, p. 754.

14. Cresap and Cresap 1987, p. 100.

Chapter 2

1. Rooney 1988, p. 133.

2. Rooney 1988, p. 5.

3. Rooney 1988, p. 88.

4. Rooney 1988, p. 137.

5. Seers and Ross 1952.

6. Rooney 1988, pp. 4–6.

7. Frempong 1982, p. 130.

8. Rooney 1988, pp. 154–168.

9. Kamarck 1967, p. 247.

10. Frempong 1982, pp. 84, 85, 87, 126.

11. *Ending the Hunger 1985*; USAID 2000.

12. Demographic Data for Development Project 1987, table 8, p. 90.

13. Rimmer 1992, p. 4.

14. UNICEF, *Progress of Nations* 1995, p. 14.

15. Domar 1957, pp. 7–8.

16. Note that the theory says that investment net of depreciation should be the relevant concept. Most economists who have used the Harrod-Domar model ever since have erroneously used gross rather than net investment.

17. Marshall 1946, p. 4.

18. Arndt 1987, p. 33.

19. Arndt 1987, p. 49.

20. Lewis 1954, p. 139.

21. Domar 1957, p. 255.

22. Kuznets 1963, p. 35. This was a rare example of actually testing the Harrod-Domar-Lewis-Rostow ICOR model. There was afterward a curious literature (e.g., Patel 1968; Vanek and Studenmund 1968) noting the strong inverse correlation between growth and the ICOR (investment/growth). Leibenstein (1966) and Boserup (1969) were clear-headed enough to point out that this negative correlation would come about mechanically if there was a low short-run correlation between growth and investment.

23. Edwards 1995, p. 224.

24. Wiles 1953, Thorp 1956.

25. Rostow 1960, p. 37.

26. Defined as members of the Organization for Economic Cooperation and Development (OECD), which includes Western Europe, North America, Australia, New Zealand, and Japan. Data are from OECD.

27. Bauer 1972, p. 127.

28. Bhagwati 1966, pp. 69, 170, 219.

29. Chenery and Strout 1966 called their model the two-gap model. The investment-savings gap was one of the two gaps; the other was the trade gap, which ex post is equal to the investment gap but ex ante might be a constraint in a shortage-prone economy with fixed prices. I'll ignore the other gap throughout this chapter, since it was less influential in development practice once market-friendly policies came into vogue and made shortage prone economies less likely.

30. Correspondence with John Holsen, December 17, 1996.

31. Correspondence with Nick Carter and Norman Hicks, December 16, 1996.

32. Meier 1995, p. 153.

33. Todaro 2000.

34. World Bank 1993a.

35. OECD data.

36. World Bank, 1993a, p. 32.

37. World Bank 1996, p. 23.

38. World Bank 1995a, pp. 10, 23.

39. Inter-American Development Bank 1995, p. 19

40. World Bank 2000b.

41. IMF 1996a, pp. 228, 239.

42. World Bank 1993b, p. 20.

43. World Bank 1997a, p. 15.

44. European Bank for Reconstruction and Development (EBRD) 1995, pp. 5, 66, 71. The EBRD's chief economist, Nicholas Stern, strongly denied any use of the Harrod-Domar model in EBRD business, these quotations notwithstanding.

45. The Soviets' own linear growth-investment relation fell apart. In the 1960s, 1970s, and 1980s, growth rates were falling even though investment rates kept rising. Easterly and Fischer 1995.

46. I am using data in domestic prices for investment, since overseas development assistance is not purchasing power adjusted. When I put all the data together I will be forced to mix purchasing power parity and domestic price data. The data on overseas development assistance are from the OECD.

47. These results are like those of Blomström, Lipsey, and Zejan 1996, who found with five-year periods that investment was a function of lagged growth, but growth was not a function of lagged investment.

48. These calculations are done with Summers and Heston 1991 data at international prices for both output and investment. However, similar results obtain using World Bank national accounts at domestic prices

49. World Bank 1998, p. 2.

50. World Bank 2000b

51. World Bank 2000c.

52. I used Summers and Heston 1991 GDP and investment rates. For aid to GDP, I used the numbers from the OECD for overseas development assistance in current prices. This is not ideal, since aid to GDP is not PPP adjusted and so how much investment it would buy could be over- or underestimated.

Intermezzo: Parmila

1. Quoted and paraphrased from Narayan et al. 2000a.

Chapter 3

1. Hadjmichael et al. 1996, p. 1.

2. Inter-American Development Bank 1995, p. 19

3. Middle Eastern Department, 1996, p. 9.

4. World Bank 1993d, p. 191.

5. United Nations, 1996, p. 8.

6. Solow 1957.

7. U.S. Statistical Abstract Calculation 1995.

8. The advantages of specialization have been emphasized by economists from Adam Smith to Paul Romer (1992).

9. Groliers on Compuserve, article on Luddites.

10. Baumol 1986 discusses data on long-run unemployment for the United Kingdom, United States, and Germany.

11. United Nations Development Programs *Human Development Report*, 1996, p. 2; 1993 HDR pp. 35–36 "Growth without employment."

12. Belser 2000.

13. United Nations Development Programs Human Development Report 1996.

14. Lucas 1990. I use a capital share of 0.4 as Lucas did. The ratio of capital stocks would have to be $(15)^{\wedge}(1/4)$, which is 871.

15. Pritchett 1997b.

16. Baumol 1986.

17. De Long 1988.

18. See also the study by Pack and Page 1994, which also gave an important role to capital accumulation and showed a fairly low total factor productivity growth estimate for Singapore.

19. Klenow and Rodríguez-Clare 1997.

20. Easterly and Levine 2000.

21. Data from King and Levine 1994.

22. Devarajan, Easterly, and Pack 1999.

23. Hsieh 1999.

24. World Bank, 1995a, p. 35.

Intermezzo: Dry Cornstalks

1. Tremblay. and Capon 1988, pp. 197–198.

Chapter 4

1. From *Bulletin: The Major Project in the Field of Education in Latin America and the Caribbean* 1990, p. 9.

2. Mayor 1990, p. 445.

3. World Bank, *World Development Report*, 1997, p. 52.

4. Verspoor 1990, p. 21.

5. The phrase is taken from Pritchett 1999.

6. Pritchett 1999.

7. One recent study (Krueger and Lindahl 1999) attributed Pritchett's findings to measurement error in educational attainment. But Pritchett carefully controls for measurement error, so his findings are not vulnerable to that charge.

8. Benhabib and Spiegel 1994.

9. Barro and Sala-i-Martin 1995 and Barro 1991 among others. For a useful survey of findings on education and growth, see Judson 1996, table 1.

10. Barro and Sala-i-Martin 1995 discuss this effect.

11. Klenow and Rodríguez-Clare 1997, p. 94. Note that Barro and Sala-i-Martin 1995 also find no relationship between growth per capita and the change in secondary schooling and higher schooling years.

12. Bils and Klenow 1998.

13. Bils and Klenow 1998.

14. Mankiw 1995, p. 295. Mankiw drew on earlier work by Barro, Mankiw, and Sala-i-Martin 1995 and by Mankiw, Romer, and Weil 1992.

15. Young 1992, 1995; World Bank 1993d.

16. Barro and Sala-i-Martin 1995, p. 431. See also Barro 1991.

17. This point was first made by Klenow and Rodríguez-Clare 1997.

18. Romer 1995. I am reproducing Romer's calculation with slightly different human and physical capital shares, using the shares assumed by Mankiw.

19. Carrington and Detragiache 1998.

20. Union Bank of Switzerland 1994.

21. Psacharopoulos 1994, p. 1332.

22. Murphy, Shleifer, and Vishny 1991.

23. Narayan et al. 2000b.

24. Talbot 1998, p. 339.

25. Husain 1999, pp. 384, 404.

26. Pritchett and Filmer 1999.

Intermezzo: Without a Refuge

1. Burr and Collins 1995, p. 15; see also Deng 1995.

2. UNICEF *State of the World's Children*, 96, p. 21.

3. http://www.reliefweb.int/irin/cea/weekly/19991119.htm#SUDAN: Refugees flee ethnic clashes to Uganda, Kenya.

4. http://www.reliefweb.int/irin/cea/countrystories/sudan/20000315.htm.

Chapter 5

1. Ehrlich 1968, pp. 74, 88.

2. World Bank World Development Indicators 2000; Simon 1995, p. 397.

3. http://www.worldbank.org/data/wdi/pdfs/tab6_4.pdf.

4. Ehrlich 1968, p. 44; World Development Indicators 2000, table 3.3.

5. Ehrlich and Ehrlich, 1990, p. 185.

6. Data from Stars World Tables on CD-ROM; http://www.worldbank.org/data/wdi/pdfs/tab2_1.pdf

7. World Bank, *World Development Report*, 1984, p. 3.

8. http://www.worldwatch.org/alerts/990408.html.

9. World Watch Institute 2000, p. 5.

10. http://www.worldwatch.org/alerts/990408.html.

11. http://www.populationaction.org/why_pop/whyfood.htm.

12. http://www.populationinstitute.org/issue.html.

13. http://www.worldwatch.org/alerts/990902.html.

14. http://www.un.org/ecosocdev/geninfo/populatin/icpd.htm#intro.

15. http://www.worldwatch.org/alerts/990902.html.

16. http://www.populationinstitute.org/thehague.html.

17. http://www.undp.org/popin/unpopcom/32ndsess/gass/state/secgeneral.pdf.

18. http://www.zpg.org/Reports_Publications/Reports/report83.html.

19. —UNICEF, *State of the World's Children*, 1992.

20. http://www.info.usaid.gov/pop_health/pop/popunmetneed.htm.

21. http://www.condoms.net/cgi-bin/SoftCart.cgi/condoms/crown.html?L+csense+ hGSb8034+948055430.

22. Pritchett 1994.

23. Kelley and Schmidt, 1995, 1996; Kling and Pritchett 1994.

24. Levine and Renelt 1992.

25. Kling and Pritchett 1994.

26. I regressed per capita growth decade averages from the 1960s through the 1990s on the black market premium, the ratio of M2 to GDP, inflation, real exchange rate overvaluation, secondary enrollment, initial income, terms of trade gain as a percentage of GDP, growth of OECD trading partners, and population growth. Population growth had a coefficient of .09 with a t-statistic of .4.

27. These facts are taken from Kling and Pritchett 1994.

28. Kremer 1993b pointed out that the Boserup idea is different from the Kuznets-Simon idea, in that the Boserup principle would predict that higher income would lower population pressure and thus slow technological change, which is contradicted by historical experience.

29. http://www.census.gov/ipc/www/worldhis.html; Kremer 1993b.

30. Population Action International, 1995.

31. The argument of the preceding paragraphs is based on Becker, Murphy, and Tamura 1990. However, many other researchers and theories suggest a negative relationship between per capita income and fertility. The idea of a low income–high population growth trap goes back to Nelson 1956.

32. Lucas 1998. My argument does not necessarily follow that of Lucas, so the text here should not be taken as an exposition of Lucas's views. I also draw on Jones 1999.

Intermezzo: Tomb Paintings

1. Critchfield, 1981, pp. 143–161.

2. Critchfield 1994, p. 136.

3. Critchfield 1994, p. 142.

Chapter 6

1. World Bank, *World Development Report*, 1983, p. 27, and *World Development Report* 1997, p. 221. I have converted GDP growth projections to per capita growth projections by dividing by the actual population growth rate.

2. World Bank and IMF 1983.

3. Clausen 1986.

4. Corbo, Goldstein, and Khan 1987.

5. Ghosh 1994.

6. Easterly 2000b.

7. Schadler et al. 1995, p. 39.

8. I took a geometric average of inflation across countries for each year, then cumu-lated geometrically across years.

9. Grosh 1991, pp. 22, 144ff.

10. p. 43 World Bank 1983.

11. World Bank 1989b, p. 11.

12. International Monetar, Fund 1996c, p. 35.

13. World Bank 1988c, vol. 1, p. 3

14. World Bank 1998b.

15. World Bank 1996, p. 4.

16. World Bank 1994c, p. 27.

17. World Bank 1983, p. 35.

18. World Bank 1979, p. 51; see also p. 17.

19. Mallet 1998.

20. Easterly 1999d.

21. Alesina and Perotti 1995 found that deficit adjustments made by cutting con-sumption were more lasting than those reduced in other ways, which is in accordance with the argument of this section.

22. The 1986 Government Finance Statistics Manual (IMF 1986, p. 31) recommended cash rather than accrual accounting. Current practice uses a mixture of cash and accrual accounting. When arrears become a serious problem, the conventional approach to deficits in developing countries will often show them explicitly as a financing item for an accrual-based deficit target. The 1996 Government Finance Statistics Manual (IMF 1996d, p. 16) recommended accrual accounting. However, arrears still can be used to temporarily meet a gross public debt target, since they are not included in the gross public debt.

23. Kee 1987, p. 11.

24. Kopits and Craig 1998.

25. White and Wildavsky 1989, p. 514.

26. Luis Serven suggested the state enterprise subsidy-to-loan conversion idea to me. The Egyptian example is from World Bank 1995a, p. 84.

27. Mackenzie and Stella 1996.

28. Pension reserves are also used to cover health costs of workers covered by social insurance programs. This further depletes the reserves. The Venezuelan government invested between 10 and 30 percent of pension reserves in the hospitals of the social security system. Now the government must face the rising expenditures on both health and pensions as the population ages with a depleted pension reserve fund (World Bank 1994b, p. 47).

29. World Bank 1994b, p. 128.

30. Sargent and Wallace 1985.

31. This section was based on Svensson 1997.

32. *Economist*, August 19, 1995.

Chapter 7

1. World Bank 1998a, p. 56

2. Dupuy 1988, p. 116; Lundahl 1992, pp. 39, 41, 244.

3. Dommen 1989; Winkler 1933, p. 22; Wynne 1951, pp. 5–7.

4. *International Herald Tribune*, June 14, 1999, p. 1; *Financial Times*, June 21, 1999. 3. See the World Bank web site on the HIPC Initiative: www.worldbank.org/hipc.

5. http://www.jubilee2000uk.org/main.html.

6. The quote is from UNCTAD 1967, p. 3.

7. World Bank 1979, pp. 7–8; UNCTAD 1983, p. 3.

8. World Bank 1981, p. 129.

9. World Bank 1984, p. 46.

10. World Bank 1986, p. 41.

11. World Bank 1988a, p. xix. The general literature started noticing low-income African debt at about the same time. See Lancaster and Williamson 1986; Mistry 1988; Greene 1989; Parfitt and Riley 1989; Humphreys and Underwood 1989; Husain and Underwood 1991; Nafziger 1993. For more recent compilations of analysis, see Iqbal and Kanbur 1997; Brooks et al. 1998.

12. World Bank 1991a, p. 176.

13. World Bank 1988b, p. xxxviii.

14. World Bank 1989, p. 31.

15. World Bank 1990, p. 29.

16. World Bank 1991b, p. 31.

17. World Bank 1993c, p. 6.

18. World Bank 1994a, p. 42.

19. Boote et al. 1997, pp. 126, 129.

20. World Bank 1999, p. 76, and the web site www.worldbank.org/hipc. The seven countries are Bolivia, Burkina Faso, Côte d'Ivoire, Guyana, Mali, Mozambique, and Uganda. According to the Bank's web site, "Ethiopia, Guinea-Bissau, Nicaragua, Mauritania and Tanzania have completed a preliminary review and could qualify for billions more in debt relief."

21. World Bank 1988c, vol 2, p. 78.

22. Chamley and Ghanem, 1994.

23. International Monetary Fund 1998, p. 29.

24. World Bank 1988c, vol 1.

25. site http://www.worldbank.org/afr/ci2.htm.

26. International Monetary Fund 1999.

27. Economist Intelligence Unit 1999.

Intermezzo: Cardboard House

1. Gonzales de la Rocha 1994, pp. 94–95, 122–123, 236–237, 241, 248.

Chapter 8

1. I have in mind most directly the AK model of Rebelo 1991.

2. See Romer 1986, 1990, 1992, 1993.

3. Employment in 1978–1979 according to Bangladesh Bureau of Statistics 1985, p. 418 (production workers Wearing Apparel except footwear). World Bank 1987 gives the following as averages in millions for Bangladeshi ready-made garment exports over 1972–1975 and 1975–1980: respectively, −0.00 and 0.17.

4. Rhee and Belot 1990, p. 8.

5. 1980 exports from International Monetary Fund, International Finance Statistics yearbook, series 77aa d.

6. World Bank 1996b, p. 14: 54 percent of $3.45 billion in exports in 1994–1995.

7. Rhee and Belot 1990, pp. 6–7.

8. Rhee and Belot 1990, p. 12.

9. Rhee and Belot 1990, p. 17.

10. From their web site at http://www.empire-capital.com/maxpages/Back_to_Back_LCS.

11. The O-ring metaphor and the accompanying theory are due to Kremer 1993a. Shuttle information from http://www.ksc.nasa.gov/shuttle/missions/51-l/mission-51-l.html.

12. Values and rankings of richest and poorest (according to personal income per capita) from U.S. Census Bureau City and County Databook.

13. Lucas 1988, p. 39.

14. Rauch 1993.

15. Grubel and Scott 1977.

16. World Bank, *World Development Report*, 1995, p. 11.

17. *Statistical Abstract of the United States*, 1995, figures for 1992, current dollar GDP 6020 billion, agriculture, forestry and fishing $116 billion.

18. World Bank, *World Development Report*, 1996, p. 210 (data for 1994). Just to confirm droughts and terrain, see p. 34 World Bank 1987b.

19. World Bank, *World Development Report*, 1996, p. 88 (data for 1995).

20. This kind of self-fulfilling discrimination has long been postulated before by distinguished economists like Kenneth Arrow and Glen Loury, but Kremer was the first to apply it more generally to skill matching and economic growth.

21. *Statistical Abstract of the United States*, 1995, tables 52, 724.

22. Kosmin and Lachman 1993, p. 260.

23. Lipset 1997, pp. 151–152.

24. Psacharopoulos and Patrinos 1994, p. 6.

25. Psacharopoulos and Patrinos 1994, p. 37.

26. Patrinos 1997.

27. Narayan et al. 2000a.

28. *New York Times*, September 18, 1999.

29. Easterly and Levine 2000.

30. Easterly and Levine 2000. See also Brookings Institution Center on Urban and Metropolitan Policy 1999.

31. Narayan et al. 2000a.

32. Other stories of poverty traps come from Azariadis and Drazen 1991; Becker, Murphy, and Tamura 1990; and Murphy, Shleifer, and Vishny 1989.

Intermezzo: War and Memory

1. Critchfield, 1994, pp. 169–189.

Chapter 9

1. http://econ161.berkeley.edu/E_Sidebars/E-conomy_figures2.html.

2. http://www.duke.edu/~mccann/q-tech.htm#Death of Distance.

3. http://econ161.berkeley.edu/OpEd/virtual/technet/An_E-conomy.

4. World Bank, *World Development Report*, 1998–1999, pp. 3–5, 57.

5. The following history is taken from Nordhaus 1994.

6. Jovanovic 2000. See also Mokyr 1990, p. 22.

7. Mokyr 1990, pp. 21–22, 29.

8. Mokyr 1990, p. 161.

9. See Jones 1999 for a description of growth in ancient empires. He notes that Sung China apparently had both technical progress and rising per capita income from the tenth to the thirteenth centuries, but then stagnation followed in Ming China and its successor to the nineteenth century (see also Young 1993). Mokyr 1990 is the source of the general description of Chinese technological prowess.

10. Hall and Jones 1999.

11. Davis and Haltiwanger 1998, fig. 6.

12. Schumpeter 1942, p. 82.

13. Aghion and Howitt 1992, 1999.

14. http://www-groups.dcs.st-and.ac.uk/~history/Quotations/Newton.html.

15. Greenwood and Jovanovic 1998.

16. David 1990.

17. http://econ161.berkeley.edu/E_Sidebars/E-conomy_figures2.html.

18. http://www.preservenet.com/endgrowth/EndGrowth.html.

19. Benfield, Raimi, and Chen, 1999.

20. Kennedy 1993, pp. 13, 15.

21. Daly 1992; Zolotas 1981; Douthwaite 1992; Trainer 1989; Wachtel 1983; Mishan 1967.

22. Mokyr 1990, p. 263.

23. Mokyr 1990, pp. 142–143.

24. Mokyr 1990, pp. 263–265.

25. This paragraph is based on Aghion and Howitt 1999, pp. 313–316.

26. Yonekura 1994, p. 207.

27. Mokyr 1990, p. 118.

28. Yonekura 1994, pp. 219–222.

29. Lieberman and Johnson 1999.

30. UNIDO, Industrial statistics at 3-digit level, World Bank on-line database.

31. D'Costa 1999, p. 3.

32. Jovanovic and Nyarko 1996. The "advantages of backwardness" is an idea that goes back to Alexander Gerschenkron.

33. Borensztein, de Gregorio, and Lee 1998; Blomström, Lipsey, and Zejan 1994.

34. Blomström and Sjöholm 1998.

35. Lee 1995.

36. http://www.wired.com/wired/archive/4.02/bangalore_pr.html.

37. Stremlau 1996.

38. Mokyr 1990, p. 162.

39. Mokyr 1990, p. 164.

40. http://www.teleport.com/~samc/hdtv/.

41. This possibility was noted by Young 1993.

42. Brad de Long, http://econ161.berkeley.edu/E_Sidebars/E-conomy_figures2.html.

Intermezzo

1. Quoted and paraphrased from Narayan et al. 2000a.

Chapter 10

1. This and previous paragraphs paraphrased from Narayan et al. 2000a.

2. World Bank, *World Development Report*, 2000–2001, consultation draft, p. 6.24.

3. http://www.worldbank.org/html/today/archives/html/sep13-17-99.htm#9-14.

4. http://www.worldbank.org/aids-econ/africa/fire.htm.

5. http://www.worldbank.org/aids-econ/africa/fire.htm.

6. UNAIDS 1999.

7. Red Cross 1995, pp. 99, 104.

8. Income per capita is from Summers and Heston 1999; growth per capita data are from World Bank on-line data.

9. http://wb.eiu.com/search_view.asp?from_page=composite&doc_id=EI541397&topicid=VE.

10. *New York Times*, December 20, 1999.

11. Easterly et al. 1993, pp. 468–469.

12. Wanniski, 1998 pp. 255, 260.

13. See Slemrod 1995 and Easterly and Rebelo 1993. For the formal sector, see Chamley and Ghanem 1995.

14. Dunn and Pelecchio 1990 still show a top rate of 40 percent in 1986, compared to Wanniski's 37 percent. Gwartney and Lawson 1995 shows 45 percent from 1979 to 1989.

15. Per capita growth 1979–1994 from World Bank national accounts.

16. Quotes from Easterly 1995.

17. Peters and Waterman 1982, p. 23.

18. Peters and Waterman 1982, pp. 26, 318.

19. Peters and Waterman 1982, p. xxi.

20. *Los Angeles Times*, October 2, 1995.

21. The other was Akeem Olajuwon, who did become a star player but has yet to bring his team a championship—in contrast to the six championships the Bulls won with Michael Jordan.

22. Lincoln 1989, p. 384.

23. Terms of trade loss is calculated as: (Percentage change in export prices) × (exports/GDP) − percentage change in import prices × (imports/GDP).

24. Brundtland Commission 1987, pp. 67, 131.

25. Lipsey 1994.

26. Easterly 2000.

27. Rescher 1995, pp. 8–9.

28. Narayan et al. 2000b.

Intermezzo: Favela Life

1. Critchfield 1981, pp. 13–15.

Chapter 11

1. Bruno 1993, p. 32.

2. Bruno 1993, p. 101.

3. Bruno 1993, p. 32.

4. Bruno 1993, p. 117.

5. Listing all high-inflation episodes 1970–1994 for Bruno and Easterly 1998, excluding those with obvious wars.

6. Bruno and Easterly 1998, pp. 8–9.

7. World Currency Yearbook (for 1985, 1990–1993); Wood 1988 (filling in missing observations in the entire sample).

8. Little et al. 1993, p. 195.

9. Reuters, August 9, 1982; World Bank, World Debt Tables 1996, p. 314.

10. Many authors have found a correlation between severely negative real interest rates and growth. See King and Levine 1992; Gelb 1989; Easterly 1993; and Roubini and Sala-i-Martin 1992.

11. I am following Edwards 1993 in describing this history.

12. This is the median least-squares growth from 1960 to 1998 in the terms of trade of sixty-three low- and middle-income countries that have at least thirty years of observations.

13. Lipsey 1994.

14. See Easterly 1993.

15. Sachs and Warner 1995.

16. Dollar 1992.

17. Lee 1993.

18. Lee 1995.

19. Harrison 1996.

20. Edwards 1998.

21. Frankel and Romer 1999.

22. Rodriguez and Rodrik 2000.

23. This was shown by Levine and Renelt 1992.

24. Husain 1999, p. 74.

25. World Bank 1997b.

26. Reinikka and Svensson 1999.

27. Maier 2000.

28. World Bank, *World Development Report*, Private Sector Survey, 1997.

29. Loayza 1996.

30. World Bank, *World Development Report*, 1977, pp. 30, 31.

31. World Bank, *World Development Report*, 1997, p. 31.

32. Jha, Ranson, and Bobadilla 1996.

33. Easterly and Rebelo 1993.

34. Easterly and Levine 1997; Canning 1999.

35. World Bank, *World Development Report*, 1997, p. 17.

36. Gyamfi 1992.

37. Rebelo and Stokey 1995.

38. Easterly, Loayza, and Montiel, 1997; Barro 1997.

39. Easterly and Levine 1997.

40. Easterly, Loayza, and Montiel 1997.

Intermezzo: Florence and Veronica

1. *New York Times*, September 18, 1998, p. A12.

Chapter 12

1. Easterly and Fischer 2000.

2. Ray 1998.

3. Narayan et al. 2000a, chap. 6, p. 11.

4. Theobald 1990, p. 55.

5. Theobald 1990, p. 68.

6. *New York Times*, August 14, 1998.

7. Dow Jones International News Service, July 29, 1998.

8. *New York Times*, July 17, 1998.

9. Wade 1982, pp. 292–293, 305.

10. Alfiler and Concepcion 1986, p. 38.

11. *Financial Times*, August 1, 1998 p. 3; Associated Press, August 2, 1998.

12. Alfiler and Concepcion 1986, p. 42.

13. Theobald 1990, p. 97.

14. *Washington Post*, June 9, 1998 p. A1, August 17, 1998 p. A13.

15. Rose-Ackerman 1997b, p. 13.

16. Theobald 1990, p. 97.

17. Mauro (1995, 1996) was the first in the recent literature to document the links between corruption and investment or growth. He found the association between corruption and growth, and between corruption and investment, to be robust to the inclusion of other control variables and to controlling for the possible endogeneity of corruption.

18. This analysis is based on Shleifer and Vishny 1993.

19. Svensson 2000.

20. Mauro 1996 also notes this link.

21. Ades and Di Tella 1994.

22. The data on institutions are from Knack and Keefer 1995, who found a link between institutional quality and growth.

Intermezzo: Discrimination in Palanpur

1. Drèze and Sharma 1998.

Chapter 13

1. Mikell 1989.

2. Wetzel 1995, p. 197.

3. Bates 1981.

4. Frimpong-Ansah 1991, p. 95.

5. The source for the Ghana story is Easterly and Levine 1997; consult them for further references.

6. Leith 1974.

7. The measure of inequality is the Gini coefficient. The data and results on land inequality and growth are from Deininger and Squire 1998; others who have found a negative relationship between inequality and growth include Alesina and Rodrik 1994; Persson and Tabellini 1994; Perotti 1996; and Clarke 1995. A contrarian positive inequality and growth result is found by Forbes 1998, 2000, using fixed effects to remove country averages; however, Deininger and Olinto 2000 find a negative effect of *land* inequality on growth even using fixed effects.

8. Easterly, 1999b. This result comes from a regression of democracy (political rights measured by the Gastil index) and civil liberties on the share of the middle class and ethnic heterogeneity.

9. Husain 1999, p. 359.

10. Easterly 1999b, 2000b.

11. Bell-Fialkoff 1996, pp. 10–11

12. Bell-Fialkoff 1996, pp. 10–11.

13. Gurr 1994.

14. *New York Times*, February 22, 2000.

15. The foregoing paragraphs are paraphrased from Narayan et al. 2000b.

16. Miguel 1999.

17. Easterly, 1999b.

18. Alesina, Baqir, and Easterly 1999. Sample of 1,397 counties with populations greater than 25,000.

19. Alesina, Baqir, and Easterly 1999. See also Luttmer 1997.

20. Poterba 1998.

21. Goldin and Katz 1998.

22. Gould and Palmer 1988, p. 427.

23. Wilson 1996, pp. 193, 202.

24. Athukorala and Jayasuriya, 1994.

25. http://flag.blackened.net/revolt/mexico/reports/five_years.html.

26. Benjamin 1996, pp. 246–247.

27. Benjamin 1996, pp. 223, 242, 249.

28. Talbot 1998, p. 24.

29. Litwack 1999, pp. 281, 286.

30. Litwack 1999.

31. Alesina and Summers 1993; Cukierman, Webb, and Neyapti 1992.

32. Alesina 1996.

33. Easterly 2000b.

34. Easterly December 1999b.

35. This figure refers to the population of either Rome itself or Italy, at the time of Augustus. See http://www.ucd.ie/%7Eclassics/96/Madden96.html.

36. http://www.sscnet.ucla.edu/southasia/History/Mughals/mughals.html   and http://pasture.ecn.purdue.edu/~agenhtml/agenmc/china/scengw.html.

37. Anand and Kanbur 1993; Ravallion 1997.

Intermezzo: Violent for Centuries

1. Critchfield, 1981, chap. 5, pp. 51–60.

References and Further Reading

Ades, Alberto, and Rafael Di Tella. 1994. "Competition and Corruption." Oxford University Institute of Economics and Statistics Discussion Paper 169.

Aghion, P., and P. Howitt. 1992. "A Model of Growth Through Creative Destruction." *Econometrica* 60, no. 2 (March).

Aghion, P., and P. Howitt. 1999. *Endogenous Growth Theory*. Cambridge, Mass.: MIT Press.

Ajayi, S. Ibi. 1997. "An Analysis of External Debt and Capital Flight in the Severely Indebted Low-Income Countries." In Z. Iqbal and R. Kanbur, eds., *External Finance for Low-Income Countries*. Washington, D.C.: International Monetary Fund.

Alesina, Alberto. 1996. "Fiscal Discipline and the Budget Process." *American Economic Review, Papers and Proceedings* 86 (May): 401–407.

Alesina, A., R. Baqir, and W. Easterly. 1999. "Public Goods and Ethnic Divisions." *Quarterly Journal of Economics* 114, no. 4 (November): 1243–1284.

Alesina, Alberto, and Roberto Perotti. 1995. "Fiscal Expansions and Adjustments in OECD Countries." *Economic Policy* 20:205–248.

Alesina, Alberto, and Dani Rodrik. 1994. "Distributive Politics and Economic Growth." *Quarterly Journal of Economics* 109, no. 2 (May): 465–490.

Alesina, Alberto, and Lawrence H. Summers. 1993. "Central Bank Independence and Macroeconomic Performance: Some Comparative Evidence." *Journal of Money, Credit and Banking* 25 (May): 151–162.

Alfiler, Ma., and P. Concepcion. 1986. "The Process of Bureaucratic Corruption in Asia: Emerging Patterns." In Ledivina V. Carino, ed., *Bureaucratic Corruption in Asia: Causes, Consequences, and Controls*. Quezon City, Philippines: JMC Press.

Anand, Sudhir, and S. M. R. Kanbur. 1993. "The Kuznets Process and the Inequality-Development Relationship." *Journal of Development Economics* 40, no. 1 (February): 25–52.

Arndt, H. W. 1987. *Economic Development: The History of an Idea*. Chicago: University of Chicago Press.

Athukorala, Premachandra, and Sisira Jayasuriya. 1994. *Macroeconomic Policies, Crises, and Growth in Sri Lanka, 1969–1990*. Washington, D.C.: World Bank.

Avramovic, Dragoslav. 1955. *Postwar Economic Growth in Southeast Asia*. E.C. 48, International Bank for Reconstruction and Development. Washington, D.C. October 10.

Ayittey, George B. N. 1998. *Africa in Chaos*. New York: St. Martin's Press.

Azariadis, Costas, and Allan Drazen. 1990. "Threshold Externalities in Economic Development." *Quarterly Journal of Economics* 105, no. 2 (May): 501–526.

Bailey, Kenneth P. 1944. *Thomas Cresap, Maryland Frontiersman*. Boston: Christopher Publishing House.

Bangladesh Bureau of Statistics. 1985. *Statistical Yearbook of Bangladesh 1984–85*. Government of the People's Republic of Bangladesh. Dhaka.

Bank for International Settlements 1995/96. 1996. *66th Annual Report*. Basel. 1996.

Barro, Robert J. 1991 "Economic Growth in a Cross Section of Countries." *Quarterly Journal of Economics* 106 (May): 407–443.

Barro, Robert. 1997. *Determinants of Economic Growth: A Cross-Country Empirical Study*. Cambridge, Mass.: MIT Press.

Barro, Robert J., N. Gregory Mankiw, and Xavier Sala-i-Martin. 1995. "Capital Mobility in Neoclassical Models of Growth." *American Economic Review* 85, no. 1 (March): 103–115.

Barro, Robert J., and Xavier Sala-i-Martin. 1992. "Convergence." *Journal of Political Economy* 100, no. 2 (April): 223–251.

Barro, Robert, and Xavier Sala-i-Martin. 1995. *Economic Growth*. New York: McGraw-Hill.

Barro, Robert J., and Xavier Sala-i-Martin. 1997. "Technological Diffusion, Convergence." *Journal of Economic Growth* 2, no. 1 (March): 1–26.

Bates, Robert H. 1981. *Markets and States in Tropical Africa: The Political Basis of Agricultural Policies*. Berkeley: University of California Press.

Bauer, P. T. 1972. *Dissent on Development: Studies and Debates in Development Economics*. Cambridge, Mass.: Harvard University Press.

Baumol, William J. 1986. "Productivity Growth, Convergence, and Welfare: What the Long Run Data Show." *American Economic Review* 76, no. 5 (December): 1072–1085.

Bayoumi, Tamim, David T. Coe , and Elhanan Helpman. 1999. "R&D Spillovers and Global Growth." *Journal of International Economics* 47:399–428.

Becker, Gary S., Kevin M Murphy, and Robert Tamura. 1990. "Human Capital, Fertility, and Economic Growth." *Journal of Political Economy* 98, no. 5 (October): S12–37.

Bell-Fialkoff, Andrew. 1996. *Ethnic Cleansing*. New York: St. Martin's Press.

Belser, Patrick. 2000. "Vietnam: On the Road to Labor-intensive Growth." World Bank Policy Research Paper 2389. July.

Benfield, F. Kaid, Matthew D. Raimi, and Donald D. T. Chen. 1999. *Once There Were Greenfields: How Urban Sprawl Is Undermining Americas's Environment, Economy, and Social Fabric*. New York: Natural Resources Defense Council.

Benhabib, Jess, and Mark Spiegel. 1994. "Role of Human Capital in Economic Development: Evidence from Aggregate Cross-Country Data." *Journal of Monetary Economics* 34 (October): 143–173.

Benjamin, Thomas. 1996. *A Rich Land, a Poor People: Politics and Society in Modern Chiapas*. Albuquerque: University of New Mexico Press.

Berthelemy, Jean-Claude, and François Bourguignon. 1996. *Growth and Crisis in Côte d'Ivoire*. Washington, D.C.: World Bank.

Bhagwati, Jagdish. 1966. *The Economics of Underdeveloped Countries*. New York: McGraw-Hill.

Bils, Mark, and Peter Klenow. 1998. "Does Schooling Cause Growth or the Reverse?" NBER Working Paper 6393.

Blanchard, Olivier, and Stanley Fischer. 1989. *Lectures on Macroeconomics*. Cambridge, Mass.: MIT Press.

Blomstrom, Magnus, Robert Lipsey, and Mario Zejan. 1994. "What Explains the Growth of Developing Countries?" In William Baumol, Richard Nelson, and Edward Wolff, eds., *Convergence and Productivity: Cross-National Studies and Historical Evidence*. Oxford: Oxford University Press.

Blomstrom, Magnus, Robert E. Lipsey, and Mario Zejan. 1996. "Is Fixed Investment the Key to Economic Growth?" *Quarterly Journal of Economics* 111, no. 1 (February): 269–276.

Blomström, Magnus, and Frederik Sjöholm. 1998. "Technology Transfers: Does Local Participation with Multinationals Matter?" *European Economic Review* 43 (April): 915–923.

Boone, Peter. 1994. "The Impact of Foreign Aid on Savings and Growth." Mimeo. London School of Economics.

Boote, Anthony, Fred Kilby, Kamau Thugge, and Axel Van Trotsenburg. 1997. "Debt Relief for Low-Income Countries and the HIPC Debt Initiative." In Z. Iqbal and R. Kanbur, eds., *External Finance for Low-Income Countries*. Washington, D.C.: International Monetary Fund.

Borensztein, Eduardo, José de Gregorio, and Jong-wha Lee. 1998. "How Does Foreign Direct Investment Affect Growth?" *Journal of International Economics* 45 (June): 115–135.

Borner, Silvio, Aymo Brunetti, and Beatrice Weder. 1995. *Political Credibility and Economic Development*. New York: St. Martin's Press.

Boserup, Mogens. 1969. "Warning Against Optimistic ICOR Statistics." *Kyklos* 22:774–776.

Brookings Institution Center on Urban and Metropolitan Policy. 1999. *A Region Divided: The State of Growth in Greater Washington*. Washington, D.C.: Brookings Institution.

Brooks, Ray, Mariano Cortes, Francesca Fornasari, Benoit Ketchekmen, Ydahlia Metzgen, Robert Powell, Saqib Rizavi, Doris Ross, and Kevin Ross. 1998. "External Debt Histories of Ten Low-Income Developing Countries: Lessons from Their Experience." IMF working paper WP/98/72.

Bruno, Michael. 1993. *Crisis, Stabilization, and Economic Reform: Therapy by Consensus.* Oxford: Oxford University Press.

Bruno, Michael. 1995. "Does Inflation Really Lower Growth?" *Finance and Development* 32 (September): 35–38.

Bruno, Michael, and William Easterly. 1998. "Inflation Crises and Long-Run Growth." *Journal of Monetary Economics* 41 (February): 3–26 .

Burnside, Craig, and David Dollar. 2000. "Aid, Policies, and Growth." *American Economic Review.* Forthcoming.

Burr, J. Millard, and Robert O. Collins. 1995. *Requiem for the Sudan: War, Drought, and Disaster Relief on the Nile.* Boulder, Colo.: Westview Press.

Canning, David. 1999. "Infrastructure's contribution to aggregate output." World Bank Policy Research Working Paper 2246.

Carrington, William J., and Enrica Detragiache. 1998. "How Big Is the Brain Drain?" International Monetary Fund working paper 98/102.

Center for International Development, Harvard University. 1999. "Implementing Debt Relief for HIPCs." Mimeo. August.

Chamley, Christophe, and Hafez Ghanem. 1994. "Côte d'Ivoire: Fiscal Policy with Fixed Nominal Exchange Rates." In W. Easterly, C. Rodriguez, and K. Schmidt-Hebbel, eds., *Public Sector Deficits and Macroeconomic Performance.* Oxford: Oxford University Press.

Chenery, Hollis B., and Alan M. Strout. 1966. "Foreign Assistance and Economic Development." *American Economic Review* 56, no. 4, part I (September).

Clarke, George R. G. 1995. "More Evidence on Income Distribution and Growth." *Journal of Development Economics* 47, no. 2 (August): 403–427.

Clausen A. W. 1986. *Adjustment with Growth in the Developing World: A Challenge for the International Community: Excerpts from Three Addresses.* Washington, D.C.: World Bank.

Cohen, Daniel. 1996. "The Sustainability of African Debt." World Bank policy research paper 1621.

Collier, Paul, Anke Hoeffler, and Catherine Patillo. 1999. "Flight Capital as a Portfolio Choice." World Bank policy research paper 2066, February.

Corbo, Vittorio, Morris Goldstein, and Mohsin Khan, eds. 1987. *Growth-Oriented Adjustment Programs.* Washington, D.C.: International Monetary Fund.

Cresap, Bernarr, and Joseph Ord Cresap. 1987. *The History of the Cresaps.* Rev. ed. Gallatin, Tenn.: Cresap Society.

Critchfield, Richard. 1981. *Villages.* New York: Doubleday.

Critchfield, Richard. 1994. *The Villagers.* New York: Anchor Books.

Cukierman, Alex, Steven B. Webb, and Bilin Neyapti. 1992. "Measuring the Independence of Central Banks and Its Effect on Policy Outcomes." *World Bank Economic Review* 6 (September): 353–398.

D'Costa, Anthony P. 1999. *The Global Restructuring of the Steel Industry: Innovations, Institutions, and Industrial Change.* London: Routledge.

Dadush, Uri, Ashok Dhareshwar, and Ron Johannes. 1994. "Are Private Capital Flows to Developing Countries Sustainable?" World Bank policy research working paper 1397.

Daly, Herman. 1992. "Sustainable Development Is Possible Only If We Forgo Growth." *Earth Island Journal* 7, no. 2 (spring).

David, Paul A. 1990. "The Dynamo and the Computer: An Historical Perspective on the Modern Productivity Paradox." *American Economic Review* 80, no. 2 (May).

Davis Steven J., and John Haltiwanger. 1998. "Measuring Gross Worker and Job Flows." In J. Haltiwanger, M. Manser, and R. Topel, eds., *Labor Statistics Measurement Issues*. Chicago: University of Chicago Press.

De Long, J. Bradford. 1988. "Productivity Growth, Convergence, and Welfare: Comment." *American Economic Review* 78, no. 5 (December): 1138–1154.

De Long, J. Bradford, and Lawrence H. Summers. 1991. "Equipment Investment and Economic Growth." *Quarterly Journal of Economics* 106, no. 2 (May): 445–502.

De Long, J. Bradford, and Lawrence H. Summers. 1993. "How Strongly Do Developing Economies Benefit from Equipment Investment?" *Journal of Monetary Economics* 32 (December): 395–415.

Deininger, Klaus, and Lyn Squire. 1998. "New Ways of Looking at Old Issues: Inequality and Growth." *Journal of Development Economics* 57, no. 2 (December): 259–287.

Deininger, Klaus and Pedro Olinto. 2000. "Asset distribution, inequality, and growth." World Bank Policy Research Working Paper 2375.

Delors, Jacques, ed. 1996. *Learning: The Treasure Within*. Report to UNESCO of the International Commission on Education for the Twenty-first Century. New York: UNESCO Publishing.

Demographic Data for Development Project. 1987. *Child Survival: Risks and the Road to Health*. Columbia, MD.: Institute for Resource Development/Westinghouse.

Demographic and Health Services. 1994. *Women's Lives and Experiences*. Calverton, Md: Macro International, Inc.

Deng, Francis M. 1995. *War of Visions: Conflict of Identities in the Sudan*. Washington, D.C.: Brookings.

Devarajan, Shanta, Vinaya Swaroop, and Heng-fu Zou. 1996. "The Composition of Public Expenditure and Economic Growth." *Journal of Monetary Economics* 37 (April): 313–344.

Devarajan, S., W. Easterly, and H. Pack. 1999. "Is Investment in Africa Too High or Too Low?" Mimeo. World Bank.

Dollar, David. 1992. "Outward-Oriented Developing Economies Really Do Grow More Rapidly: Evidence from 95 LDCs, 1976–1985." *Economic Development and Cultural Change* 40, no. 3 (April): 523–544.

Dollar, David, and Roberta Gatti. 1999. "Gender Inequality, Income, and Growth: Are Good Times Good for Women?" Mimeo. World Bank.

Dollar, David, and Aart Kraay. 2000. "Growth Is Good for the Poor." Mimeo. World Bank.

Domar, Evsey. 1946. "Capital Expansion, Rate of Growth, and Employment." *Econometrica* 14 (April): 137–147.

Domar, Evsey. 1957. *Essays in the Theory of Economic Growth*. Oxford: Oxford University Press.

Dommen, Edward. 1989. "Lightening the Debt Burden: Some Sidelights from History." *UNCTAD Review* 1, no. 1:75–82.

Douthwaite, R. J. 1992. *The Growth Illusion: How Economic Growth Has Enriched the Few, Impoverished the Many, and Endangered the Planet*. Dublin: Resurgence.

Drazen, Allan, and William Easterly. 1999. "Do Crises Induce Reform? Simple Empirical Tests of Conventional Wisdom." Mimeo. University of Maryland and World Bank.

Drèze, Jean, and Naresh Sharma. 1998. "Palanpur: Population, Society, Economy." In Peter Lanjouw and Nicholas Stern, eds., *Economic Development in Palanpur over Five Decades*. Oxford: Clarendon Press.

Dunn, David and Anthony Pellechio. 1990. "Analyzing taxes on business income with the marginal effective tax rate model." World Bank Discussion Paper 79.

Dupuy, Alex. 1988. *Haiti in the World Economy: Class, Race, and Underdevelopment Since 1700*. Boulder, Colo.: Westview Press.

Easterly, William. 1993. "How Much Do Distortions Affect Growth?" *Journal of Monetary Economics* 32:187–212.

Easterly, William. 1994. "Economic Stagnation, Fixed Factors, and Policy Thresholds." *Journal of Monetary Economics* 33:525–557.

Easterly, W. 1995. "Explaining Miracles: Growth Regressions Meet the Gang of Four." In Takatoshi Ito and Anne Krueger, eds., *Growth Theories in Light of East Asian Experience*. Chicago: University of Chicago Press.

Easterly, W. 1999a. "Life During Growth." *Journal of Economic Growth* 4, no. 3 (September): 239–76.

Easterly, W. 1999b. "The Middle-Class Consensus and Economic Development." Mimeo. World Bank, December.

Easterly, W. 1999c. "The Ghost of Financing Gap: Testing the Growth Model of the International Financial Institutions." *Journal of Development Economics* 60, no. 2 (December): 423–438.

Easterly, William. 1999d. "When Is Fiscal Adjustment an Illusion?" *Economic Policy* no. 28 (April): 57–86.

Easterly, W. 2000a. "Can Institutions Resolve Ethnic Conflict?" Forthcoming. *Economic Development and Cultural Change*.

Easterly, W. 2000b. "The Lost Decades: Explaining Developing Country Stagnation 1980–98." Mimeo. World Bank, January.

Easterly, W., and S. Fischer. 1995. "The Soviet Economic Decline." *World Bank Economic Review* 9, no. 3:341–371.

Easterly, William, and Stanley Fischer. 2000. "Inflation and the Poor." *Journal of Money, Credit, and Banking*, forthcoming.

Easterly, W., and R. Levine. 2000. "It's Not Factor Accumulation: Stylized Facts and Growth Models." World Bank. Mimeo.

Easterly, W., M. Kremer, L. Pritchett, and L. Summers. 1993. "Good Policy or Good Luck: Country Growth Performance and Temporary Shocks." *Journal of Monetary Economics* 32, no. 3 (December): 459–483.

Easterly, W., and R. Levine. 1997. "Africa's Growth Tragedy: Policies and Ethnic Divisions." *Quarterly Journal of Economics* 112, no. 4 (November): 1203–1250.

Easterly, William, Norman Loayza, and Peter Montiel. 1997. "Has Latin America's Post-Reform Growth Been Disappointing?" *Journal of International Economics* 43 (November): 287–311.

Easterly, W., and S. Rebelo. 1993. "Fiscal Policy and Economic Growth: An Empirical Investigation." *Journal of Monetary Economics* 32, no. 3 (December).

Economist Intelligence Unit. 1999. Côte d'Ivoire Country Report, Fourth Quarter.

Edwards, Sebautian. 1990. "Openness, Trade Liberalization, and Growth in Developing Countries." *Journal of Economic Literature* 31 (September).

Edwards, Sebastian. 1995. *Crisis and Reform in Latin America: From Despair to Hope*. New York: Oxford University Press for the World Bank.

Edwards, Sebastian. 1998. "Openness, Productivity, and Growth: What Do We Really Know." *Economic Journal* 108 (March): 383–398.

Ehrlich, Paul R. 1968. *The Population Bomb*. New York: Ballantine Books.

Ehrlich, Paul R., and Anne H. Ehrlich. 1990. *The Population Explosion*. New York: Simon and Schuster.

European Bank for Reconstruction and Development. 1995. *Transition Report*. London.

Filmer, Deon, and Lant Pritchett. 1997. "Child Mortality and Public Spending on Health: How Much Does Money Matter?" World Bank Policy research Working Paper 1864, December.

Fischer, David Hackett. 1991. *Albion's Seed: Four British Folkways in America*. New York: Oxford University Press.

Forbes, Kristin. 1998. "Growth, Inequality, Trade, and Stock Market Contagion: Three Empirical Tests of International Economic Relationships." Ph.D. dissertation, MIT.

Forbes, Kristin. 2000. "A Reassessment of the Relationship Between Inequality and Growth." *American Economic Review*, forthcoming.

Frankel Jeffrey, and David Romer. 1999. "Does Trade Cause Growth?" *American Economic Review* 89, no. 3 (June): 379–399.

Frempong, Agyei. 1982. "Multinational Enterprise and Industrialization in Developing Countries: An Assessment of Ghana's Volta River Project." Ph.D. dissertation, University of Pittsburgh.

Frimpong-Ansah, Jonathan. 1991. *The Vampire State in Africa: The Political Economy of Decline in Ghana*. London: James Currey.

Gelb, Alan. 1989. "Financial Policies, Growth, and Efficiency." World Bank Working Paper Series 202.

Ghosh, Atish. 1994. "A Review of World Bank Projections." Mimeo. World Bank.

Gillis, Malcolm, Dwight Perkins, Michael Roemer, and Donald Snodgrass. 1996. *Economics of Development*. New York: Norton.

Goldin, C., and L. Katz. 1998. "Human Capital and Social Capital: The Rise of Secondary Schooling in America, 1910 to 1940." National Bureau of Economic Research working paper 6439.

Gonzales de la Rocha, Mercedes. 1994. *The Resources of Poverty: Women and Survival in a Mexican City*. Cambridge, Mass.: Blackwell Publishers.

Gould, Stephanie, and John L. Palmer. 1988. "Outcomes, Interpretations, and Policy Implications." In John L. Palmer, Timothy Smeeding, and Barbara Boyle Torrey, eds., *The Vulnerable*. Washington, D.C.: Urban Institute Press.

Greene, Joshua. 1989. "The External Debt Problem of Sub-Saharan Africa." *IMF Staff Papers* 36 (December): 836–874.

Greenwood, Jeremy, and Boyan Jovanovic. 1998. "Accounting for Growth." National Bureau of Economic Research working paper W6647, July.

Groliers Encyclopedia, Compuserve, article on Luddites.

Grosh, Margaret. 1991. *Public Enterprise in Kenya: What Works, What Doesn't, and Why*. Boulder, Colo.: Lynne Rienner Publishers.

Grubel, Herbert G., and Anthony Scott. 1977. *The Brain Drain: Determinants, Measurement and Welfare Effects*. Waterloo, Ont.: Wilfrid Laurier University Press.

Gurr, Ted Robert. 1994. "Peoples Against States: Ethnopolitical Conflict and the Changing World System." *International Studies Quarterly* 38:347–377.

Gyamfi, Peter. 1992. *Infrastructure Maintenance in LAC: The Costs of Neglect and Options for Improvement*. Vol. 4: *The Road Sector*. World Bank Latin America and Caribbean Technical Department Regional Studies Program report 17, June.

Gwartney, James D., and Robert A. Lawson. 19995. *Economic Freedom of the World 1975–1995*. Vancover: Fraser Institute.

Hadjmichael, Michael T., Michael Nowak, Robert Sharer, and Amor Tahari. 1996. *Adjustment for Growth: The African Experience*. Washington, D.C.: IMF, October.

Hall, Robert E., and Charles Jones. 1999. "Why Do Some Countries Produce So Much More Output per Worker Than Others?" *Quarterly Journal of Economics* 114, no. 1 (February): 83–116.

Harberger, Arnold. 1983. "The Cost-Benefit Approach to Development Economics." *World Development* 11, no. 10:864–866.

Harrison, Ann. 1996. "Openness and Growth: A Time Series, Cross-Country Analysis for Developing Countries." *Journal of Development Economics* 48:419–447.

Hayes, J. P., assisted by Hans Wyss and S. Shahid Husain. 1964. "Long-Run Growth and Debt Servicing Problems: Projection of Debt Servicing Burdens and the Conditions of Debt Failure." In Dragoslav Avramovic et al., *Economic Growth and External Debt*. Washington, D.C.: Economic Department, International Bank for Reconstruction and Development.

Herring, Ronald. 2000. "Making Ethnic Conflict: The Civil War in Sri Lanka." In Milton J. Esman and Ronald J. Herring, eds., *Foreign Aid and Ethnic Conflict*. Ann Arbor: University of Michigan Press, forthcoming.

Heywood, Paul. 1996. "Continuity and Change: Analysing Political Corruption in Modern Spain." In Walter Little and Eduardo Posada-Carbo, eds., *Political Corruption in Europe and Latin America*. New York: St. Martin's Press.

Hine, David. 1996. "Political Corruption in Italy." In Walter Little and Eduardo Posada-Carbo, eds., *Political Corruption in Europe and Latin America*. New York: St. Martin's Press.

Howitt, Peter. 1999. "Steady Endogenous Growth with Population and R&D Inputs Growing." *Journal of Political Economy* 107, no. 4 (August): 715–730.

Hsieh, Chang-Tai. 1999. "Productivity Growth and Factor Prices in East Asia." *American Economic Review* 89, no. 2 (May): 133–138.

Humana, Charles. 1992. *World Human Rights Guide*. 3d ed. New York: Oxford University Press.

Humphreys, Charles, and John Underwood. 1989. "The External Debt Difficulties of Low-Income Africa." In Ishrat Husain and Ishac Diwan, eds., *Dealing with the Debt Crisis*. Washington, D.C.: World Bank.

The Hunger Project, *Ending the Hunger: An Idea Whose Time Has Come*. 1985. New York: Praeger.

Husain, Ishrat. 1999. *Pakistan: The Economy of an Elitist State*. Karachi: Oxford University Press.

Husain, Ishrat, and John Underwood, eds. 1991, *African External Finance in the 1990s* Washington, D.C.: World Bank.

Inter-American Development Bank. 1995. *Economic and Social Progress in Latin America*. Washington, D.C.

Inter-American Development Bank. 1996. *Economic and Social Progress in Latin America*. Washington, D.C.

International Labor Organization. 1995. *World Employment*. Geneva.

International Monetary Fund. 1986. *Government Finance Statistics Manual*. Washington, D.C.

International Monetary Fund. 1992. *World Economic Outlook*. Washington, D.C.

International Monetary Fund. 1993. *World Economic Outlook*. Washington, D.C.

International Monetary Fund. 1996a. *Financial Programming and Policy: The Case of Sri Lanka*. Washington, D.C.

International Monetary Fund. 1996b. *World Economic Outlook*. Washington, D.C. October.

International Monetary Fund. 1996c. *Kenya Enhanced Structural Adjustment Facility.* April 12.

International Monetary Fund. 1996d. *Government Finance Statistics Manual.* Washington, D.C.

International Monetary Fund. 1998. *Côte d'Ivoire: Selected Issues and Statistical Appendix.* IMF Staff Country Report No. 98/46. Washington, D.C.

International Monetary Fund. 1999. "IMF Concludes Article IV Consultation with Côte d'Ivoire." Public Information Notice 99/63, July 16.

International Monetary Fund. Various years. *International Finance Statistics.* Washington, D.C.

Iqbal, Z., and R. Kanbur, eds. 1997. *External Finance for Low-Income Countries.* Washington, D.C.: International Monetary Fund.

Jacob, John J. 1881. *A Biographical Sketch of the Life of the Late Michael Cresap.* Cumberland, Md: J. J. Miller.

Jha, Prabhat, Kent Ranson, and José Luis Bobadilla. 1996. "Measuring the Burden of Disease and the Cost-Effectiveness of Health Interventions: A Case Study in Guinea." World Bank technical paper 333.

Jones, Charles I. 1999. "Was an Industrial Revolution Inevitable? Economic Growth over the Very Long Run." National Bureau of Economic Research, working paper W7375.

Jovanovic, Boyan. 2000. "Growth Theory." National Bureau of Economic Research working paper 7468.

Jovanovic B., and Y. Nyarko. 1996. "Learning by Doing and the Choice of Technology." *Econometrica* (November): 1299–1310.

Judson, Ruth. 1996. "Do Low Human Capital Coefficients Make Sense? A Puzzle and Some Answers." Board of Governors of the Federal Reserve System. Finance and Economics Discussion Series 96–13, March.

Kamarck, Andrew M. 1967. *The Economics of African Development.* New York: Praeger.

Kee, James. 1987. "President Reagan's FY88 Budget: The Deficit Drives the Debate." *Public Budgeting and Finance* 7, no. 2 (Summer): 3–23.

Kelley, Allen C., and Robert M. Schmidt. 1995 "Population and Income Change: Recent Evidence." World Bank discussion papers 0259–210X, 249.

Kelley, Allen, and Robert Schmidt. 1996. "Towards a Cure for the Myopia and Tunnel Vision of the Population Debate: A Dose of Historical Perspective." In D. Ahlburg, A. Kelley, and K. Mason, eds., *The Impact of Population Growth on Well Being in Developing Countries.* New York: Springer.

Kennedy, Paul. 1993. *Preparing for the Twenty-First Century.* New York: Vintage.

Kidron, Michael, and Ronald Segal. 1995. *The New State of the World Atlas.* New York: Simon & Schuster.

King, Robert, and Ross Levine. 1992. "Financial Indicators and Growth in a Cross-Section of Countries." World Bank Working Paper Series 819, January.

King, Robert G., and Ross Levine. 1993a. "Finance, Entrepreneurship, and Growth: Theory and Evidence." *Journal of Monetary Economics* 32 (December): 513–542.

King, Robert G., and Levine, Ross. 1993b. "Finance and Growth: Schumpeter Might Be Right." *Quarterly Journal of Economics* 108 (August): 717–737.

King, Robert, and Ross Levine. 1994. "Capital Fundamentalism, Economic Development, and Economic Growth." *Carnegie-Rochester Conference Series on Public Policy* 40:259–292.

Klenow, Peter, and Andrés Rodríguez-Clare. 1997. "The Neoclassical Revival in Growth Economics: Has It Gone Too Far?" In Ben Bernanke and Julio Rotemberg, eds., *NBER Macroeconomics Annual 1997*. Cambridge, Mass.: MIT Press.

Kling, Jeff, and Lant Pritchett. 1994. "Where in the World Is Population Growth Bad?" World Bank policy research working papers 1391.

Klitgaard, Robert. 1988. *Controlling Corruption*. Berkeley: University of California Press.

Knight, Alan. 1996. "Corruption in 20th-Century Mexico." In Walter Little and Eduardo Posada-Carbo, eds., *Political Corruption in Europe and Latin America*. New York: St. Martin's Press.

Kopits, George, and Jon Craig. 1998. "Transparency in Government Operations," International Monetary Fund occasional paper 158, January.

Kosmin Barry A., and Seymour P. Lachman. 1993. *One Nation Under God: Religion in Contemporary American Society*. New York: Harmony Books.

Kremer, Michael. 1993a. "The O-ring Theory of Economic Development." *Quarterly Journal of Economics* 108 (August): 551–575.

Kremer, Michael. 1993b. "Population Growth and Technological Change: 1 Million B.C. to 1990." *Quarterly Journal of Economics* (August).

Krueger, Alan B., and Mikael Lindahl. 1999. "Education for Growth in Sweden and the World." *Swedish Economic Policy Review* 6, no. 2 (Autumn): 289–339.

Kuznets, Simon. 1963. "Notes on the Takeoff." In W. W. Rostow, ed., *The Economics of Takeoff into Self-Sustained Growth*. London: Macmillan.

Lambsdorff, Johann Graf. 1998. "Corruption in Comparative Perception." In Arvind K. Jain, ed., *Economics of Corruption*, Recent Economic Thought Series. Vol. 65. Boston: Kluwer Academic.

Lancaster, Carol, and John Williamson, eds. 1986. *African Debt and Financing*. Washington, D.C.: Institute for International Economics.

Lee, Jong-Wha. 1993. "International Trade, Distortions, and Long-Run Economic Growth." *IMF Staff Papers* 40, no. 2 (June).

Lee, Jong-Wha. 1995. "Capital Goods Imports and Long-run Growth." *Journal of Development Economics* 48:91–110.

Leibenstein, H. 1966. "Incremental Capital-Output Ratios and Growth Rates in the Short Run." *Review of Economics and Statistics* (February): 20–27.

Leith, J. Clark. 1974. *Foreign Trade Regimes and Economic Development: Ghana*. New York: NBER/Columbia University Press.

Levine, Ross, and David Renelt. 1992. "A Sensitivity Analysis of Cross-Country Growth Regressions." *American Economic Review* 82:942–963.

Lewis, W. Arthur. 1954. "Economic Development with Unlimited Supplies of Labor." *Manchester School* 22 (May): 139–192.

Lieberman, Marvin B., and Douglas R. Johnson. 1999. "Comparative Productivity of Japanese and US Steel Producers, 1958–1993." *Japan and the World Economy* 11:1–27.

Lincoln, Abraham. 1989. *Speeches and Writings 1832–1858*. New York: Library of America.

Lipset, Seymour Martin. 1997. *American Exceptionalism: A Double Edged Sword*. New York: Norton.

Lipsey, Robert E. 1994. "Quality Change and Other Influences on Measures of Export Prices of Manufactured Goods and the Terms of Trade Between Primary Products and Manufactures." National Bureau of Economic Research working paper 4671, March.

Little, I. M. D., Richard N. Cooper, W. Max Corden, and Sarath Rajapatirana. 1993. *Boom, Crisis and Adjustment: The Macroeconomic Experience of Developing Countries*. Oxford: Oxford University Press.

Litwack, Leon. 1999. *Trouble in Mind: Black Southerners in the Age of Jim Crow*. New York: Vintage Books.

Loayza, Norman. 1996. "The Economics of the Informal Sector: A Simple Model and Some Empirical Evidence from Latin America." *Carnegie-Rochester Conference Series on Public Policy* 45 (December): 129–162.

Lucas, Robert E., Jr. 1988. "The Mechanics of Economic Development." *Journal of Monetary Economics* 22, no. 1 (July): 3–42.

Lucas, Robert E., Jr. 1990. "Why Doesn't Capital Flow from Rich to Poor Countries?" *American Economic Review* 80, no. 2 (May): 92–96.

Lucas, Robert E., Jr. 1998. "The Industrial Revolution: Past and Future." February. Mimeo. University of Chicago.

Lundahl, Mats. 1992. *Politics or Markets: Essays on Haitian Underdevelopment*. London: Routledge.

Luttmer, Erzo F. P. 1997. "Group Loyalty and the Taste for Redistribution." Mimeo. Harvard University.

Mackenzie, G. A., and Peter Stella. 1996. *Quasi-Fiscal Operations of Public Financial Institutions*. International Monetary Fund occasional paper 142, October.

Maier, Karl. 2000. *This House Has Fallen: Midnight in Nigeria*. New York: Public Affairs.

Mallet, Victor. 1998. "Telecom Investors Prepare to Dial Africa's Number." *Financial Times*.

Mankiw, N. Gregory. 1995. "The Growth of Nations." *Brookings Papers on Economic Activity* 1:275–326.

Mankiw, N. Gregory, David Romer, and David N. Weil. 1992. "A Contribution to the Empirics of Economic Growth." *Quarterly Journal of Economics* 107, no. 2 (May): 407–437.

Marshall, Alfred. 1946. *Principles of Economics*. 8th ed. New York: Macmillan.

Mauro, Paolo. 1995. "Corruption and Growth." *Quarterly Journal of Economics* 110, no. 3 (August): 681–712.

Mauro, Paolo. 1996. "The Effects of Corruption on Growth, Investment, and Government Expenditures." International Monetary Fund working paper 96/98, September.

Mayor, Federico. 1990. "Education for All: A Challenge for the Year 2000." *Prospects* 20, no. 4:441–448.

Meier, G. M., ed. 1995. *Leading Issues in Economic Development*. 6th ed. Oxford: Oxford University Press.

Meyer, Stephen Grant. 2000. *As Long As They Don't Move Next Door: Segregation and Racial Conflict in American Neighborhoods*. Lanham, Md.: Rowman and Littlefield.

Middle Eastern Department, International Monetary Fund. 1996. *Building on Progress: Reform and Growth in the Middle East and North Africa*. Washington, D.C.

Miguel, Ted. 1999. "Ethnic Diversity and School Funding in Kenya." Mimeo. Harvard University, November.

Mikell, Gwendolyn. 1989. *Cocoa and Chaos in Ghana*. New York: Paragon House.

Milesi-Ferretti, Gian Maria, and Assaf Razin, 1996. "Sustainability of Persistent Current Account Deficits." National Bureau of Economic Research working paper 5467.

Mishan, E. J. 1967. *The Costs of Economic Growth*. London: Staples Press.

Mistry, Percy S. 1988. *African Debt: The Case for Relief for Sub-Saharan Africa*. Oxford: Oxford International Associates.

Mokyr, Joel, 1990. *The Lever of Riches: Technological Creativity and Economic Progress*. Oxford: Oxford University Press.

Muhuri, Pradip, and Shea Rutstein. 1994. *Comparative Studies 9: Socioeconomic, Demographic, and Health Indicators for Subnational Areas*. Calverton, Md.: Macro International June.

Mulligan, Casey B., and Xavier Sala-i-Martin. 1993. "Transitional Dynamics in Two-Sector Models of Endogenous Growth." *Quarterly Journal of Economics* 108 (August): 739–773.

Murphy, Kevin M., Andrei Shleifer, and Robert W. Vishny. 1989. "Industrialization and the Big Push." *Journal of Political Economy* 97, no. 5 (October): 1003–1026.

Murphy, Kevin M., Andrei Shleifer, and Robert W. Vishny. 1991. "The Allocation of Talent: Implications for Growth." *Quarterly Journal of Economics* 106, no. 2 (May): 503–530.

Nafziger, E. Wayne. 1993. *The Debt Crisis in Africa*. Baltimore: Johns Hopkins University Press.

Narayan, Deepa, Robert Chambers, Meera Shah, and Patti Petesch. 2000a. *Crying out for Change: Voices of the Poor*. Vol. 2. Washington, D.C.: World Bank.

Narayan, Deepa, with Raj Patel, Kai Schafft, Anne Rademacher, and Sarah Koch-Schulte. 2000b. *Can Anyone Hear Us? Voices from 47 Countries*. Washington, D.C.: World Bank.

Nelson, Richard R. 1956. "A Theory of the Low-Level Equilibrium Trap in Under-developed Economies," *American Economic Review* 46, no. 5 (December): 894–908.

Nordhaus, William. 1994, "Do Real Output and Real Wage Measures Capture Reality? The History of Lighting Suggests Not." Yale Cowles Foundation discussion paper: 1078, September.

Obstfeld, Maurice, and Kenneth Rogoff. 1996. *Foundations of International Macroeconomics.* Cambridge, Mass.: MIT Press.

Ogaki, Masao, Jonathan D. Ostry, and Carmen M. Reinhart. 1995. "Saving Behavior in Low- and Middle-Income Developing Countries: A Comparison." IMF Working Paper WP/95/3.

Pack, Howard, and John M. Page, Jr. 1994. "Accumulation, Exports, and Growth in the High-Performing Asian Economies." *Carnegie-Rochester Conference Series on Public Policy* 40 (June): 199–250.

Parfitt, Trevor W., and Stephen P. Riley. 1989. *The African Debt Crisis.* London: Routledge.

Patel, Surendra J. 1968. "A Note on the Incremental Capital Output Ratio and Rates of Economic Growth in the Developing Countries." *Kyklos* 21:147–150.

Patrinos, Harry. 1997. "Differences in Education and Earnings across Ethnic Groups in Guatemala." *Quarterly Review of Economics and Finance* 37 (Fall): 809–821.

Perotti, Roberto. 1996. "Growth, Income Distribution, and Democracy: What the Data Say." *Journal of Economic Growth* 1, no. 2 (June): 149–187.

Persson, Torsten, and Guido Tabellini. 1994. "Is Inequality Harmful for Growth?" *American Economic Review* 84, no. 3 (June): 600–621.

Peters, Thomas J., and Robert H. Waterman, Jr. 1982. *In Search of Excellence: Lessons from America's Best-run Companies.* New York: Harper and Row.

Population Action International. 1995. *Reproductive Risk: A Worldwide Assessment of Women's Sexual and Maternal Health.* Washington, D.C.: Population Action International.

Poterba, J. 1998. "Demographic Structure and the Political Economy of Public Education." National Bureau of Economic Research working paper 5677, July.

Pritchett, Lant. 1994. "Desired Fertility and the Impact of Population Policies." *Population and Development Review* 20, no. 1 (March): 1–56.

Pritchett, Lant. 1997a. "Where Has All the Education Gone?" World Bank policy research working paper 1581, June.

Pritchett, Lant. 1997b. "Divergence, Big Time." *Journal of Economic Perspectives* 11, no. 3 (summer): 3–17.

Pritchett, Lant. 1999. "The Tyranny of Concepts: Cumulative Depreciated Investment Effort (CUDIE) Is Not the Same as Capital Accumulation." Mimeo. World Bank.

Pritchett, Lant, and Deon Filmer. 1999. "What Educational Production Functions Really Show: A Positive Theory of Education Spending." *Economics of Education Review* 18, no. 2 (April): 223–239.

Przeworski, Adam, and James Vreeland. 2000. "The Effect of IMF Programs on Economic Growth." *Journal of Development Economics*, 62, Issue 2 (August): 385–421.

Psacharopoulos, George. 1994. "Returns to Investment in Education: A Global Update." *World Development* 22:1325–1343.

Pscacharopoulos, George, and Harry Anthony Patrinos, eds. 1994. *Indigenous People and Poverty in Latin America: An Empirical Analysis*. World Bank Regional and Sectoral Study. Washington, D.C.: World Bank.

Rauch, James E. 1993. "Productivity Gains from Geographic Concentration of Human Capital: Evidence from the Cities." *Journal of Urban Economics* 34:380–400.

Ravallion, Martin. 1997. "A Comment on Rati Ram's Test of the Kuznets Hypothesis." *Economic Development and Cultural Change* 46 (October): 187–190.

Ravallion, Martin, and Shaohua Chen. 1997. "Distribution and Poverty in Developing and Transition Economies: New Data on Spells During 1981–93." *World Bank Economic Review* 11 (May).

Ray, Debraj. 1998. *Development Economics*. Princeton: Princeton University Press.

Rebelo, Sergio. 1991. "Long Run Policy Analysis and Long Run Growth." *Journal of Political Economy* 99:500–521.

Rebelo, Sergio, and Nancy L. Stokey. 1995. "Growth Effects of Flat-Rate Taxes." *Journal of Political Economy* 103, no. 3 (June): 519–550.

Red Cross, 1995. *World Disasters Report*. Dordrecht, Netherlands: Nijhoff.

Reinikka, Ritva, and Jakob Svensson. 1999. "How Inadequate Provision of Public Infrastructure and Services Affects Private Investment." World Bank working paper 2262, December.

Reno, William. 1995. *Corruption and State Politics in Sierra Leone*. Cambridge: Cambridge University Press.

Rescher, Nicholas. 1995. *Luck: The Brilliant Randomness of Everyday Life*. New York: Farrar Straus Giroux.

Rhee, Yung Whee, and Therese Belot. 1990. "Export Catalysts in Low-Income Countries: A Review of Eleven Success Stories." World Bank discussion paper 72.

Rimmer, Douglas. 1992. *Staying Poor: Ghana's Political Economy, 1950–1990*. New York: Oxford University Press.

Rodriguez, Francisco, and Dani Rodrik. 2000. "Trade Policy and Economic Growth: A Skeptic's Guide to the Cross-National Evidence." In *NBER Macroeconomics Annual 2000*. Cambridge, Mass.: MIT Press.

Rodrik, Dani. 1995a. "Getting Interventions Right: How South Korea and Taiwan Grew Rich." *Economic Policy* 20 (April): 55–107.

Rodrik, Dani. 1995b. "Trade Strategy, Investment, and Exports: Another Look at East Asia." National Bureau of Economic Research, working paper 5339, November.

Romer, Paul. 1986. "Increasing Returns and Long-run Growth." *Journal of Political Economy* 94, no. 5 (October): 1002–1037.

Romer, Paul. 1987. "Crazy Explanations for the Productivity Slowdown." In S. Fischer, ed., *NBER Macroeconomics Annual*. Cambridge, Mass.: MIT Press.

Romer, Paul. 1990. "Endogenous Technological Change." *Journal of Political Economy* 98, no. 5, part 2 (October): S71–102.

Romer, Paul M. 1992. "Growth Based on Increasing Returns Due to Specialization." In Kevin D. Hoover, ed., *The New Classical Macroeconomics*. Vol. 3. Aldershot, U.K.: Elgar.

Romer, Paul. 1993. "Idea Gaps and Object Gaps in Economic Development." *Journal of Monetary Economics* 32, no. 3 (December): 543–574.

Romer, Paul. 1994. "The Origins of Endogenous Growth." *Journal of Economic Perspectives* 8, no. 1 (winter): 3–22.

Romer, Paul. 1995. Comment on N. Gregory Mankiw, "The Growth of Nations." *Brookings Papers on Economic Activity* 1:313–320.

Rooney, David. 1988. *Kwame Nkrumah: The Political Kingdom in the Third World*. London: IB Tauris and Co.

Rorabaugh, W. J. 1981. *The Alcoholic Republic, an American Tradition*. New York: Oxford University Press.

Rose-Ackerman, Susan. 1997a. "The Political Economy of Corruption." In Kimberly Ann Elliot, ed., *Corruption and the Global Economy*. Washington, D.C.: Institute for International Economics.

Rose-Ackerman, Susan. 1997b. "The Costs and Causes of Corruption." Prepared for a panel discussion on corruption, IMF, Washington, D.C., April 3.

Rose-Ackerman, Susan, and Jacqueline Coolidge. 2000. "Kleptocracy and Reform in African Regimes." In *Corruption and Development in Africa: Lessons from Country Case Studies*, ed. Bornwell C. Chikulo and Kempe Ronald Hope, Sr. New York: St. Martin's Press.

Rostow, W. W. 1960. *The Stages of Economic Growth: A Non-Communist Manifesto*. Cambridge UK: University Press.

Roubini, Nouriel, and Xavier Sala-i-Martin. 1992. "Financial Repression and Economic Growth." *Journal of Development Economics* 39, no. 1 (July): 5–30.

Roubini, Nouriel, and Paul Wachtel. 1998. "Current Account Sustainability in Transition Economies." National Bureau of Economic Research working paper 6468.

Sachs Jeffrey, and Andrew Warner. 1995. "Economic Reform and the Process of Global Integration." *Brookings Papers on Economic Activity* 1:1–117.

Sargent, Thomas J., and Neil Wallace. 1985. "Some Unpleasant Monetarist Arithmetic." *Quarterly Review/Federal Reserve Bank of Minneapolis (U.S.)* 9 (winter): 15–31.

Schadler, Susan, et al. 1995. "IMF Conditionality: Experience Under Stand-by and Extended Arrangements." IMF occasional paper 128, September.

Schmidt-Hebbel, Klaus, and Luis Serven. 1997. "Saving Across the World: Puzzles and Policies." World Bank discussion paper 354.

Schumpeter, Joseph. *Capitalism, Socialism, and Democracy*. New York: Harper. (Originally published 1942.)

Seers, Dudley, and C. R. Ross. 1952. *Report on Financial and Physical Problems of Development in the Gold Coast*. Accra: Office of the Government Statistician.

Shleifer, Andrei, and Robert Vishny. 1993. "Corruption." *Quarterly Journal of Economics* 108 (August): 599–617.

Simon, Julian, ed. 1995. *The State of Humanity*. Oxford: Blackwell.

Slemrod, Joel. 1995. "Do Cross-Country Studies Teach About Government Involvement, Prosperity, and Economic Growth?" *Brookings Papers on Economic Activity* 10, no. 2:373–415.

Solow, Robert M. 1957. "Technical Change and the Aggregate Production Function." *Review of Economics and Statistics* 39:312–320.

Solow, Robert M. 1987. *Growth Theory: An Exposition*. New York: Oxford University Press. (Originally published 1970).

Stremlau, John. 1996. "Dateline Bangalore: Third World Technopolis." *Foreign Policy* (Spring): 152–168.

Summers, Robert, and Alan Heston. 1991. "The Penn World Table (Mark 5): An Expanded Set of International Comparisons, 1950–1988." *Quarterly Journal of Economics* 106, no. 2 (May): 327–368.

Svensson, Jakob. 1997. "When Is Foreign Aid Policy Credible? Aid Dependence and Conditionality." World Bank working paper 1740, March.

Svensson, Jakob. 1998. "Reforming Donor Institutions: Aid Tournaments." Mimeo. World Bank, April.

Svensson, Jakob. 2000. "Foreign Aid and Rent-Seeking." *Journal of International Economics* 51, no. 2 (August): 437–461.

Talbot, Ian. 1998. *Pakistan: A Modern History*. New York: St. Martin's Press.

Theobald, Robin. 1990. *Corruption, Development, and Underdevelopmen*. Durham, N.C.: Duke University Press.

Thorp, Willard. 1956. "American Policy and the Soviet Economic Offensive." *Foreign Affairs* (October).

Todaro, Michael P. 2000. *Economic Development*, 7th ed. Reading, Mass.: Addison-Wesley.

Trainer, Ted. 1989. *Developed to Death*. London: Green Print.

Tremblay, Helene, and Pat Capon. 1988. *Families of the World: Family Life at the Close of the Twentieth Century*. New York: Farrar, Straus and Giroux.

UNAIDS. 1999. *AIDS Epidemic Update*. December.

UNICEF. Various years. *Progress of Nations*. New York.

UNICEF. Various years. *State of the World's Children*. New York.

Union Bank of Switzerland. 1994. *Prices and Earnings Around the Globe*. Geneva.

United Nations Conference on Trade and Development. 1967. *The Terms, Quality, and Effectiveness of Financial Flows and Problems of Debt Servicing.* Report TD/B/C.3/35, February 2.

United Nations Conference on Trade and Development. 1983. *Review of Arrangements Concerning Debt Problems of Developing Countries Pursuant to Board Resolution 222 (XXI), Paragraph 15.* Report TD/B/945, March 23.

United Nations Development Program. Various years. *Human Development Report.*

United Nations Industrial Development Organization. Industrial Statistics, Various Years.

United Nations. 1996. *World Economic and Social Survey.*

United States Agency for International Development, Office of U.S. Foreign Disaster Assistance (OFDA). 2000, OFDA Reports Index, Washington, D.C.

United States Census Bureau, City and County Databook, Various Years.

United States Statistical Abstract, 1995, Washington, D.C.

Van Wijnbergen, Sweder, Ritu Anand, Ajay Chhibber, and Roberto Rocha. 1992, *External Debt, Fiscal Policy, and Sustainable Growth in Turkey.* Baltimore: Johns Hopkins University Press.

Vanek, J., and A. H. Studenmund. 1968. "Towards a Better Understanding of the Incremental Capital-Output Ratio." *Quarterly Journal of Economics* (August): 452–464.

Verspoor, Adriaan. 1990. "Educational Development: Priorities for the Nineties." *Finance and Development* 27 (March): 20–23.

Wachtel, Paul L. 1983. *The Poverty of Affluence: A Psychological Portrait of the American Way of Life.* New York: Free Press.

Wade, Robert. 1982. "The System of Administrative and political corruption: canal irrigation in South India." *Journal of Development Studies* 18, no. 3 (April): 287–328.

Wade, Robert. 1989. "Politics and Graft: Recruitment, Appointment, and Promotions to Public Office in India." In Peter M. Ward, ed., *Corruption, Development, and Inequality: Soft Touch or Hard Graft.* London: Routledge.

Wanniski, Jude. 1998. *The Way the World Works.* 4th ed. Washington, D.C.: Regnery.

Wetzel, Deborah L. 1995. "The Macroeconomics of Fiscal Deficits in Ghana: 1960–94." Ph.D. dissertation, Oxford University.

White, Joseph, and Aaron Wildavsky. 1989. *The Deficit and the Public Interest: The Search for Responsible Budgeting in the 1980s.* Berkeley: University of California Press.

Wiles, Peter. 1953. "Soviet Economy Outpaces the West." *Foreign Affairs* (July): 566–580.

Wilson, W. 1996. *When Work Disappears: The World of the New Urban Poor.* New York: Knopf.

Winkler, Max. 1933. *Foreign Bonds: An Autopsy.* Philadelphia: Roland Swain Company.

Wood, Adrian. 1988. "Global Trends in Real Exchange Rates: 1960–84." World Bank discussion paper 35.

World Bank. 1975. *Kenya: Into the Second Decade*. Baltimore, Md.: Johns Hopkins University Press.

World Bank. 1979. *World Debt Tables 1979*. Washington, D.C.

World Bank. 1981. *Accelerated Development in Sub-Saharan Africa: An Agenda for Action*. Washington, D.C.

World Bank. 1983. *Kenya Country Economic Memorandum*. Red Cover. Washington, D.C.

World Bank. 1984. *Toward Sustained Development in Sub-Saharan Africa: A Joint Program of Action*. Washington, D.C.

World Bank. 1986. *Financing Adjustment with Growth in Sub-Saharan Africa, 1986–90*. Washington, D.C.

World Bank. 1987a. *Bangladesh Country Economic Memorandum*. Report 6616-BD, March 10.

World Bank. 1987b. *Ethiopia Country Economic Memorandum*. Report 5929-ET. February 25.

World Bank. 1988a. *World Debt Tables 1987–88*, Vol. 1. Washington, D.C.

World Bank. 1988b. *World Debt Tables 1988–89*, Vol. 1. Washington, D.C.

World Bank 1988c. *Côte d'Ivoire: Mobilizing Domestic Resources for Stable Growth*. Report 7372-RCI, vols. 1 and 2. Washington, D.C.

World Bank. 1988d. *Côte d'Ivoire: Mobilizing Domestic Resources for Stable Growth*. 7372-RCI. Washington, D.C.

World Bank. 1989a. *World Debt Tables 1989–90*, Vol. 1. Washington, D.C.

World Bank. 1989b. *Kenya Public Expenditure Review*, April 14.

World Bank. 1990. *World Debt Tables 1990–91*, Vol. 1. Washington, D.C.

World Bank. 1991a. *Sub-Saharan Africa: From Crisis to Sustainable Growth*. Washington, D.C.

World Bank. 1991b. *World Debt Tables 1991–92*, Vol. 1. Washington, D.C.

World Bank. 1991c. *World Development Report*. Washington, D.C.

World Bank. 1993a. *Guyana: From Economic Recovery to Sustained Growth*. Washington, D.C.

World Bank. 1993b. *Lithuania: The Transition to a Market Economy*. Washington, D.C.

World Bank. 1993c. *World Debt Tables 1993–94*, Vol. 1. Washington, D.C.

World Bank. 1993d. *The East Asian Miracle*. New York: Oxford University Press.

World Bank. 1994a. *World Debt Tables 1994–95*, Vol. 1. Washington, D.C.

World Bank. 1994b. *Adjustment in Africa: Reforms, Results, and the Road Ahead*. Oxford: Oxford University Press.

World Bank. 1994c. "Lao People's Democratic Republic." Country Economic Memorandum. Report 12554. March 24.

World Bank. 1995a. *Bureaucrats in Business*. Oxford: Oxford University Press.

World Bank. 1995b. *Latin America After Mexico: Quickening the Pace*. Washington, D.C.

World Bank. 1995c. *RMSM-X Model Building Reference Guide*. Washington, D.C. July.

World Bank. 1996a. *Uganda: The Challenge of Growth and Poverty Reduction*. Washington, D.C.

World Bank. 1996b. *Bangladesh Country Economic Memorandum*. Report 15900-BD. Washington, D.C.

World Bank. 1997a. *Croatia: Beyond Stabilization*. Washington, D.C.

World Bank. 1997b. Report No. 15310-PAK *Staff Appraisal Report Pakistan National Drainage Program Project*. September 25, 1997.

World Bank. 1998a. *Global Development Finance 1998*, Vol. 1. Washington, D.C.

World Bank 1998b. *Assessing Aid: What Works, What Doesn't, and Why*. Oxford: Oxford University Press.

World Bank 1998c. *Egypt in the Global Economy*. Washington, D.C.

World Bank. 1999. *Global Development Finance 1999*, Vol. 1. Washington, D.C.

World Bank. Various years. *World Development Report*. Washington, D.C.

World Bank and International Monetary Fund. 1983. "Adjustment and Growth; How the Fund and Bank Are Responding to Current Difficulties." *Finance and Development* 20, no. 2 (June): 13–15.

World Bank. 2000a. *World Development Indicators*. Washington, D.C.

World Bank. 2000b. *Thailand: Social and Structural Review*, Report 19732-TH. Washington, D.C.

World Bank. 2000c. *Can Africa Claim the 21st Century?* Washington, D.C.

World Commission on Environment and Development (Brundtland Commission), *Our Common Future*, (New York: Oxford University Press), 1987.

World Conference on Education for All. 1990. "World Declaration on Education for All." *Bulletin: The Major Project in the Field of Education in Latin America and the Caribbean*, no. 21, Santiago, Chile, April.

World Currency Yearbook. Various Years. Brooklyn: International Currency Analysis Inc.

World Watch Institute. 2000. *State of the World 2000*. New York: Norton.

Wynne, William H. 1951. *State Insolvency and Foreign Bondholders: Selected Case Histories of Governmental Foreign Bond Defaults and Debt Readjustments*. New Haven, Conn.: Yale University Press.

Yonekura, Seiichiro. 1994. *The Japanese Iron and Steel Industry, 1850–1990*. New York: St. Martin's Press.

Young, Alwyn. 1992. "A Tale of Two Cities: Factor Accumulation and Technical Change in Hong Kong and Singapore." In Olivier Blanchard and Stanley Fischer, eds., *NBER Macroeconomics Annual*. Cambridge, Mass.: MIT Press.

Young, Alwyn. "Substitution and Complementarity in Endogenous Invention." *Quarterly Journal of Economics* 108, no. 3 (August 1993): 775–807.

Young, Alwyn. 1995. "The Tyranny of Numbers: Confronting the Statistical Realities of the East Asian Growth Experience." *Quarterly Journal of Economics* (August): 641–680.

Zolotas, Xenophon. 1981. *Economic Growth and Declining Social Welfare*. Athens: Bank of Greece.

Index